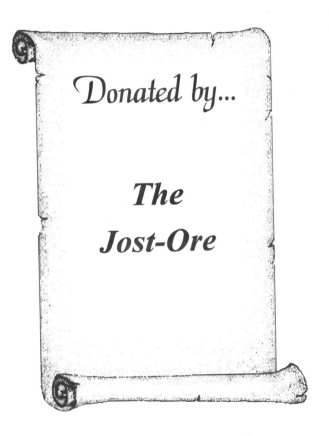

Donated by...

The
Jost-Ore

INTELLECTUAL CRAFTSMEN

INTELLECTUAL CRAFTSMEN

Ways and Works in American Scholarship

1935-1990

Steven Weiland

Transaction Publishers
New Brunswick (U.S.A.) and London (U.K.)

Library of Congress Catalog Number: 89-49251
ISBN: 0-88738-339-4
Printed in the United States of America

Library of Congress Cataloging-in-Publication Data

Weiland, Steven.
    Intellectual craftsmen : ways and works in American scholarship /
Steven Weiland.
        p.   cm.
    ISBN 0-88738-339-4
    1. United States—Intellectual life—20th century.   2. Learning and
scholarship—United States—History—20th century.   3. Psychoanalysis and
culture—United States.   4. Universities and colleges—United States—
History—20th century.   5. Intellectuals—United States—History—20th
century.   I. Title.
    E169.12.W4   1990
    306'.0973—dc20   89–49251
                                                              CIP

Contents

Preface

Readers of this book will observe the influence of anthropologist Clifford Geertz, also the subject of the last chapter. When I met Geertz shortly after the publication of his *Local Knowledge* (1983) and asked him to sign my copy he wrote in it simply: "In gratitude for a reader." I was impressed of course by his modesty, he being perhaps today's most widely cited scholar in the humanities and social sciences. And though I have played no role myself in Geertz's work I understand how colleagueship can help to transform ideas and intentions into print.

Accordingly, I want to recognize the following for their contributions to what intellectual craftsmanship this book displays and to professional opportunities that have made it possible for me to maintain a scholarly career side by side with an administrative one: Valborg Anderson, Cynthia Buckingham, Charles Cole, Cheryl Dickson, Roderick French, David Grossman, David Hamilton, Jay Kaplan, Richard Lewis, Geri Malandra, Betsy McCreight, Harold Miller, Sondra Myers, Horace Newcomb, John Raeburn, David Riesman, Martin Schwartz, Morton Seiden, Michael Sherman, Bruce Sievers, James Smith, Milton Stern, B. J. Stiles, Barbara Stuhler, Catharine Stimpson, Stuart Tave, Robert Vaughan, and James Veninga. Laurence Goldstein, Donald Gray, and Robert Fogarty (all editors of periodicals) encouraged me to write outside my nominal area of specialization. Irving Louis Horowitz of Transaction Publishers proposed that I present my work as a statement on intellectual history. He also guided me toward an expeditious reworking of the essays for their publication here.

I am grateful for all that has been provided to me by my parents, Florence and Harold Weiland, and for all that I have gained from my son Matthew, now himself a student of intellectual craftsmanship. My daughter Anna, only a nascent reader right now, is nonetheless the audience, so to speak, for all those activities that add to the pleasure of intellectual work. This book is dedicated to my wife, Deborah Silverman Weiland. She knows why.

Earlier versions of the chapters in this book appeared in the following periodicals and are used here with permission:

Chapter 2: *South Atlantic Quarterly* 86 (Summer 1987).

Chapter 3: *American Studies* 23 (Fall 1982).

Chapters 4 and 10: *Michigan Quarterly Review* 18 (Summer 1979) and 24 (Spring 1985).

Chapters 5 and 8: *Antioch Review* 44 (Fall 1986) and 46 (Fall 1988).

Chapter 6: *North Dakota Quarterly* 5 (Winter 1983).

Chapter 7: *Georgia Review* 37 (Fall 1983).

Chapter 9: *Northwest Review* 19 (1981).

Chapters 11 and 12: *College English* 44 (December 1982) and 49 (November 1987). Copyright by the National Council of Teachers of English.

1

Introduction:
Intellectuals, Scholars, Craftsmen

Intellectuals and Scholars

According to some of its critics, American academic life houses too many intellectuals, too many teachers and scholars who are adept at broad and deep reflection (to use Allan Bloom's definition) but who have adopted an adversarial stance toward literary and other scholarly traditions, and toward bourgeois culture. Paradoxically, another criticism of the university is that it supports too few intellectuals, the true adversarial temperament and method being incompatible with the demands, much less the prerogatives, of a fully institutionalized profession. There is a political disagreement here about the uses of liberal education and the learned professions, and about the role of learning in democratic society, one that also reveals how the use of the term intellectual itself can be counted on to move reflective men and women to deep discord.[1] Intellectuals are appealing if often vexing objects of inquiry precisely because they appear to embody American ideals even as they express skepticism about them.

Historians, critics, and other observers of intellectuals also make seemingly contradictory claims about them because they understand the term *intellectual* to have different or even irreconcilable meanings. Intellectual was originally a synonym for intelligent. But since the early nineteenth century it has often been used nearly as that term's opposite.[2] Indeed, in the mass

1

media intellectual is often a term of derision, used to stigmatize bookish—or campus- and library-bound—work for its remoteness from the putative realities of business, social, and political life. Among other things, this view reflects complex historical and social resentment against the self-proclaimed elites (from the point of view of their populist antagonists) who create, criticize, theorize, and even just reflect about ideas. The making and consequences of this resentment is what prompted historian Richard Hofstadter to defend intellectuals, and of course himself, as my chapter about him explains.

But even within academic life *intellectual* can be a term of approbation designating generalists, while in most fields legitimacy depends on specialization. Modern scholarship is understood by many contributors to it to represent the fruits of specialization, as intellectual work is thought by some to be a kind of protest against specialization on behalf of integration, synthesis, or even public understanding or policy-making. Hence in the university the opposite of intellectual is not merely the man or woman of action but the scholar engaged in a well- (some might say narrowly) defined area of inquiry or the pragmatic professor of engineering, accounting, or social work. And off campus, where teachers and scholars have not been as active as those who worry about public discourse and the popular arts would have them be, the habits of generalizing carry their own burdens. As has been said of the famous New York Intellectuals, most of whom did not hold academic appointments early in their careers, "they abhorred specialization so they became specialists in every subject."[3]

My use of intellectual and scholar as near synonyms is meant to bring the sometimes competing practices they represent closer together, as demonstrated by many of the subjects in this book. Within these terms, as recent decades have shown, disagreements abound over the proper objects and forms of inquiry and even its audience. Intellectual history as an academic specialty itself illustrates these tensions in the criticism mounted against it by the social historians of the 1960s and 1970s. The work of intellect was set against all other forms of working and living as a measure of the democratization and pluralization of historical interests generally. Intellectual historians have had to respond not just on behalf of their scholarship but on behalf of their subjects.[4] Intellectual history, to which *Intellectual Craftsmen* is intended to contribute, seems now to have recovered its place in the field. Nonetheless, few intellectuals seem to accept the term happily. And even within the group I designate intellectuals (they are scholars also) there is considerable variety. Pluralist in its own way, intellectual life invites historical, institutional, and comparative accounts, biography, textual criticism, and even a form of ethnography as anthropologist Clifford Geertz has proposed.[5]

The many ways to think about intellectual life in part reflect fresh perspectives in the disciplines inspired by the debate over critical theory and postmodernism. Between John Dollard, the first subject of *Intellectual Craftsmen,* and Geertz, the last, there is a distance not merely in time but also in the proliferation of styles and intentions of academic discourse. In the past decade or so both intellectuals and specialized scholars—and in this case there is little difference between them—have been the medium for the influence of critical theory, a group of ideas about the institutions and languages of the arts, the academic disciplines, and the professions. Paradoxically, they have also been its target since many postmodernists, perhaps the best known of today's theorists, promote the view that the instability of discursive practices and institutions—like the classroom or the book—chastens whatever intentions (much less traditions) reside in the roles of intellectuals and scholars.[6] Nonetheless, many in America have taken up this position for its interpretive utility (or novelty). So too do they value both its apparent candor in describing what they feel to be the paradoxes of their institutional circumstances and its uses in resisting the conventions of their roles.

Yet some scholars retain a nostalgia for forms of discourse outside the old and the new conventions. As Dominick LaCapra (whose efforts on behalf of postmodern historiography are the subject of an essay in this book) has proposed:

> The intellectual historian should . . . recognize his or her audience as a tensely divided one made up of both experts and a generally educated public. The intellectual historian is required to come as close as possible to an "expert" knowledge of the problems being investigated. But a goal of intellectual history should be the expansion of the "class" of the generally educated and the generation of a

better interchange between them and the "experts." This means helping to put the generally educated in a position to raise more informed and critical questions. It also means attempting to prevent expertise from becoming enclosed in its own dialect or jargon. In these senses, intellectual history faces complex problems of "translation," and its own concerns bring it into contact with larger social and cultural questions.[7]

This is an argument more in line with John Dewey than with the deconstructionist Jacques Derrida, who holds a leading place in the postmodern pantheon; it is somewhat surprising, however, that the American philosopher too is a hero for what might be called the neo-pragmatist version of postmodernism. LaCapra studies other intellectuals of the past century, but he feels the pressure of the role strongly enough himself to wonder about the uses of ideas in a culture as diffuse as the United States. For him, speaking from a relatively remote site like the academic research library, one of the large questions is still "how to resist the establishment of common culture on a relatively uncritical level and to further the creation of a more demanding common culture that, within limits, is genuinely open to contestation." The question of what formats are available for intellectual careers and their products, their "ways" and "works," that would satisfy such lofty goals is one theme of *Intellectual Craftsmen*.

Craftsmanship According to Mills

With these problems of vocation as backdrop, two recent studies of post World War II American intellectual life have found their hero in C. Wright Mills, a fact that would have pleased him and surprised his academic friends, many of whom felt sure that he had sacrificed his reputation with the ideological polemics of his last few years.[8] But despite his skepticism about or even ridicule of the organized intellectuals of the university, Mills thought carefully and personally about the nature of intellectual work and its consequences. Concealed within his unacademic manners was someone very serious about the intellectual and scholarly vocations. Mills's first major study was on the question of intellectual and scholarly careers (among the philosophers of pragmatism) and several early essays took up questions of language and audience as part of the problems in the sociology of knowledge. In *White Collar* (1951) he tried to salvage the traditions of the independent-minded scholar from the intellectual suburbs of public relations, journalism, and other anti-intellectual careers.

It was in "On Intellectual Craftsmanship," which appeared as an "appendix" to Mills's *The Sociological Imagination* (1959), that Mills supplied his best statement on the subject. As Mills's biographer Irving Louis Horowitz notes of the term "white collar," my own use of "intellectual craftsmen" is meant to describe the vocations of my subjects without imposing unity on a diverse group.[9] Mills wrote a first draft of "On Intellectual Craftsmanship" just after *White Collar* appeared.[10] The urgency of his statement in this scholar's guide is conveyed by his reassertion of the theme of that book, that is "the hollowness of the work which men in general do." By contrast, intellectual work, at least as Mills defines it, has the capacity to satisfy its practitioners while it meets timely scholarly and social goals.

The attributes of such work are considered in some detail in "On Intellectual Craftsmanship." They might be grouped under three headings. First, there is research itself or what Mills calls "the context of discovery."[11] Mills means by this mainly reading since he was admittedly ambivalent (at best) about empirical work. Second are matters of writing and rhetoric or the "context of presentation." He notes that the activity of intellectual craftsmanship is the moving back and forth between these two contexts and "whenever you move it is well to know where you might be going."

Mills insisted on attention not merely to the subject of research but to the entire aim of scholarly activity, the third theme of "On Intellectual Craftsmanship." It is an area Mills himself did not name but which can be called, in the spirit of Mills's own interest in American pragmatism, the "context of results." Chief among these are the personal consequences of craftsmanship as Mills understood it. For he insisted that "scholarship is a choice of how to live as well as a choice of a career; whether he knows it or not, the intellectual workman forms his own self as he works toward the perfection of his craft; to realize his own potentialities, and any opportunities that come his way, he constructs a character that has as its core the qualities of the good workman" (*IC*, 196). I take the subjects of *Intellectual Craftsmen* to have such characters and to be exemplary practitioners in the essential domains of scholarship as outlined by Mills. And like him each has influenced intellectuals and scholars in other fields, in effect helping to define the intellectual vocations and discourses beyond the boundaries of a single discipline.

The making of Mills himself as a scholar is the subject of "On Intellectual Craftsmanship," in which he puts his own work habits on display. He valued most the maintenance of a "file," one subject of my essay on Mills in *Intellectual Craftsmen*. Yet the bureaucratic sounding metaphor of the "file" (an irony apparent when you consider his use in *White Collar* of the epithet "the enormous file" for modern office work) vies with Mills's interest in "discovery" or even of creativity and innovation, terms only awkwardly applied to scholarship in the social sciences and the humanities as it is conducted in academic departments. Indeed, in a note to "On Intellectual Craftsmanship" Mills casually cites some work on "insight" by the little-known Eliot Dole Hutchinson, which suggests his interest in the psychologizing of scholarship.

The tale of an assistant to Thomas Edison must have amused and impressed Mills. M. A. Rosanoff had worked for more than a year in the trial-and-error mode of his boss to find a more effective formula for softening the wax of the original phonographic cylinders when the solution came to him quite suddenly while he was lying on a couch at home trying to recover from a headache. "It come without effort" he says, "after a year of the Edisonian blind groping that had led nowhere." And he offers this explanation for his research success: "I had learned to think waxes."[12] Or as Hutchinson puts it, summarizing the experiences of insight across many fields and with more moral import than one might associate with the case of the wax: "One never has a choice. And [the person with insight] not only produces something; he becomes something as well."[13]

The point for Mills, and for Rosanoff and Hutchinson, was that for the craftsman his or her subject becomes part of the self. Personal identity comes to include the devotion to a scholarly craft as I think is apparent for the subjects of *Intellectual Craftsmen*. Work was a crucial subject for Mills as it was for David Riesman and other postwar sociologists. The essay on Riesman in *Intellectual Craftsmen* is aimed at bringing the making of his unusual career forward as part of our understanding of his authority on the question of intellectual work. Still, the psychoanalyst Erik H. Erikson noted in his pathmaking *Young Man Luther* (which acknowledges a debt to Riesman) that "the problem of work" was the great neglected theme in his field. He took up the question in biography, as Mills did in more modest form in "On Intellectual Craftsmanship." But they agreed on a utopian psychology of work among people for whom ideas are paramount. As Mills put it: "You do not really have to *study* a topic you are working on . . . once you are into it, it is everywhere. You are sensible to its themes; you see and hear them everywhere in your experience, especially, it always seems to me, in apparently unrelated areas" (*IC*, 210). Accordingly, Mills offers later in his essay a metaphor, to complement the file, that captures the habit of the intellectual craftsman to seek out variability in viewpoint and unexpected combinations of ideas: "let your mind become a moving prism catching light from as many angles as possible" (*IC*, 214).

The particularity of Mills's prescriptions for intellectual work— notetaking, filemaking, outlining and the like—derives from the audience for the first draft of "On Intellectual Craftsmanship," his graduate students. They must have welcomed his candid advice about reading just parts of books, for Mills not a sign of laziness but of the pragmatics of scholarship with large goals and diverse sources: "You are *using* this particular idea, this particular fact, for the realization of your own projects" (*IC*, 199). By the time the essay appeared in *The Sociological Imagination* its purpose had been enlarged to strengthen the argument about consequences, how the scholar's work shapes his or her life. Hence intellectual craftsmanship came to rely on traditional notions of craft, that is the practice of a skill over a significant period of time in such a way that the products display elements of tradition and artistry as well as some sign of the identity of the craftsman. This was an important theme in *White Collar* where Mills lamented—as he evoked the Victorian ideals of William Morris—that within the conditions of modern work "the model of craftsmanship has become an anachronism."

It is by no means to deflate this historical ideal to note that Mills himself was an inveterate gadgeteer and tinkerer, that he had pride in his talent for automobile mechanics and carpentry, and that he built two homes for himself.[14] There is in his use of the term craft vestiges of the ideals of handiwork, seemingly a remote aspect of academic scholarship only if we don't recognize the idiosyncratic prose forms that distinguish truly intellectual work across the disciplines from, for example, the scholarly but standardizing formats of the American Psychological Association. One need only observe the innovative short forms favored by the physician Lewis Thomas or the ornate style of Geertz, intellectuals who differ in their practice of the rhetorical crafts even as they resemble one another in their skepticism of professional conventions. The other subjects of *Intellectual Craftsmen* are each in their fashion self-conscious writers within the traditions of their fields as they too discover forms of expression suited to their particular habits of "discovery" and hopes for "results."

Ways, Works, and Texts

Accordingly, the "ways" and "works" of my title must also rely on considerable variability in order to suggest how both constitute the intellectual craftsman. By *ways,* of course, I mean more than merely methods—the forms for practicing a particular discipline— but also in several essays the career and setting of which that practice is a part. In the cases of Dollard, Coles, Riesman, Mead, and Thomas, the pursuit of a career came to include the necessity of redefining how the vocation of an academic or medical specialist might be modified by the unique experience of the practitioner.

The term *works* is more problematic, especially in light of demands of recent theorizing in literature and what is often now called, on the European model, the human sciences. One might say simply, as a leading scholar of intellectual life has, that "a work is an objectively existing pattern of symbols of remote reference which record the 'state of mind' of the producer."[15] But for Roland Barthes, one of the leading theorists, the idea of the work, the object in the library with a recognizable set of intentions, meanings, and uses must give way to that of the "text" which is "a methodological field" where the activities of writers and readers are relativized, freed from tradition and liberated by association, contiguity, and contradiction. "The Text . . . decants the work . . . from its consumption and gathers it up as play, activity, production, practice."[16]

All of the books discussed in *Intellectual Craftsmen* might be read profitably from this point of view and indeed, even an essay like "On Intellectual Craftsmanship," with its insistence on the activities of composition and their meaning for the personal identity of the scholar (and hence also the reader) invites such an approach. In Barthes' view "the Text requires that one try to abolish (or at the very least to diminish) the distance between writing and reading, in no way by intensifying the projection of the reader into the work but by joining them in a single signifying practice" (*WT*, 162). Mills and others discussed in this book sought and seek readers in this spirit but with greater confidence than Barthes' approach allows in the independent standing of scholarly expression and its representation of a recognizable world.

Hence I have retained the older term *work* in this book's title in recognition of the need for limits (as LaCapra suggests) to the radical skepticism characteristic of postmodernism. For Barthes again, "the discourse of the Text should itself be nothing other than text, research, textual activity, since the Text is that *social* space which leaves no language safe, outside, nor any subject of the enunciation in position as judge, master, analyst, confessor, decoder. The theory of the text can coincide only with a practice of writing" (*WT*, 164). The roles dismissed by Barthes are those of the subjects of *Intellectual Craftsmen*, though not the only ones.

It has been one aim of recent theorists to reveal the limits (chiefly misguided optimism about language and representation) of an intellectual generation, largely the one considered in *Intellectual Craftsmen*. Yet it has also been defended recently for its liberalism and for its aspirations on behalf of public discourse. The portraits in this book recognize the problem of intellectual authority and of the relations between the scholar and society. My goal, prompted by Mills, is simply to display a variety of intellectual "ways" within critical categories of intellectual life. One of today's leading theorists has warned that postmodernism will mean the return of all the old anti-modernist prejudices, and I suspect that I share with my largely tradition-minded subjects some of what yet another theorist has called "the fantasy to seize reality."[17]

The modernist preoccupation with epistemological instability has now been transferred onto language itself, making *textuality* a problem as compelling as the historical, social, and psychological themes that works have heretofore represented. Efforts to convey the relations between what we know about language and what we think we have always known about the world and experience—for Geertz, the need to speak Wittgenstein—reflect the sort of paradox that binds scholarly and intellectual roles even among figures remote from the debates of critical theory. And if the classification of methods and ideologies is to get beyond the binary form of modernism-postmodernism, then attention to such figures will do more than fill out the historical record. It will supply images of intellectual and scholarly work, making questions of continuity as important as those of rupture and reorganization. It is not necessary to claim for intellectuals like Dollard, Riesman, and Margaret Mead—and indeed for Mills—that they anticipated elements of postmodernism or that they are now important as models of resistance to it. They are figures who represent ideals of craftsmanship that appear to animate even those who aspire to surpass them.

An Itinerary

The chapters of *Intellectual Craftsmen* are grouped under three headings. Erikson has called *Childhood and Society* a "conceptual itinerary," a phrase that suggests to me, thinking of my own ways, that the diverse contents of *Intellectual Craftsmen* have at least the continuity of thematic relations as I have brought them together as a reader, teacher, and scholar. This reflects more than the choices and accidents of a single career. Their unity lies in the possibilities today of seeing how subjects, disciplines, careers, and history intersect—how rhetoric has now been claimed as a subject for historians and anthropologists, how the careers of exemplary scholars can compete for importance with the works they produce, and how the history of a profession (like psychoanalysis) comes to reflect historical imperatives as well as professional prerogatives.

Psychoanalysis and the American Child

Part one of *Intellectual Craftsmen* considers some relations between psychoanalysis and society. Psychoanalytic study and treatment of children intensified with the migration to the United States in the 1930s and early 1940s of many scholars and intellectuals threatened by Nazism. As a vocation in the European tradition it had attracted scholars, social workers, and even artists as lay analysts. As a medical specialty in America psychoanalysis has sometimes foresworn these elements of its origins even as it has, of course, sought to amplify the habits of the founders: sympathy for children and powers of direct observation. American child psychoanalysts, and scholars in other fields with psychoanalytic training (like Dollard), adopted what Freud hoped would be its "widening scope" via applications in the social sciences and humanities.

Despite the example of Freud, defining the psychoanalyst as an intellectual means highlighting his or her resistance to the narrowing tendencies of the profession as it has institutionalized itself in American medicine. Medical psychoanalysis has been notably sectarian in its interests in comparison with the ideals Freud had in mind.[18] And American academic psychology was slow to assimilate psychoanalysis (when it has at all).[19] Still, most child psychiatrists and psychoanalysts, and then of course psychoanalytically oriented social scientists interested in children, have society in some form as their subject precisely because they rely on direct observation as well as on the discourse (or play) of their subjects. Inevitably their clinical crafts reflect their interest in theoretical and methodological themes that include psychoanalytic technique but have the "widening scope" of cultural and institutional formations as well. In effect, the child as an object of inquiry has prompted variations in psychoanalytic thought that have helped to maintain Freud's original intentions about the psychoanalytic vocation. Dollard, Erikson, and Coles are loyal Freudians even as they are rebels of a kind within their professions.

Academic Attitudes

In part two, "Academic Attitudes," the subject is forms of intellectual craftsmanship as they appear in the careers of a group of influential scholars closely identified with the American university as it developed after World War II. The postwar decades in the United States have been described as "proud" ones, with the nation on a "high," while intellectual life during this period is generally understood to have been "disconnected."[20] According to one participant-observer, "the main characteristic of our time is its kaleidoscopic quality, its shattering into literally dozens of currents, its rapid changes, its endless contradictions, its amnesia, its cultisms—on the whole, its appearance of dispersion, like a galaxy of stars moving in all directions."[21] Intellectuals typically take their times to be characterized by disorder and transition, perhaps justifying their synthesizing and sometimes moralizing habits in doing so. Mills certainly asked for as much; he would not accept mere craftsmanship as a substitute for history and politics in scholarship.

Still, after Mills himself the scholars I discuss in "Academic Attitudes" cannot be called partisans of the kind he relished, especially late in his career, and indeed Mills's personal relations with his more temperate Columbia colleagues Lionel Trilling and Hofstadter inevitably soured. The latter has been called a representative of the "mature American Modernist sensibility" for his pluralist methods and efforts to reconcile conflicting historical ideas and social and professional ideals.[22] I take this characterization to suggest my own view of Hofstadter's (and Trilling's and Riesman's) intellectual development which displayed, contra Mills, a more conciliatory middle way in the intellectual and political discord of the postwar decades. Hofstadter's "attitude," and also Riesman's, was a scholarly form of what Trilling took to be the prophetic element (perhaps even of postmodernism) in American novelists of the nineteenth century: they "contained both the yes and the no of their culture."[22]

Ways with Words

The intellectuals considered in part three, "Ways with Words," share with the subjects of the book's other essays the self-consciousness about form Mills took to be indispensable to crafts-manship. The notion of craft should of course be readily if not most observable in formal or rhetorical inventiveness. And Mills can be said to have anticipated current attention to rhetorical aspects of scholarship even if the durability of his own books does not depend on their form.[24] One might even say that the detailed advice of "On Intellectual Craftsmanship" has effects very differ-ent from the ones Mills intended, that is, it appears to make "textuality" the cornerstone of scholarship rather than ideas and ideological commitment.

It will be one of the tasks of postmodern scholarship to give structure to the relations between these aspects of works or texts, to interpret the "interpretive turn" for the purposes of those sympathetic to it and even those who are not (as LaCapra cited above would have it).[25] And Geertz's recent study of what might be called "pre-postmodernism" in anthropology grapples with the problem of "facing the page." He too prefers the standard term "work" and he presents scholarly writing as a search for a "signa-ture" or "writerly identity" and for "a way of putting things—a vocabulary, rhetoric, a pattern of argument—that is connected to that identity in such a way that it seems to come from it as a remark from a mind."[26]

For Margaret Mead the themes of ethnography were very different from those that interest Geertz, but her scholarly voca-tion also came to include recognition of its expressive elements and their significance. Thomas is an exemplary stylist as well but in a field where anything but exacting clinical writing seems an oddity altogether, vying with the demanding skills of the labora-tory or operating room but (mistakenly, as other medical authors assert) thought to have no relation to them. LaCapra is a student of the ways of history and historiography yet the clarity of his own prose provides an impressive instance of counterpoint to the historians and philosophers he admires but does not emulate. This has to do, as I suggest above, with a nascent interest in the public or at least the interdisciplinary responsibilities of history, but its effect is also to demonstrate—as Geertz does—how concern with the problems of language and rhetoric does not inevitably have to be expressed in forms that appear to compete with their subjects in striving for discursive ambiguity.

Though its intentions are in part historical, *Intellectual Crafts-men* is not a history of the postwar period. I believe that any intellectual history of the past fifty years would have to account for the themes, figures, and texts I discuss in these essays, but the gaps (in the same categories) are also plain.[27] An itinerary is the record of a journey but also a plan for one. The opening essay in *Intellectual Craftsmen* begins with an influential query of 1940, "knowledge for what?" In the closing essay the issue is very much "what can we know?" The second question has not of course displaced the first but it has dramatized for intellectuals and scholars the problem of making a vocation out of the plural and now we may even say competing ideals of craftsmanship.

Notes

1. See Allan Bloom, *The Closing of the American Mind: How Higher Education Has Failed Democracy and Impoverished the Souls of Today's Students* (New York: Simon and Schuster, 1987) and Russell Jacoby, *The Last Intellectuals: American Culture in the Age of Academe* (New York: Basic Books, 1987). The scholarly and public controversy surrounding Bloom's book is well known. It is summarized, from Bloom's point of view, by Peter Shaw in "The Academic Assault on Allan Bloom" *(The War Against Intellect: Episodes in the Decline of Discourse* [Iowa City: University of Iowa Press, 1989], 173–81). A different form of discord is observable in Jacoby's exchange with reviewer Lynn Garafola in the *New Left Review* no. 169 (May/June 1988): 122–8 and no. 172 (Nov/Dec 1988): 125–8.
2. Raymond Williams, *Keywords: A Vocabulary of Culture and Society,* rev. ed. (New York: Oxford University Press, 1983), 169–71. The literature on intellectuals, if one considers biography and criticism, is as large as the word is difficult to define. The term has even reached clarinetist and band leader Artie Shaw because, according to Barnett Singer, he satisfies Richard Hofstadter's criterion, the ability to play creatively with ideas ("Becoming an Intellectual: The Strange Saga of Artie Shaw," *Biography* 4 (Fall 1981): 326–39). Paul Johnson's subjects in *Intellectuals* (New York: Harper and Row, 1988) are a mixture of novelists, poets and critics chosen to demonstrate his belief that liberal artists and intellectuals are poor moral guides for society. Highlights of the historical and critical literature on the subject are: the comprehensive collection of commentaries on intellectuals, mainly from the twentieth century, in George B. de Huszar, ed., *The Intellectuals: A Controversial Portrait* (Glencoe, IL: The Free Press, 1960) and the comparative views

of Edward Shils, *The Intellectuals and the Powers, and Other Essays* (Chicago: University of Chicago Press, 1972). For a comprehensive survey of the American case see Lewis Perry, *Intellectual Life in America: A History* (New York: Franklin Watts, 1984). See also, especially on the sociological aspects of American intellectual life, Charles Kadushin, *The American Intellectual Elite* (Boston: Little, Brown, 1974) and Daniel Bell, "The 'Intelligentsia' in American Society," *The Winding Passage: Essays and Sociological Journeys, 1960–1980* (New York: Basic Books, 1980), 119–37. In addition to Jacoby's *The Last Intellectuals* another timely and more comprehensive study of the politics of American intellectual life is: Richard Pells, *The Liberal Mind in a Conservative Age: American Intellectuals in the 1940s and 1950s* (New York: Harper and Row, 1985).

3. Pells, *Liberal Mind in a Conservative Age,* 75.
4. See Laurence Veysey, "Intellectual History and the New Social History" and David Hollinger, "Historians and the Discourse of Intellectuals," in *New Directions in American Intellectual History,* ed. John Higham and Paul K. Conkin (Baltimore: Johns Hopkins University Press, 1979), 3–26 and 42–63. Hollinger pursues this theme also in *In the American Province: Studies in the History and Historiography of Ideas* (Baltimore: Johns Hopkins University Press, 1985). Donald Kelley finds the American case somewhat parochial; see "Horizons of Intellectual History: Retrospect, Circumspect and Prospect," *Journal of the History of Ideas* 48 (1987): 143–69.
5. Clifford Geertz, "The Way We Think Now: Toward an Ethnography of Modern Thought," in *Local Knowledge: Further Essays in Interpretive Anthropology* (New York: Basic Books, 1983), 147–63.
6. Two widely cited statements are: Fredric Jameson, "Postmodernism, or the Cultural Logic of Late Capitalism," *New Left Review* no. 146 (July/August 1984): 54–92 and Jean-Francois Lyotard, *The Postmodern Condition: A Report on Knowledge,* trans. Geoff Bennington and Brian Massumi (Minneapolis: University of Minnesota Press, 1984). Jameson considers the competing versions of postmodernism in "The Politics of Theory: Ideological Positions in the Postmodernism Debate," *New German Critique* 33 (1984): 53–66.
7. Dominick LaCapra, *Rethinking Intellectual History: Texts, Contexts, Language* (Ithaca: Cornell University Press, 1983), 65n. Edward Shils has a different view, as the thinly veiled preference in this comment suggests: "There is probably a process of selection which separates those who can create and who are strongly impelled to do so from those who, having been trained in a discipline, devote themselves to making its results intelligible to the inexpert instead of adding to its results" *(The Intellectuals and the Powers,* 108).
8. See Jacoby, *The Last Intellectuals,* and Pells, *The Liberal Mind in a Conservative Age.*

9. Irving Louis Horowitz, *C. Wright Mills: An American Utopian* (New York: Macmillan, 1983), 227. Hollinger finds fault with Christopher Lasch's otherwise admirable *The New Radicalism in America, 1889–1963: The Intellectual as a Social Type* (New York: Knopf, 1965) for its abstract effort to define a collectivity made up of a "type" (Hollinger, *In the American Province,* 203). I take Horowitz's and Hollinger's points to be in line with my grouping the subjects of *Intellectual Craftsmen* within the suggestive but certainly not definitive criteria proposed by Mills.

10. See "On Intellectual Craftsmanship (1952)," *Transaction/Society* (January/February 1980): 63–70. Mills made several changes in organization and wording from the first to the second draft. A long closing section on composing and rhetoric was added for the version that appeared in *The Sociological Imagination* (see following note).

11. C. Wright Mills, "On Intellectual Craftsmanship," in *The Sociological Imagination* (New York: Oxford University Press, 1959), 222. Subsequent references to this essay are incorporated into the text with the abbreviation *IC.* Mills credits the philosopher and historian of science Hans Reichenbach with the phrase "context of discovery."

12. Eliot Dole Hutchinson, "Varieties of Insight in Humans," in Patrick Mullahy, ed., *A Study of Interpersonal Relations: New Contributions to Psychiatry* (1949; reprint, New York: Science House, 1967), 391.

13. Hutchinson, "The Nature of Insight," in Mullahy, *A Study of Interpersonal Relations,* 445.

14. Harvey Swados, "C. Wright Mills: A Personal Memoir," *Dissent* 10 (Winter 1963): 35–42.

15. Edward Shils, "Intellectuals, Tradition and the Traditions of Intellectuals: Some Preliminary Considerations," *Daedalus* 101 (1972): 21.

16. Roland Barthes, "From Work to Text," *Image-Music-Text* (New York: Hill and Wang, 1977), 162. Subsequent references are incorporated into the text with the abbreviation *WT.*

17. Fredric Jameson, "Foreword," in *The Postmodern Condition,* by Jean-Francois Lyotard, xvii. The remark about seizing reality was made by Lyotard himself in the closing sentences of *The Postmodern Condition:* "We have paid a high enough price for the nostalgia of the whole and the one, for the reconciliation of the concept and the sensible, of the transparent and the communicable experience. Under the general demand for slackening and for appeasement, we can hear the mutterings of the desire for a return of terror, for the realization of the fantasy to seize reality. The answer is: Let us wage a war on totality; let us be witnesses to the unpresentable; let us activate the differences and save the honor of the name" (81–2).

18. See Nathan G. Hale, Jr., "From Bergasse XIX to Central Park

West: The Americanization of Psychoanalysis, 1919–1940," *Journal of the History of the Behavioral Sciences* 14 (1978): 229–315.

19. See Marie Jahoda, "Some Notes on the Influence of Psychoanalytic Ideas on American Psychology," *Human Relations* 16 (1963): 111–29 and "The Migration of Psychoanalysis: Its Impact on American Psychology," *Perspectives on American History* 2 (1968): 420–45.

20. John Patrick Diggins, *The Proud Decades: America in War and Peace, 1941–1960* (New York: Norton, 1988); William L. O'Neil, *American High: The Years of Confidence: 1945–1960* (New York: The Free Press, 1986); Perry, *Intellectual Life in America,* 381–449.

21. William Phillips, *A Partisan View: Five Decades of the Literacy Life* (New York: Stein and Day, 1983), 169.

22. David Joseph Singal, "Towards a Definition of American Modernism," *American Quarterly* 39 (1987): 20.

23. Lionel Trilling, "Reality in America," *The Liberal Imagination* (New York: Anchor Books, 1954): 21. Philosopher Richard Rorty has expressed a view similar to Trilling's but framed by the debates of postmodernism. He favors the "liberal ironist," the critic who combines commitment with awareness of its contingency. See *Contingency, Irony, and Solidarity* (Cambridge: Cambridge University Press, 1989), 61–8. Rorty has made a related statement that in effect seeks points of contact between the "mature modernists" with the postmodernists: "Postmodern Bourgeois Liberalism," *Journal of Philosophy* 80 (1983): 583–9.

24. See John S. Nelson, Allan Megill, and Donald N. McCloskey, eds., *The Rhetoric of Inquiry: Language and Argument in Scholarship and Public Affairs* (Madison: University of Wisconsin Press, 1987).

25. See Paul Rabinow and William M. Sullivan, eds., *Interpretive Social Science: A Second Look* (Berkeley: University of California Press, 1987). The introduction offers a timely discussion of the relations between the "interpretive turn" and the several varieties of postmodernism. See also Kelley, "Horizons of Intellectual History" (cited above) and its citations.

26. Clifford Geertz, *Works and Lives: The Anthropologist as Author* (Stanford: Stanford University Press, 1988), 9.

27. Most notably of female scholars. The choice of craftsmen for this book's title, however, reflects its source in Mills's essay and the awkwardness of "craftsperson."

Part One

PSYCHOANALYSIS AND THE AMERICAN CHILD

2

John Dollard: Life History, Psychoanalysis, and Social Science

No less than today's social scientists their forerunners complained about the isolation of the disciplines from one another, questioned the limits of methodological conventions, and feared the social marginality of scholarship. In 1940 Robert Lynd, coauthor with Helen Merrell Lynd of the pathbreaking "Middletown" studies, attacked the biases in orthodox academic inquiry for the "manageably known" and the "fencing off" of the disciplines from each other and society. "Each social science," he said, "tends to be a floating island of more or less internally coherent but partially unreal theoretical and factual certainties in the vast sea of living uncertainty. What we tend to teach our students is the limited cartography of our respective islands, paying scant attention to the *mare incognitum* of surrounding behavior." Lynd sought to apply the sense of urgency brought about by domestic and international crises—the Depression and World War II—to scholarly work, insisting that the social sciences did not merely observe the national culture but were a part of it. "It is the precise character of a culture and the problems it presents as an instrument for furthering men's purposes," he claimed, "that should determine the problems and to some extent, the balance of methods of social science research.[1]

In the generation that followed Lynd's, few social scientists worked as hard to bind theoretical, empirical, and social interests as Yale's John Dollard, a teacher and scholar in several fields whose work reflects the quest for a unified social science based on

what Dollard himself called a "blend structure" of research principles. Author and coauthor of several books on problems, methods, and applications in psychology and social relations, Dollard
exemplified the sort of scholar Lynd proposed was needed in the
social sciences which, he pointed out in full rhetorical splendor,
"deal with the white-hot core of current controversy, where pas-
sions are most aggravated and counsel most darkened."[2] Dollard
indeed understood the force of social problems even as he pursued
concrete methodological themes in his allied fields of study. Justifiably remembered for his pioneering work in community studies,
he also contributed to the redefinition of the scholarly vocation by
advancing academic and public uses of psychology. And he helped
to explore how psychoanalysis, as a resource within the social
sciences, might be applied to the problem of "caste and class"
faced by American children.

The Living Context

During the 1930s and 1940s, the definition of social science itself
appeared to depend on the problems and opportunities posed by
depth psychology, especially psychoanalysis. Yet as Kenneth
Burke once said, "The reading of Freud I find suggestive almost to
the point of bewilderment."[3] As a literary critic Burke certainly
had the resources now recognized as important for work in psychoanalysis, for apart from its clinical achievements it has also
produced an authentic critical literature. But the suggestiveness of
psychoanalysis not only prompts textual criticism, it also explains
Freud's impact on other disciplines. In his authoritative history of
sociology, for instance, Edward Shils admits, albeit somewhat
grudgingly, that psychoanalysis has been assimilated into his discipline. According to Shils, particular psychoanalytic propositions,
like the Oedipus complex and Freudian ideas about aggression,
anxiety, and repression, may be found to be untrue or at least
impossible to prove scientifically, but "the naming and description
of these phenomena has made sociologists more aware of them,
more realistic in their perception of them, more able to assess
their magnitude and to estimate the probability of their occur-
rence under certain conditions."[4] Many social scientists have
shared Shils's ambivalence; some because of their doubts about

the scientific status of psychoanalysis, others because they were skeptical about the claims made on its behalf as a unifying research format.

Burke also was alert to related problems in method. Writing about the Lynds' work on Middletown, he praised it as an exemplary effort of description and admonition. The Lynds, he says, show us a community that knows that "man's proper enterprise must be expended in developing modes of thought that enable him to accept the world but who is tragically engaged in trying to extend such modes of acceptance to institutions that can and should be rejected." Nonetheless, the Lynds' ideological achievements do not, for Burke at least, entirely compensate for two methodological flaws. The first is the presentation of the community as "a study in cultural conflict," as *Middletown in Transition* was subtitled. This approach is rejected by Burke not because it is untrue but because it is unoriginal. The conflict between opposing tendencies is more convenient than analytic, for "all moral journeys go between Scylla and Charybdis." Even more important is what was to Burke the fundamental problem in much social science, the search for "the typical" as the essential resource for generalization. In his view the typical is inert, ahistorical, and the goal only of survey research. He acknowledges that history is "moved by quantities" but asks about the capacity of social scientists to accommodate the "qualities" as well. "Might not the single song of one poet, under certain conditions, put us on the track of something that the typical platitudes of a group could give us no inkling of?"[5]

Burke's question cannot be dismissed as merely the revenge of literature on sociology—or of the humanities on the social sciences—though he might be charged with sidestepping the problems faced by actual scholars who presumably would be responsible for deciding under which conditions their data would change so radically. Yet many social scientists shared Burke's skepticism about their methods. During the 1930s and 1940s many saw that gains in the power to quantify, to make their work more scientific and hence in their view more usable, were often at the expense of the qualities peculiar to individuals: the songs not necessarily of poets but of ordinary people, the actual subjects whose habits, ideals, expectations, and anxieties were the material for research.

The quest for synthesis based on the formative power of society sometimes concealed the fullest potential of the data.

Yet at the same time one of the great achievements of social science during this period was its dialectical tendency, its robust self-consciousness. The name given to one influential self-correcting device was "culture and personality." Its leading proponent, the linguist and anthropologist Edward Sapir, proposed in 1934 that social scientists refuse to confine themselves to the procedures of orthodox ethnography. He offered, in the manner of Henry James, this summary of the problem: "If we make the test of imputing the contents of an ethnological monograph to a known individual in the community which it describes, we would inevitably be led to discover that, while every single statement in it may, in the favorable case, be recognized as holding true in some sense, the complex of patterns as described cannot, without considerable absurdity, be interpreted as a significant configuration of experience, both actual and potential, in the life of the person appealed to." Cultures, according to Sapir, are "abstract configurations of idea and action patterns," whose meanings differ enormously for different individuals.[6] Like Burke, Sapir values attention to particulars—even a single gesture or word can carry great meaning—but speaking as a professional social scientist who has to organize and report his data, he resists the critic's appealing call for methodological simplicity.

To rectify the tendency toward abstraction, Sapir proposed that ideas about the origin, structures, and meanings of cultures must, "if they are to build up into any kind of significant psychic structure, whether for the individual or the small group or the larger group, be set in relation to each other in a complex configuration of evaluations, inclusive and exclusive implications, priorities, and potentialities of realization." This new and demanding research agenda could be achieved by reviewing the purposes of sociology, anthropology, psychology, psychiatry, and psychoanalysis. From the point of view of the tasks he outlines, Sapir praises these disciplines as "preliminary" ones, useful in gathering and sifting the data and phrasing the major problems. He foresees a time when they will be justified largely by their joint efforts, "which will bring every cultural pattern back to the living context from which it has been abstracted in the first place and, in parallel fashion, bring every fact of personality formation back to its social matrix."[7]

Sapir's optimism reflected his own multidisciplinary talents and the promise of "culture and personality" as a format for the new styles of research. He also had the advantage of a suitable institutional setting, Yale's Institute of Human Relations, which was a crucible for landmark work in the social sciences, often derived from Sapir's approach and variations on it. Erik H. Erikson, who was affiliated with the institute for a time, was influenced by Sapir, Dollard, and others in the work that finally appeared as *Childhood and Society*. The best-known psychologist at the institute was the behaviorist Clark Hull, but he welcomed psychoanalysis as a subject for one of his renowned seminars out of the interest he shared with colleagues in formulating a comprehensive and systematic view of human behavior. The institute never achieved this lofty goal, but psychoanalysis appears to have demonstrated to the Yale scholars (from medicine, law, and the social sciences) the limits of behaviorism and the difficulty of integrating their diverse interests.[8]

Open Country

The institute's leading psychoanalytic scholar was Dollard, who arrived at Yale's anthropology department in 1932 after completing graduate work at the University of Chicago and taking a training analysis with Freud's close colleague Hans Sachs at the Berlin Psychoanalytic Institute. Dollard's two major interests formed the title of a paper published in that year by Sapir in which he urged scholars in the cultural and psychological fields to "follow tangible problems of behavior rather than the selected problems set by recognized disciplines."[9] Dollard understood the fertility of such thinking and, as he put it twenty-five years later in a new preface to *Caste and Class in a Southern Town* (first published in 1937), "I headed for this open country."[10]

In *Caste and Class* Dollard sought to illustrate how psychoanalytic ideas could be used to bring to life the underlying dynamics of a community. While he acknowledged the traditions in which he was working, cultural anthropology and the study of social structure, he also reiterated in 1957 what psychoanalysis could contribute: "I see man . . . as Freud saw him. If . . . Durkheim sees man poised and timeless in the frieze of structure, Freud sees him the ambitious beast, shivering in the high wind of culture. Seen close, he smokes" (*CC,* ix). Dollard sought a form of social science which not only classified types of behavior in society but which offered an emotionally significant account of personal relations. In addition to *Caste and Class* he wrote an unjustly ignored methodological statement, *Criteria for the Life History* (1935), several important works on learning theory and social psychology, and he collaborated with Allison Davis in a second book on the South, *Children of Bondage* (1940), which focused his methods on the problems of race, caste, and adolescence.

After a year of teaching anthropology, Dollard joined the institute where he worked from 1932 until its demise twenty years later when he became professor of psychology. The mixture of interests that made the nascent enterprise of "culture and person-ality" so compelling to Dollard and others is clear from his admiration of the institute's "steady behavioral heart, culturalist lungs and Freudian guts."[11] From this unlikely combination came the motive for *Criteria for the Life History* in which Dollard sought to help "culture and personality" earn the name discipline.

His work originates modestly enough in a restatement of Sapir's major themes. As soon as we "take the post of observer on the cultural level," Dollard says, "the individual is lost in a crowd and our concepts never lead us back to him."[12] Accordingly, for Dollard the proper goal for social science is the one for "culture and personality" studies: "The element for which we are perenni-ally seeking is a significant concept of the person to set off against our valuable formal descriptions of social life" (*LH,* 1). To advance such work Dollard invites sociologists, biographers, psy-choanalysts, historians, and even literary critics—especially those interested in autobiography and its problems—to participate in a common task, the development of evaluative principles serving the cultural and psychological fields.

The collaborative approach would take as its data life history, defined by Dollard as a "deliberate attempt to define the growth of a person in a cultural milieu and make theoretical sense of it" (*LH,* 3). Any life history is an account of cultural transmission, of how a person meets the traditional expectations of his society by becoming an adult. Dollard sees that by focusing on life history it is possible to create a "long section" view of culture where the subjects of study retain their particularity and presence while serving as data or evidence. "The culture forms a continuous connected wrap for the organic life. From the standpoint of the life history the person is viewed as an organic center of feeling moving through a culture and drawing magnetically to him [its] main strands. In the end the individual appears as a person, as a microcosm of the group features of his culture" (*LH*, 4). Community studies that depend on life histories, therefore, avoid the faults of what Dollard calls "pure" cultural studies, and the real person does not disappear in favor of an abstracted person identified largely if not solely by his or her relation to the cultural pattern. Individual experience and meaning can be restored to social research by recasting its goals; a culture and personality problem can be identified in every case by observing whether "the person is 'there' in full emotional reality" (*LH*, 5). The most suitable material for the study of such problems is the life history, and the best technique for its making and interpretation is psychoanalytic psychology.

Dollard's proposed criteria are designed to replace the "consoling methodologies" which in his view have given only "refuge" to those despairing of orderly development in the study of social and personal life. As a remedy he called for "a psychology workable from the standpoint of systematic cultural knowledge" (*LH*, 288) and favored a style that is familiar today but that was novel just a few decades ago. It was in *Criteria for the Life History* that Dollard established his program for social and historical research. He predicted that what is now called psycho-historical method will "most likely emerge from the continuous refinement of our observations on the individual life and especially from treating this life as a unit event and beginning our studies with the problems that people actually have in current life situations. If we can stimulate a number of people to cling bitterly to this problem, we shall very likely blaze one of the valuable paths in social science research" (*LH*, 288).

Stated formally in his text (in the conditional passive), Dollard's seven criteria are more accessible put this way: 1) show the subject as a specimen in a cultural series, as a group plus one, as a link in the chain of cultural transmission; 2) give organic factors their due regard, including social influence on physical functioning and the role of physical change in psychological development throughout the life cycle; 3) stress the family's peculiar role in transmitting culture in the way it forecasts and forecloses certain kinds of social participation; 4) show how the individual's specific traits and attitudes are learned, i.e., his or her path of social learning; 5) stress the continuous related character of experience through childhood to adulthood (the life cycle); 6) specify the social situation carefully and continuously; and 7) work toward a coherent, objective set of necessary terms.[13]

Its principles are so widely agreed upon now that Dollard's method, and his role as an innovator, are easy to ignore. Erikson thanked Dollard for "remarkable interdisciplinary stimulation," and his widely cited essay on "The Nature of Psycho-Historical Experience" is also animated by the search for systematic criteria.[14] By directing attention to life histories and their evaluation for use in social research, Dollard demonstrated where sociology, anthropology, and psychology assimilate essential elements of one another. He also helped to free applied psychoanalysis from exclusive reliance on the drive theory in favor of a social perspective, as psychoanalysis itself has directed the cultural disciplines to the unconscious. In Dollard's words, we do not have to "beat the devil of the instinct theory around the stump . . . since scientific reports from other cultures have shown the extreme variability of human action and the great importance of vested tradition in determining the action of any new member" (*LH*, 16). As Dollard and his successors find many ways of saying, the essence of "culture and personality" is the shared strength of its components.

The examples offered in *Criteria* are judged rigorously, if sometimes mechanically, according to Dollard's standards: case studies by Freud, Adler, the little-known Jessie Taft, Thomas and Znaniecki's "Life Record of an Immigrant" from *The Polish Peasant in Europe and America,* Clifford Shaw's ethnography of crime in Chicago, *The Jack Roller,* and H. G. Wells's autobiography. None meet all the criteria completely; each has its uses as a life history. The priority given Freud is apparent though not because his technique for life history is ideal. Orthodox psychoanalysis is accused of not paying enough attention to external life. Moreover, Dollard charged, psychoanalysts often accept uncritically the society they share with patients. He thus anticipates Marxist uses of Freud and Burke's comment on *Middletown in Transition* by proposing that "the adequate theoretical definition of the current situation and the difference between it and the patient's private view of the same situation is an important step in acculturating such a psychology as Freud's to social science uses" (*LH,* 139). The intrinsic advantages of Freudian theory are its "singular consistency and beauty" and its adaptability and timeliness.

Dollard apparently felt some urgency as well in the unfolding of his own career. In a coda to *Criteria* he restates again their lessons. He protests that he has no theory of psychological and social growth, only some suggestions about what must be the essential items covered by such a theory. His ideas modestly extend to a momentary questioning of the "culture and personality" program which, he admits, can be vague, merely an attempt to freshen up old problems, or worst of all perhaps, a "banal attempt to sit astride of conduits which lead from fund-giving agencies to ambitious and impecunious scholars" (*LH,* 271). Yet Dollard finally puts aside the possibilities for opportunism and identifies the genuine opportunity before him as a scholar: "It is important to be able to say to oneself in a slow and significant way how a culture-personality problem looks when you meet it in nature" (*LH,* 281). It was, therefore, intellectual zeal and academic cabin fever that moved Dollard from New Haven to the deep South.

Caste and Personality

Equipped with at least the raw material for a theory and a strong desire to take the first steps in a project in applied psychoanalysis, Dollard went in the fall of 1935 to Indianola, Mississippi, where he stayed for five months. His goal was to record a few life histories in order to learn something about black personality development. Not surprisingly, he quickly decided to study the community. He had no choice, he says, since to ignore the fact that in "Southerntown" (the name he gives Indianola) the lives of blacks and whites are "so dynamically joined and fixed in one system" would be to collect the life histories in a void. Yet while he has sacrificed his original objective, showing the actual linear development of a few Southerntown black subjects, there remains one major theme: "the attempt to see the social situation as a means of patterning the affects of white and Negro people, as a mold for love, hatred, jealousy, deference, submissiveness, and fear. Only in the individual life can one see these emotional forces surging against the barriers and outlets of the governing social order" (CC, 2). For this reason Dollard defends the importance of the psychoanalytic method even though the life histories are not presented in full.

Like other field workers Dollard found that the "crucial problem was to objectify the life of Southerntown by participating and reacting in it" (CC, 9). Needless to say, he met with considerable apprehension and fear, largely associated with suspicions by whites about his real purpose (i.e., social change), and with uneasiness among black informants about his unusual method. Looking back on his study Dollard notes the intractability of these research problems even in the late 1950s. "The significant, truly explanatory, data on the South is hidden behind great sets of defensive habits. Much of the relevant material can appear only in intimate relations where fear is reduced. The relation of friendship is such a one; the psychoanalytic relation, another. Where friendships must be formed or patients acquired in order to sample adequately, the difficulties are grave indeed. Not every person can be a friend. One cannot find people willing to accept the psychoanalytic condition of free association by routine picking from the city directory" (CC, viii). Nevertheless, as he outlined his research method in 1937, the formative influence of Dollard's psychoanalytic training was plain: "People may not tell [the researcher] directly what he wants to know, perhaps may not know how to, and they will certainly not be able to give him a theory of their culture. What they will do is illustrate it for him, act it out, and in the best case be their true selves before his eyes" (CC, 19). Dollard credits his reluctance to question his informants aggressively with the fact that their biases were aroused only minimally. Hence the material is "all set in a natural context, it is implicative, it points before and after and has in every case a concrete setting" (CC, 19).

As for his own biases, Dollard cites the psychoanalytic transference which he terms "mediation" or "reflection" on the inner meaning of one's field experience and contacts with informants. Such uncensored reactions are often clues to understanding his own and others' behavior. Learning about the community therefore meant learning about himself, and accordingly Dollard notes at the opening of *Caste and Class* that he will use the pronoun "I," though his reasons seem paradoxical: "It will show the researcher as separated from his data and it will give the reader a more vivid sense of the research experience" (*CC*, 2n). The technique makes sense to Dollard because it represents in fieldwork or participant observation the clinical situation of psychoanalysis where the two subjects of interest move together through the process of reconstruction and inquiry while they organize and articulate the differences between their psychological lives.

Yet the psychoanalytic method, Dollard admits, had to be adapted to local circumstances. The nine blacks who offered their life histories to Dollard (among more than two hundred informants) did so, he asserts, because they had hopes of gaining insight into their own personalities and because they became convinced that Dollard's research would ultimately contribute to better public understanding of their circumstances and hence their improvement. He had no white life histories of comparable detail, a fact that troubled him somewhat more than the small black sample. For Dollard's confidence in the life history technique carried out with psychoanalytic tools convinced him that "in the field of mores and collective life any person is a good sample of his culture. In every life history of a Negro will be found the dilemmas typical of his caste and class position. It is exactly the function of any culture to pattern its objects characteristically and to leave on every single individual the mark of the mores" (*CC*, 26). No plainer statement of the lesson of Sapir's seminar could be cited. At the same time the dangers of the "abstract typical" are overcome, he assumed, in his own form of intimate social research. Yet Dollard includes his psychoanalytic training as one of the biases he brought to his work (the others are his status as a Yankee on "the old northern errand" and as a middle-class, academic social scientist). He notes again that the analyst is concerned mainly with individual meaning. That is one part of Dollard's own project. The other is to unearth these meanings through personal encounters shaped by psychoanalytic technique. As an analyst he was "trained to watch for the reservations with which people carry out formally defined social actions, the repression required by social conformity, and in general to see behind the surface of a smooth social facade, the often unknown and usually unacknowledged emotional forces which drive and support social action" (*CC*, 38).

In *Caste and Class,* therefore, Dollard generally eschews formal psychoanalytic interpretation. Discussions of the economic, social, and prestige gains of the white middle class, of caste patterning of education, politics, and religion, and of aggression among blacks and whites rarely rely on psychoanalytic diction. Freudian theory is decidedly in the background. There are occasional dream analyses, and Dollard does invoke the Oedipus complex to explain elements of white aggression. He also suggests "libido outflow" as a source of the ease in some black personal relations. However, his clear restraint makes the discussion of complex and volatile topics accessible as well as psychologically credible. The chapter on "The Defensive Beliefs of the White Caste," for instance, begins with the assertion that "the function of defensive beliefs is to make the actions of white caste members toward negroes seem expedient and in line with current ideals; if this cannot be done satisfactorily, then at least these acts can be made to seem inevitable" (*CC*, 364). Psychoanalytic reasons lie behind the suggestions of expediency and inevitability, but Dollard's explanations stay close to the social and historical circumstances of Indianola culture and its role in the making of personality. Moreover, Dollard was concerned about both reductionism in psychoanalytic interpretations and the meaning of point of view. He advised the open study of incidents since they "tend to have leading lines to all major social configurations; what varies is the standpoint of the observer and classifier who moves in cautious circles around the complex event" (*CC*, 369).

The Limits of Social Learning

Neither the scope, in subject or method, of *Caste and Class,* nor the social ideals it embodied, made Dollard very confident about its reception or durability.[15] He saw himself as the practitioner of an evolving method, reliant on the complementary (but sometimes contradictory) settings of the psychological laboratory and the living community. Another chance to reconcile the two came in *Children of Bondage* (1940), the study of child development in New Orleans and Natchez that he wrote with the anthropologist Allison Davis. Each contributed a prefatory note, and while Davis stresses the integration in their text of psychoanalytical and sociological understanding Dollard underlines their meliorative intentions. "We want to know what forces are at work in training a child to participate in social life and what variables operate when the attempt is made to re-socialize, that is, to alter the habits of adults." Accordingly, *Children of Bondage* is aimed at helping Americans (blacks *and* whites Dollard insists) "to assume conscious control of their society's development."[16]

By titling the book's theoretical chapter "The Mystery of Personality" Davis and Dollard (the latter was, I think, the principle, even perhaps the sole author) offer a sign of how ambivalent they were about the resolute positivism of Hull and his other experimentalist colleagues at Yale. While they had indeed absorbed on their terms the Freudian program for the study of childhood, Dollard was never satisfied with their approach. Their preoccupation with the drives, aggression, sublimation, and other Freudian essentials needed to emerge from the experimental settings of the Institute of Human Relations and into the social settings that helped to shape personality and behavior. While Dollard was in the South his sometime Yale colleague Erikson was undertaking a series of psychoanalytic and ethnographic studies that would yield the definitive, mid-century study of the child in society. And psychiatrist Robert Coles, Erikson's student and biographer, later made the lives of southern (and then northern and other) children part of the progressive racial and social climate of the 1960s and 1970s. Both have acknowledged debts to Dollard's point of view, which was like their's of a very different kind than that of the psychoanalytic community allied to medicine. Moreover, Dollard's Freudianism (however modified), fieldwork among the black and poor, and case-study methods with their documentary overtones helped to free developmental psychology and the study of children from the "scientism" of the academic laboratory.

Yet true to his search for a comprehensive method Dollard was only a skeptical behaviorist. "Let no one out of vanity despise what we have discovered about human learning from the rat," he says (*CB*, 5) just before he announces his dedication to Freud in the study of childhood. He thought that psychoanalysts and behaviorists could be brought together via mutual recognition of their interest in different elements of the same research problem, even the demanding one of the developmental crises of black children in the segregated South. "Where behaviorists saw the problem box, the action sequence and the bar, Freud saw the hungry rat and the food pellet." Psychoanalysis, he adds, "gives vitality and body to our conception of behavior" (*CB*, 9). The problem, in his view, is the presentation of essential Freudian ideas in behaviorist terms, the mingling of Freud's emphasis on origins understood as the universal dynamics of early childhood, and the social anthropologist's interest in origins to signify the role of local institutions in personality formation. Indeed, "Culture and Personality" once more.

But the problem Davis and Dollard pursued was not one that could, I think, be solved within the limits of a study like *Children of Bondage,* which despite its self-conscious Freudianism begins with a behaviorist premise: "Social learning takes place only where there is a dilemma. People must be in some kind of squeeze to learn; no squeeze, no learning" (*CB*, 4-5). The "squeeze" that Dollard and Davis studied was "status controls" across a cross section of black adolescents, a few from each of three social classes. As Dollard admits regretfully, the children were interviewed by hastily trained assistants.

The opening of the very first case suggests how the "mystery of personality" vied with behaviorist habits in the minds of the authors: "Julia Wilson is one of those individuals who seems to have an insatiable claim against life. Driven by strange and unpredictable animosities and by equally mysterious and uncontrollable fears, these individuals are the children of wrath and self-love" (*CB*, 23). Dollard and Davis conclude, in this and the seven other cases they present, that it is not only origins, in the Freudian sense again, that count in the personality development of the child, but class or caste as well. And even as they moved toward identification of developmental psychopathology, and in a few cases survival and even apparent hardiness, as historical and social phenomena, they retained the biologism of the laboratory and the ahistorical side of psychoanalysis (the Freud who was ready to generalize across time and cultures). Hence, despite the fact that their study of black children emerged from a national project aimed at consolidating opinion on the priority of race and class in development, Davis and Dollard assert that their young subjects were not "culturally patterned" in the manner of youth in homogenous primitive societies (or so at least as the latter were often presented by social anthropologists at the time). "It is simply held," they say instead, "that [the adolescents they studied] reveal the interplay of personality formation between those factors which arise from the general family, age, and sex controls, and those which are systematically reinforced by the class or caste environment" (*CB*, 16).

Consequently, what *Children of Bondage* demonstrated was that social learning could not account by itself for the mysteries of personality. Without taking social learning theory out into the field, into society itself and indeed into the "fields" of ethnography and psychoanalysis, social learning could never supply the genuinely integrated approach its adherents hoped for. Those who turned out to be most successful in this endeavor, like Erikson and Coles, approached the problem from psychoanalysis and psychiatry without Dollard's commitment to experimental methods. In effect Dollard had two hurdles to overcome or two complex projects of methodological integration: of Freudian psychoanalysis with the behavioral models he was loyal to and, within his pyschoanalytic interests, of the methods of observation and discourse that were emerging in child psychoanalysis in the 1930s and 1940s. Preoccupied with the first of these he ignored the second (despite his relations with Erikson) and that is one reason, I think, why his work has not turned out to be as durable as it might have been. To be sure, in the history of the study of child development psychoanalysis has been admitted at times only grudgingly, but Erikson's influence at least illustrates the lines of scholarly progress and fateful choice made by his colleague Dollard.[17]

Conclusion: Frontiers of Social Science

In the preface to *Caste and Class* Dollard said of that book what he might have said also of his collaboration with Davis: "[It is] part of the exploratory work of science, of the fumbling and fiddling out of which more authoritative descriptions of reality will emerge" (*CC*, viii). This sounds as if he anticipated that his work would someday be the subject of a chapter in a study of criteria for the uses of psychoanalysis in the social sciences. Such criteria, like Dollard's for the life history, would stress the capacity of psychoanalysis to illuminate the myriad interests associated with "culture and personality." They would be included, in other words, in Abram Kardiner's prescription in the mid-1940s for a psychology suitable to the needs of sociology. It must, he said, be "holistic. . . . It must be able to follow change and motion. . . . It must be dynamic. . . . It must be a genetic psychology. . . . It must be able to account for complex motivations and the adaptive role of fantasy (and) to recognize the influence of various drives . . . and it must be able to analyze values, ideals, and religion for these are the currency of the social life of man."[18] That is only a partial list, but Kardiner still proposes psychoanalysis as the only all-purpose psychology available. He stops short of promising a social transformation based on psychoanalysis, but then Freud himself was skeptical about the future of social psychology: "What would be the use of the most correct analysis of social neuroses," he asked in *Civilization and its Discontents* (1930), "since no one possesses authority to impose such a therapy upon the group."[19]

Nonetheless, generous ideas of the applicability of psychoanalysis animated scholars and clinicians during the middle of this century when Freudian and other versions of psychoanalysis achieved wide scholarly and popular recognition. It was the period that proved the truth of W. H. Auden's poetic tribute, "In Memory of Sigmund Freud": "To us he is no more a person/Now but a whole climate of opinion." The past two decades have brought a predictable backlash.[20] Yet even some of today's strongest advocates of psychoanalysis—many of whom favor Jacques Lacan and the French style—see its primary uses in the study of the structure of thinking and language rather than in the behavioral sciences (not to mention plainspoken literary criticism and historical narrative), where understanding the social sources and meanings of individual psychology is the goal.

Near the end of his career Freud himself showed signs of ambivalence about the case to be made for psychoanalysis as a new science modeled on the older ones. Especially in its applied forms, he proposed, serious methodological problems were likely, especially gaps in evidence and seemingly unstructured inferences. The problem for practitioners, as well as for lay readers and scholars in other fields, was that in a very short time psychoanalysis had assumed the burden of its own history and renown which suggested comparisons with other fields. Hence when Freud resumed his *Introductory Lectures on Psychoanalysis* in 1932 (the original set had appeared fifteen years before) he included this rueful defense of his efforts:

> In no other field of scientific work would it be necessary to boast of such modest intentions. They are universally regarded as self-evident; the public expects nothing else. No reader of an account of astronomy will feel disappointed and contemptuous of the science if he is shown the frontiers at which our knowledge of the universe melts into haziness. Only in psychology is it otherwise. There mankind's constitutional unfitness for scientific research comes fully into the open. What people seem to demand of psychology is not progress in knowledge, but satisfaction of some sort; every unsolved problem, every admitted uncertainty is made a reproach against it."[21]

Freud devoted the last of the *Lectures* to the reasons for subordinating the development of a unique self-justifying psychoanalytic Weltanschauung to the general aims and habits of scholarship in the sciences and the humanities.

Dollard's psychoanalytic social science does not confront the technical problems now often regarded as crucial to psychoanalytic interpretation, like the reliability of language and narrative in the patient's life history or problems in the sociology of knowledge related to the analysts' case-study techniques.[22] Nor did Dollard ever employ, beyond his ethnographic ventures, the techniques figures like Erikson and then Coles came to employ: the study of children's play and drawings. Yet what Dollard gives up in relation to post-Freudian psychoanalysis, in the domains of adult and child therapies, he gains with regard to psychoanalytic ideology. For he never fully absorbed what Phillip Rieff calls the "analytic attitude." Rieff finds psychoanalysts and the scholars they influence "charter members of the Negative Community," instinctive opponents of authority and tradition. "Psychoanalysis," he says, "is yet another method of learning how to endure the loneliness produced by culture."[23] Though Dollard maintained his interest in behaviorism and learning theory throughout his career, he believed in the meliorative powers of depth psychology, especially as a resource in strengthening our understanding of life in society, and hence its capacity to fortify "culture and personality" as facts and as a subject.[24] No less bewildered by Freud than Kenneth Burke perhaps, he made of his encounter with psychoanalysis a novel and influential encounter with the possibilities of social science.

Notes

1. Robert S. Lynd, *Knowledge for What? The Place of Social Science in American Culture* (Princeton, NJ: Princeton University Press, 1940), 118; ix.
2. Ibid., 8.
3. Kenneth Burke, *The Philosophy of Literary Form* (Baton Rouge: Louisiana State University Press, 1941), 221.
4. Edward Shils, "Tradition, Ecology and Institution in the History of Sociology," *Daedalus* 99 (Fall 1970): 805. See also: Peter Berger, "Toward a Sociological Understanding of Psychoanalysis," *Social Research* 32 (Spring 1965): 26–41; Robert J. Wallerstein and Neil J. Smelser, "Psychoanalysis and Sociology: Articulations and Applications," *International Journal of Psychoanalysis* 50 (1969): 693–710; Fred Weinstein and Gerald M. Platt, *Psychoanalytic Sociology: An Essay on the Interpretation of Historical Data and the Phenomenon of Collective Behavior* (Baltimore: Johns Hopkins University Press, 1973); Fred Weinstein, "The Sociological Endeavor and Psychoanalytic Thought," *American Quarterly* 28 (1976): 343–59.
5. Burke, *Philosophy,* 411; 409. Lynd himself appears to have arrived at a similar position. He says in *Knowledge for What?:* "Psychology is unique among the social sciences in that, its announced field being the study of individuals, it has not been tempted as have its fellows to overlook individual differences and to concentrate upon derivative generalizations of the by-and-large-and-other-things-being-equal sort. With its field thus fortunately concentrated on the central powerhouse of culture, individuals, it is in the strategic position of having the other social sciences turn increasingly to it for the solution of realistic problems" (160).
6. Edward Sapir, *Culture, Language and Personality: Selected Essays of Edward Sapir,* ed. David G. Mandelbaum (Berkeley: University of California Press, 1961), 200.
7. Ibid., 199–201.

8. See David Shakow and David Rapaport, "The Influence of Freud on American Psychology," *Psychological Issues* IV (1964): 135–42; J. G. Morawski, "Organizing Knowledge and Behavior at Yale's Institute of Human Relations," *ISIS* 77 (1986): 219–42.

9. Sapir, *Selected Essays*, 151.

10. John Dollard, *Caste and Class in a Southern Town*, 3d ed. (New York: Anchor Books, 1957), vii. Future references are incorporated into the text with the abbreviation *CC*.

11. Quoted by A. F. Davies, "Criteria for the Political Life History," *Historical Studies* 13 (October 1967): 76.

12. John Dollard, *Criteria for the Life History* (New Haven: Yale University Press, 1935), 7. Future references are incorporated into the text with the abbreviation *LH*.

13. My paraphrase relies on Davies, "Criteria," 78–9.

14. Erikson's essay appears in *Life History and the Historical Moment* (New York: Norton, 1975), 113–68. Erikson's approach and others' are the subject of William M. Runyan, *Life Histories and Psychobiography: Explorations in Theory and Method* (New York: Oxford University Press, 1982).

15. The book was well received by Dollard's colleagues (Margaret Mead for example) with the exception of a long review featuring hostile treatment of Freudianism in social research, especially in the South: "He packed these concepts into his research kit and proceeded to use them on the perceptual material, with the confidence one would expect of a plumber using pipe wrenches. And the results are about as difficult to appraise, from the point of view of scientific methodology, as if Mr. Dollard had himself used pipe wrenches" (Lyle H. Lanier, "Mr. Dollard and Scientific Method," *Southern Review* 3 [1938]: 665–6).

16. Allison Davis and John Dollard, *Children of Bondage: The Personality Development of Negro Youth in the Urban South* (New York: Harper and Row, 1964), vi. Subsequent references are incorporated into the text with the abbreviation *CB*.

17. Psychoanalysis merits only a very brief section in the otherwise comprehensive essay that appears in the most widely used reference work on child development: see Robert Cairns, "The Emergence of Developmental Psychology," in *Handbook of Child Psychology,* ed. Paul H. Mussen, vol. 1 (New York: Wiley, 1983). It plays a more prominent role in Robert Sears, "Your Ancients Revisited: A History of Child Development," in *Review of Child Development Research,* ed. E. M. Hetherington, vol. 5 (Chicago: University of Chicago Press, 1975) and David Elkind, "Child Development Research," *A Century of Psychology as a Science,* ed. Sigmund Koch and David E. Leary, (New York: McGraw-Hill, 1985), 472–88.

18. Abram Kardiner, *The Psychological Frontiers of Society* (1945; reprint New York: Columbia University Press, 1963), 21–2.
19. Sigmund Freud, *Civilization and its Discontents,* trans. and ed. James Strachey (New York: Norton, 1961), 91.
20. The most comprehensive recent example is Adolph Grünbaum, *The Foundations of Psychoanalysis: A Philosophical Critique* (Berkeley: University of California Press, 1984). In the form and substance of his study, Grünbaum grants more to psychoanalysis than other critics. A favorable view of Freudian tradition can be found in Steven Marcus, *Freud and the Culture of Psychoanalysis* (Winchester, MA: Unwin, 1984).
21. Sigmund Freud, *New Introductory Lectures on Psychanalysis,* trans. and ed. James Strachey (New York: Norton, 1964), 6.
22. Roy Schafer, for instance, claims that "the primary narrative problem of the analyst is not how to tell a narrative chronological life history; rather it is how to tell the several histories of each analysis" ("Narrative in the Psychoanalytic Dialogue," in *On Narrative,* ed. W. J. T. Mitchell [Chicago: University of Chicago Press, 1981], 49). A useful study of this theme is Donald P. Spence, *Narrative Truth and Historical Truth: Meaning and Interpretation in Psychoanalysis* (New York: Norton, 1982).
23. Phillip Rieff, *The Triumph of the Therapeutic: The Uses of Faith After Freud* (New York: Harper and Row Torchbooks, 1968), 32.
24. Dollard's best-known later work, written with Neal E. Miller, is the ambitious *Personality and Psychotherapy: An Analysis in Terms of Learning, Thinking and Culture* (New York: McGraw-Hill, 1950). Dollard still claimed an interest in psychoanalysis but not now without the "rigors of the natural science laboratory" in demonstrating the relations of individual neuroses and the "facts of culture" (3).

3

Erik H. Erikson on America:
Childhood and Society
and National Identity

Psychoanalysts are not known for their humor, but Erik H. Erikson sometimes seeks a laugh in order to make a point. He tells, for instance, of encountering an elderly chassidic Jew in the streets of Jerusalem who asked simply, "An American?" Erikson nodded "yes" and his questioner replied with sympathy, *"We* know where we are and *here* we stay."[1] Questions of place and identity, immigration and roots have dominated Erikson's work since he arrived in America from Vienna over four decades ago. In books and essays devoted equally to clinical observations and to theory, American identity has been to Erikson a motivating idea and psychological example. His influential biographies of Luther and Gandhi, and briefer studies of Shaw, Hitler, and Gorky reflect the study of national identity as it appeared in his early work on America. And *Dimensions of a New Identity* (1973) is dedicated to the role of Jefferson in formulating a distinctly American style of politics and learning.

The choice of American themes was perhaps inevitable for a psychoanalyst with Erikson's clinical style and theoretical disposition, not to mention his flight with many other psychoanalysts from European capitals threatened by Nazism. His own awareness of the adaptation of his work to a new setting became in turn a central scholarly theme. His and other psychoanalysts' relation to Freudian tradition and his enthusiastic acceptance of American

41

clinical opportunities as well as the distinctive features of our regional and national cultures are important aspects of Erikson's own intellectual biography. *Childhood and Society* is the complex realization of these interests, the most radical and inclusive example of the psychoanalytic style for which Erikson is justly admired.

The Single Endeavor in America

It is typical of psychoanalysts, whatever their clinical preferences, to state the relation of their work to Freud's. And loyalty to the Freudian canon, of course, is a persistent issue in psychoanalytic writing. In his own comments on Freud, Erikson has concentrated less on the interpretation of texts than on Freud's philosophical and epistemological orientation. While he writes and treats patients firmly within the Freudian tradition—he was trained by Anna Freud and other distinguished second generation psychoanalysts—Erikson is frank in recognizing some weaknesses in the original structure of psychoanalytic thought.

According to Erikson, Freud and his first colleagues in psychoanalysis focused on "a single endeavor: introspective honesty in the service of self enlightenment."[2] Emphasis on the drives, defenses, and neuroses, however, meant neglect of those aspects of the mind which synthesize a functional style of behavior consistent with the traditions and expectations of particular cultures. As essentially students of the id rather than the ego, early psychoanalysts reflected Freud's disposition to clarify and classify the etiology of sexual and other neuroses, and to make society more hospitable to those who suffered from them. Freud saw the social, economic, and political environment of his patients as just that, a setting in which the instincts developed their own relation to the other parts of the mind. "The alliance of the superego with a high sense of cultural identity," Erikson says, "remained neglected: ways by which a given environment permits and cultivates self-abandonment in forms of passion or reason, ferocity or reserve, piety or skepticism, bawdiness or propriety, gracefulness or sternness, charity or pride, shrewdness or fair play" (*CS*, 282). Within the shelter of Viennese intellectual life, the earliest psychoanalysts, in their preoccupation with the origins of adult disorder in childhood events, underestimated a complementary or allied dependency of the structure of mental life on the character of the society in which it unfolds.

Erikson's inclusive conception of cultural development required still another addition to traditional psychoanalytic theory. Freudian concentration on the earliest stages of life had denied to both theoretical and clinical work the advantages of insight into the ways in which later stages display their developmental tasks, including the assumption or reflection of particular domestic, social, occupational, and intellectual initiatives. Emphasis on potentially debilitating aspects of the inner lives of infants and young children concealed from early psychoanalysts the equally powerful potential for society to meliorate the difficulties of youth in collective habits of family and social organization. Erikson writes:

> Psychoanalysis has consistently described the vicissitudes of instincts and of the ego only up to adolescence, at which time rational gentility was expected to absorb infantile fixations and irrational conflicts or to admit them to repeat performances under manifold disguises. The main recurrent themes thus concerned the shadow of frustration which falls from childhood on the individual's later life and on his society. [I] suggest that to understand either childhood or society, we must expand our scope to include the study of the way in which societies lighten the inescapable conflicts of childhood with a promise of some security, identity and integrity. In thus reinforcing the values under which the ego exists, societies create the only condition under which human growth is possible. (*CS*, 277)

Attention to adolescence and succeeding stages, Erikson claims, not only completes our understanding of individual development but reveals how each generation, in its movement through adolescence and adulthood, revitalizes the very institutions that shape its growth.

Recognizing that his point of view entails a major shift in theoretical and clinical emphasis, Erikson proposes its condensation into a formula: "The patient of today suffers most under the problem of what he should believe in and who he should—or indeed might—be or become; while the patient of early psychoanalysis suffered most under inhibitions which prevented him from being what and who he thought he knew he was" (*CS*, 279). He claims that the study of identity is therefore especially timely, a contemporary counterpart of the Freudian study of sexuality. Yet Erikson by no means proposes that his efforts represent progress in psychoanalytic thought. His version of psychoanalysis, like Freud's, is expressive of *his* time and place as well as an account of timeless human qualities. Progress in psychoanalysis, as in other disciplines, is a function of collaboration and of recognition of fundamental continuities in intention and technique despite differences in orientation and results.

> Historical relativity in the development of a field . . . does not seem to preclude consistency of ground plan and continued closeness to observable fact. Freud's findings regarding the sexual etiology of the neurotic part of a mental disturbance are as true for our patients as they were for his; while the burden of identity loss which stands out in our consideration probably burdened Freud's patients as well as ours, as reinterpretations would show. Different periods thus permit us to see in temporary exaggeration different aspects of essentially inseparable parts of personality. (*CS,* 283)

Erikson's interest in identity is therefore a response to the historical imperatives of his time and to the place he chose in which to develop a clinical method.

Periodically throughout his career Erikson has commented on Freud's achievement, the fate of his legacy among succeeding analysts, especially those in the United States.[3] All of the citations above, however, come from a single source, a forceful statement of the meaning and limits of Freudian tradition. It is the compact preface to Erikson's well-known "Reflections on the American Identity" which is itself the first section in a comparative study of national identity in his first and still most important book, *Childhood and Society.*

By its position in the text the statement on psychoanalytic tradition suggests that Erikson's strategy for supplementing Freud's orientation is the analysis of national character. America is the touchstone against which chapters on Germany and Russia are presented, not because of the natural supremacy of American values, but because it is the purpose of *Childhood and Society,* beyond presenting the interaction of the two elements of its title, to locate the American identity in a post-World War II world. We will never know if Erikson, an immigrant to America in 1933, would have written the same book had he remained in Europe or emigrated to another country. He thought, for a time, of settling in Denmark. As a work of psychoanalytical theory of course *Childhood and Society* proposes—by no means to the satisfaction of all psychologists and psychoanalysts—a universal series of developmental formulae. In its clinical evidence, however, *Childhood and Society* is distinctly American, incorporating, in and out of the chapters on American identity, the observations of a new American on the traditions, cultural imperatives, and opportunities now likely to become a part of his own identity. Devoting an introductory section to Freud, therefore, is Erikson's way of acknowledging the psychoanalytical point of view he left behind and the terms in which his own contribution to psychoanalysis needs to be understood. Freud, he reminds us, was largely aloof from the world revolutions of the nineteenth and twentieth centuries and from the development of the industrial culture of America. In Freud's view, according to Erikson, "any organized group was a latent mob and a potential enemy to the spirit of individuation and reason" (*CS,* 281). Erikson accepts America as a subject of study, most obviously, but also as a nation whose collective struggle for identity and whose typical citizens display the representative themes of modern society.

Erikson saw these themes in a personal way. Addressing the plight of emigrants and refugees nearly three decades after his own emigration, he reviewed the special burdens of the *Vertrieben,* those who have been driven from their homelands. Their plain need to identify with a national culture is revealed in symptoms that suggest a loss in mastery as well as of the nourishment of community life. Hence initiative, as well as wholeness, central attributes of identity according to Erikson, require participation in a national culture in which one feels at home. The tendency of early psychoanalysts to consider identity formation as a one-way process, in which individuals identify themselves with others, limited psychoanalytic recognition of those processes of identity formation that represent elements provided by national cultures. Societies, says Erikson, "confirm the individual in all kinds of ideological frameworks and assign roles and tasks to him in which he can recognize himself and feel recognized."[4] Though when he emigrated to America he was well beyond the stage when decisive events in identity formation take place, Erikson himself had to incorporate into the appropriate tasks of middle age the opportunities for adopting a new national identity.

Indeed, Erikson admits in his only autobiographical essay that his initial use of the terms "identity" and "identity crisis" seemed to emerge naturally from his experience of emigration and Americanization.[5] In *Childhood and Society,* however, Erikson also admitted the "deep hesitation" with which he approached the study of American identity. One reason was the expansion of scholarship on national character that followed World War II; another was the "precariousness" of the subject, especially with respect to a complex society like the United States. "It is impossible (except in the form of fiction)," Erikson says, "to write *in* America *about* America *for* Americans." Some detachment is necessary. Lifelong citizens can travel and return with the required perspective, but immigrants and visitors have no special advantages. It is inevitably the very processes of Americanization which dominate the observations of all writers on the American identity. An enthusiastic traveler as a youth and young adult, he himself settled in America with gratitude and admiration, but also with some detachment. "In the end," Erikson says, "you always write about the way it feels to arrive or leave, to change or to get settled" (*CS,* 283).

Yet looking back on his career two decades after the initial publication of *Childhood and Society,* Erikson could speak with considerably more confidence about the relation of American themes to the clinical responsibilities and theoretical orientation of an emigré psychoanalyst like himself:

> In the Roosevelt era, we immigrants could tell ourselves that America was once more helping to save the Atlantic world from tyranny; and were we not hard at work as members of a healing profession which—beyond the living standards it accustomed us to—contributed to a transforming enlightenment apt to diminish both the inner and outer oppression of mankind? What now demanded to be conceptualized, however, called for a whole new orientation which fused a new world image (and, in fact, a New World image) with traditional theoretical assumptions.[6]

Such fusion is one of the goals of *Childhood and Society,* as Erikson's attention to orthodox Freudian theory at a critical place in the text suggests. Further, with the advantage of hindsight

Erikson is even more deeply convinced that in choosing a particular stage of life for analysis in *Childhood and Society* and later books and essays he had located a distinctive feature of American life in relation to universal themes of human development. "If something like an identity crisis gradually appeared to be a normative problem in adolescence and youth, there also seemed to be enough of an adolescent in every American to suggest that in his country's history fate had chosen to highlight identity questions together with a strangely adolescent style of adulthood—that is, one remaining expansively open for new roles and stances—in what at the time was called a 'national character.' "[7] As a work of fusion, and an attempt to unify psychological and social themes and historical and psychoanalytical methods, *Childhood and Society* is Erikson's effort to enhance Freudian theory, to illustrate the applicability of American themes to national cultures, and to fortify his own identification with American society.

Childhood and Society: Mothers, Autocrats, and Adolescents

Like other analysts of the national character, Erikson proposes the organization of psychological traits into a series of polarities. Recognizing that it is a commonplace indeed to suggest that each American trait has its equally characteristic opposite, Erikson nonetheless proposes that a national identity is "derived from the ways in which history has, as it were, counterpointed certain opposite potentialities; the way in which it lifts this counterpoint to a unique style of civilization or lets it disintegrate into mere contradiction" (*CS,* 285). In America, moreover, the peculiarly dynamic quality of the polarities means for its citizens, in contrast to the other older industrialized nations, abrupt changes and extreme contrast time and again during individual lifetimes.

Erikson's own catalogue of American polarities is in effect a summary of many familiar previous efforts to distill an American character.[8] According to him, Americans face these choices and others in establishing and maintaining their own and shared identities: "Open roads of immigration and jealous islands of tradition; outgoing internationalism and defiant isolationism; boisterous competition and self effacing cooperation" (*CS,* 285). As each American finds an appropriate combination of such attitudes he or she also builds an ego identity from a synthesis of these additional dynamic polarities: movement vs. stasis, individuation vs. standardization, competition vs. cooperation, piety vs. freethinking, responsibility vs. cynicism. Like other cultures America gains its special flavor from the interplay of contrasts.

The polarities can be invigorating, as behavioral choices or as subjects of study, but they usually pose, Erikson claims, a clinical problem for which we have had an habitual if unappealing solution. For rigid adherence to one attribute or another includes an implied defense against its opposite which is feared but also sometimes desired. The defense, in turn, forces Americans to live with two sets of truths: "a set of religious principles or religiously pronounced political principles of a highly puritan quality, and a set of shifting slogans which indicate what, at a given time, one may get away with on the basis of not more than a hunch, a mood, or a notion" (*CS*, 286). The coordination of such defenses with experiments in daily living, adaptations to the particulars of time and place and stage of life, is one of the tasks of identity formation. And societies themselves express in their unique national identities the results of polar organization, since "a living culture has its own balances which make it durable and bearable to a majority of its members" (*CS*, 292). Balance and durability can also be said to be the goals of each of the eight stages in human development Erikson outlines in *Childhood and Society*.

In this pathmaking theory Erikson proposes that each life gradually but inevitably organizes itself epigenetically around a series of complementary needs and virtues. He first suggested the stages through adolescence and then, a few years prior to the publication of *Childhood and Society,* extended the groundplan through the rest of the life cycle. Its inclusiveness is certainly one reason for its appeal. Yet some clinicians (as well as scholars in other fields) have declared their skepticism *because* epigenesis appears to explain too much or on the grounds that in the theory clinical or social goals appear at times to dominate empirical evidence. The eight stages may appear to be prescribed attributes. Erikson himself, however, has warned against taking the stages as a definitive "inventory," a standard against which to judge actual lives. "I only speak of a developing capacity to perceive and to abide by values established by a particular living system."[9]

In the case of America the system lends itself to Erikson's bipolar style of thought, his habit of expressing through contrasting imagery the structure of psychological, social, and historical phenomena. Oddly enough, however, in *Childhood and Society* Erikson's presentation of the bipolar American character has three elements. First *Mom,* then an attitude toward work represented by the legend of John Henry, and finally the influence on adolescence of the machine, organizational routine, and *bossism* are chosen to illustrate American efforts to build a satisfying identity.

> [Mom] is unquestioned authority in domestic mores and morals yet is vain in her appearance and infantile in her emotions. She is demanding yet hypochondriacal, puritanical yet exhibitionist, loyal to tradition yet fearful of aging. Above all she [artificially maintains] the discontinuity between the child's and the adult's status without endowing this differentiation with the higher meaning emanating from superior example. Mom is the victor and the victim. (*CS,* 290)

Belief that excessive concern about her role as mother is her prime potential fault has produced the opposite of what she wants. She is feared, mistrusted and blamed, likely to feel that her life was a waste. Erikson is unsparing in characterizing this American type, "a woman in whose life cycle remnants of infantility join advanced senility to crowd out the middle range of mature womanhood, which thus becomes self absorbed and stagnant" (*CS,* 290).

True to his method, Erikson finds the formative components of *Mom* in the psychological history of American culture; she embodies a timely response to the demands of the newly settled continent. "It was up to the American woman to evolve one common tradition, on the basis of many imported traditions, and to base on it the education of her children and the style of her home life . . . it was up to her to establish new habits of sedentary life on a continent originally populated by men who in their countries of origin, for one reason or another had not wanted to be fenced in" (*CS,* 292). In order to do so, American mothers developed methods of child rearing appropriate to the demands of continuous settlement and resettlement along the frontier and to the requirements of moral and domestic orthodoxy known as Puritanism.

The result of the adaptation was the debilitation of mothers and sons alike. Mothers needed to avoid weakening potential frontiersmen with excessive protective maternalism. In struggling to be fair (and to get beyond the limits of his understanding of the psychology of women) Erikson terms this rejective attitude a "modern fault based on a historic virtue." Well suited to its time and circumstances, such deliberate rejection enabled sons to fit into the ceaseless movement and competitiveness of American life. Similarly, and inevitably, mothers were forced to convey the essential tenets of puritanism as a check on the aggressively secular influences of industrialization and urbanization. In doing so, Erikson says, they introduced into the tasks of pregnancy, childbirth, nursing, and childrearing the frigid point of view of puritanism. And "men were born who failed to learn from their mothers to love the goodness of sensuality before they learned to hate its sinful uses. Instead of hating sin, they learned to mistrust life. Many became puritans without faith or zest" (*CS,* 293). Erikson has little to say about American daughters except in so far as they fulfill their potential as willing American mothers. Since men were largely identified with the frontier ethos of exploration and conquest, sons always appear ready to take up an identity built on necessary skills and attitudes.

To illustrate one central adaptive trait, Erikson turns to the legend of John Henry as the second representative image of the American identity, an occupational model who is determined to master the rigors of the frontier and then the new industrial technology. Americans needed to marshal their strength and independence in order to confront two "autocrats": the continent and the machine. Mastery of the first yields frontier boosterism, aggressive independence nurtured by the unique circumstances and structure of American child-rearing patterns, especially in the historically determined and specialized role of Mom. The second autocrat, the machine and industrial culture, also requires a particular approach to parental tasks. Children and adolescents must be taught the virtues of regularity and routine, willing adaptation to the needs of machine technology and large organizations.

Therefore, in his summary of adolescence, the third of the three central images of the American identity, Erikson poses the struggle between critical developmental tasks and social needs. His subject is the typical male child in America:

> In his early childhood he was faced with a training which tended to make him machinelike and clocklike. Thus standardized, he found chances, in his later childhood, to develop autonomy, initiative and industry, with the implied promise that decency in human relations, skills in technical details, and knowledge of facts would permit him freedom of choice in his pursuits, that the identity of free choice would balance his self-coercion. As an adolescent and man, however, he finds himself confronted with superior machines, complicated, incomprehensible, and impersonally dictatorial in their power to standardize his pursuits and tastes. (*CS*, 323)

In family life childhood is understood to have a social meaning in the need to prepare adolescents to establish their identities in light of the prevailing political and economic ideologies. As Erikson argued in a paper written just a few years before *Childhood and Society* and its elaboration of the eight ages theory, adolescents gain relief from their developmental burdens by discovering a self in context, by accepting the historical necessity which contributes to what they are. "The individual feels free when he learns to apply that which is given to that which must be done. Only thus can he derive ego strength (for his generation and the next) from the coincidence of this one and only life cycle with a particular segment of human history."[10] What must be done, of course, is only partly the work of the culture as it is expressed in a national identity. In America, Erikson claims, occupational choices are dominated by routine, standardization, and organization. Choosing domestic and occupational initiatives satisfying to the self, reflecting an ego in society but also in control, is thus the task of adolescence and the stages that follow it.

Erikson's reason for placing adolescence at the center of his analysis of the American character is a sign of his interest in gaining wider clinical recognition for this stage. "Adolescence is the age of the final establishment of a dominant positive ego identity. It is there that a future within reach becomes part of the conscious life plan" (*CS*, 306). In so characterizing adolescence, Erikson helped to redirect psychoanalytic interest in that stage from emphasis on physical changes and sexuality to questions of domestic, social, and occupational identity. In these matters, of course, parents play a critical role, helping the adolescent to translate the national identity into a workable format for individual growth. The balance between a nascent ego identity and social conventions is at stake in family life. "The more idiosyncratic this relationship and the less adequate the parent in reflecting the changing cultural prototypes and institutions, the deeper the conflict between ego identity and superego will be" (*CS*, 312).

In America, however, Erikson claims the adolescent is spared much of the potential difficulty in the process because of an "ingenious arrangement," the diffusion of the father ideal. Our "decaying paternalism" leaves a gap filled by "fraternal images" and by adolescent confidence in the power of youth in a rapidly changing society. In fact, Erikson says, "because of their greater affinity with the tempo and with the technological problems of the immediate future children are in a sense 'wiser' than their parents" (*CS*, 314). Overenthusiastic perhaps about the virtues of adolescence, Erikson also suggests that some of the energy of this stage is found in the belief that children may more nearly approach ideal types than did their parents.

Other features of American family life also fortify adolescence. Erikson finds an important analogy between the spirit of compromise in American politics and the balance of different interests within the family. He asks, "How does his home train [the adolescent] for democracy?" As Erikson's argument proceeds, it is clear that the question might also be reversed. Each system, political or domestic, is organized to prevent autocracy and inequality by producing people willing to bargain and adapt. And they make it improbable that the American adolescent will become what his peers in other large industrialized nations sometimes become, "uncompromising ideologists." The American system, therefore, as it is found in public and private life, is a "rocking sea of checks and balances in which uncompromising absolutes must drown." It also has a related danger, "that such absolutes may be drowned in all-around acceptable banalities, rather than in productive compromises." In the family especially, the spirit of compromise may mean that large areas of the "unacceptable" are displaced by "parallel daydreaming." Real issues then, are neglected, and mutual responsibilities denied which may "empty the pattern of majority concurrence of its original indignation, and thus of its dignity" (*CS*, 318). According to Erikson, the American family may be without conflict but also without the passion needed for important parts of adolescent identity to take shape.

In summarizing the situation of the American adolescent, Erikson supplements his typical evenhandedness with some impatience and irony.

> This American adolescent then, is faced, as are adolescents of all countries who have entered or are entering the machine age, with the question: freedom for what, and at what price? The American feels so rich in his opportunities for free expression that he often no longer knows what it is he is free from. Neither does he know where he is not free; he does not recognize his native autocrats when he sees them. He is too immediately occupied with being efficient and being decent.
>
> This adolescent will make an efficient and decent leader in a circumscribed job, a good manager or professional worker and a good officer, and will most enjoy his recreation with the boys in the organizations to which he belongs. As a specimen, he illustrates the fact that in war or in peace, the fruit of American education is to be found in a combination of native mechanical ability, managerial autonomy, personalized leadership, and unobtrusive tolerance. These young men are truly the backbone of the nation. (*CS*, 321)

The psychological economy of American organizations and institutions has produced in its "bosses" individuals convinced they are the "crown of democracy" but who are in fact the "ideal autocracy of irresponsibility." It is precisely this ethical deficit which is to Erikson the chief threat to young workers since it represents the worship of "functioning" at the expense of human values. Erikson is most bitter in his condemnation of those who manage the American corporate economy and the legislative bureaucracy. "That these men run themselves like machinery is a matter for the doctor, psychiatrist or undertaker. That they view the world and run people as machinery becomes a danger to man" (*CS*, 322). The power and danger of *bossism* is finally illustrated in a manner typical among World War II emigré writers to America, suggesting that certain national tendencies are allied to fascism and other forms of totalitarianism. The chapters in *Childhood and Society* that follow the one on America are certainly meant to reflect on the traits Erikson found harmful in American society.

In the case of Nazi Germany, the central conflict of adolescent development, a split between "precocious individualistic rebellion and disillusioned, obedient citizenship" meant persistent political immaturity. Culturally fragmented as a nation, reflecting and resenting the influence of the several cultures that surround it, Germany could not resist Hitler's fairy tales of unification, autonomy, and omnipotence. Whatever the defects in the frontier and industrial family systems in America they pale beside the "desparate paradoxes" in the German character as they appeared in Nazism.

In America an identity emerges from a selection among neuroses-producing but fundamentally ethical traits. Germany of the 1920s and 1930s, however, demonstrated the underside of the processes of identity formation. For "every person and every group has a limited inventory of historically determined spatial-temporal concepts, which determine the world image, the evil and ideal prototypes, and the unconscious life plan. These concepts dominate a nation's strivings and can lead to high distinction; but they also narrow a people's imagination and thus invite disaster" (*CS*, 345). Americans, in their tendency not only to reflect but also to transcend dominant national traits like conformity and competitiveness, compare favorably with the Germans and also the Russians. The latter, identified by Erikson as "our cold and dangerous adversaries," are in his view still struggling, like Americans albeit at a different stage and rate, to manage the energy released by industrialization, as well as the political rigidities entailed in consolidation of the 1917 Revolution. Perhaps reflecting post-World War II optimism (some would say naivete), Erikson finds in the Russian identity a form of "delayed protestantism"—sectarian, individualistic and industrial—remarkably like our own.

Avoiding war, therefore, will depend on the recognition of what mutually activates and binds national identities as well as on what inevitably makes them differ. By concentrating on youth and adolescence in his comparative study of American and other national identities, Erikson has illustrated the grounding of character in culture not as a formula for easy categorization and social forecasting but as a way of emphasizing that identity formation entails ideological and ethical choices crucial to the growth of individuals at critical stages of life and also to the future of nations.

While American adolescence, and its relation to the authority of routine and organization, or bossism, is an image of national character with international significance, so also are the American Indian tribes whose child-rearing customs are outlined in *Childhood and Society*. Pleased to capitalize on the opportunities offered by anthropologists Alfred Kroeber and Scudder Mekeel to add ethnographic evidence to his nascent theories of child development, Erikson spent several months of 1938 and 1939 among the Oglala Sioux on the Pine Ridge Reservation in South Dakota and among the Yurok of Northern California. He found them to be complete cultures, especially in their complex and purposeful styles of child rearing. Part of the dismal American story of exploited minorities, American Indians also demonstrated to Erikson the integration of psychological traits manifested in particular child-rearing patterns into a discernible group identity.

The durability of native American cultures, in fact, suggested to Erikson that seemingly primitive people can maintain an "elastic mastery" in psychological matters, often impossible in more sophisticated social systems. Speaking, for instance, of the ways in which the Sioux manage the early oral instincts of children and the maintenance of tribal ethical ideals like generosity and fortitude, Erikson offers this statement of the structure of a national character, American, Indian, or any other.

> We are speaking of goals and values and the energy put at their disposal by child-training systems. Such values persist because the cultural ethos continues to consider them "natural" and does not admit of alternatives. They persist because they have become an essential part of an individual's sense of identity, which he must preserve as a core of sanity and efficiency. But values do not persist unless they work, economically, psychologically, and spiritually; and I argue that to this end they must continue to be anchored, generation after generation, in early child training; while child training, to remain consistent, must be embedded in a system of continued economic and cultural synthesis. For it is a synthesis operating within a culture which increasingly tends to bring into close-knit thematic relationship and mutual amplification such matters as climate and anatomy, economy and psychology, society and child training. (*CS*, 138).

Mindful, however, of the responsibilities of clinical approaches to the disciplines of national character study, Erikson admits candidly, "How can we show this?" His answer is simply a summary of the structure and intentions of *Childhood and Society*. "Our proof must lie in the coherent meaning which we may be able to give to seemingly irrational data within one culture and to analogous problems in comparable cultures" (*CS*, 138). "Reflections on the American Identity," therefore, has a purpose all its own. Yet its meaning can also be found in its relation to other parts of the text, including lessons to be derived from the examination of the child-rearing practices of representative American Indian tribes, and from myths of childhood, adolescence, and national character associated with other nations.

Evidence, Inference, and National Character

Still, proof is elusive. And whatever the virtues of Erikson's portrait of American identity, it now coexists with a bewildering array of other equally ambitious national character studies. Rights to this subject have been disputed among the disciplines, and the appropriate scholarly techniques debated *within* the disciplines. Historians, anthropologists, sociologists, and psychologists have worked within their own fields and also sought a synthesis of intentions, methods, and results. That none agreeable to all now exists is no reflection on the capabilities of our scholars but testimony to the elusiveness of the subject. Erikson himself termed "obscure" several passages of his "Reflections" and wondered what he "dreaded" so that he could not state directly the elements in the national identity needing preservation and those that should be changed.

If "Reflections" is sometimes obscure then perhaps it is a sign of the division of purpose implicit in *Childhood and Society*. The period of Erikson's emigration and early clinical, ethnographic, and scholarly work in America was dominated by particular themes in statements on the national identity.[11] In the 1930s anthropologists and psychoanalysts, many of them also emigrés in the United States, promoted the interaction of culture and personality as the decisive aspect of national character. Edward Sapir, Abram Kardiner, and others employed psychoanalytic ideas to state their belief that individuals are molded by their cultures and express the values of its institutions, its prevailing styles of social and economic organization.

World War II stimulated national character studies in the international setting, to suggest what values bound the United States to its allies and distinguished it from its enemies. Like national character studies in other periods, these efforts were usually more literary than scientific, concerned less with detailed evidence than with interpretive generalizations. For some writers, like Margaret Mead, influencing American attitudes toward the war, even enhancing morale, was a goal allied to historical analysis. Mead, an early American friend to Erikson and strong influence on him, applied the spirit of her ethnographic work, if not its rigor, to the question of national identity in *And Keep Your Powder Dry* (1942). An attempt to evaluate the strengths and weaknesses of American society, this book stressed, as Erikson does, the debilitating psychological effects of materialism and single-minded economic competition. Postwar America, and its relations with other countries, Mead hoped, would be based on values reflecting charity in the social system and restraint in world affairs.

With the advent of the Cold War, studies of national character often concentrated on foreign policy and the need to have a distinctly American ideology based on fundamental but functional beliefs that would demonstrate the differences between the democratic and totalitarian systems. The search for an ideology is apparent in *Childhood and Society* as is Erikson's sensitivity to the dangers of not building a workable relationship with the Soviet Union. He expresses this idea in terms that, at the time of the publication of *Childhood and Society,* were fresh and, perhaps inevitably, scientific.

> Whether or not a few men on the Eurasian continent or some nervous council of ministers will plunge us into war—we do not know. But it may well be that the future—with or without war—will belong to those who harness the psychological energies freed from the wasteful superstitions of ancient agricultural moralities on the European, Asiatic and African continents. Physics, in learning to split the atom, has released new energy, for peace and for war. With the help of psychoanalysis we can study another kind of energy which is released when the most archaic part of our conscience is "split." As civilization enters into an industrialized era, such a split is inevitable. The

enormous energy thus released can be benevolent, and it can be malevolent. In the end, it may be more decisive than material weapons. (*CS*, 401)

No more inclined to propaganda than scholars in other fields, Erikson nonetheless reflects in *Childhood and Society* the political environment in which studies of national character came to be seen. And one additional aspect of this environment needs to be cited in any consideration of the American background of his first book: the loyalty oath controversy at the University of California.

At the time *Childhood and Society* was published the regents of the University required faculty members to sign an oath affirming that the signer was not a member of the Communist party or any other organization that advocated the overthrow of the government by force or violence and had "no commitments in conflict with [his or her] responsibilities with respect to impartial scholarship and free pursuit of truth."[12] Erikson and a number of colleagues refused to sign but most were reappointed and simply given a warning. Yet when other instructors were dismissed for refusing, Erikson resigned his post. A statement he prepared in June 1950 borrows some of the ideas and diction from the concluding chapter of *Childhood and Society,* especially its suggestion that "judiciousness" is the quality needed by those who in "quiet work and in forceful words" can reveal to the public the oversimplifications in arguments favoring the loyalty oath. And speaking as a psychoanalyst but also as a scholar and teacher, Erikson stressed the need to marshall certain professional virtues in the Cold War struggle facing America.

> My field includes the study of "hysteria," private and public in "personality" and "culture." It includes the study of the tremendous waste in human energy which proceeds from irrational fear and from the irrational gestures which are part of what we call "history." I would find it difficult to ask my subject of investigation (people) and my students to work with me, if I were to participate without protest in a vague, fearful and somewhat vindictive gesture devised to ban an evil in some magic way—an evil which must be met with much more searching and concerted effort.[13]

Erikson's complete identification with America is clear as is his intention, in *Childhood and Society,* to synthesize the interests and methods of studies of national character in the preceding few decades.

While advancing the view of culture and personality theorists, Erikson also suggests the meaning of totalitarianism in its German and Russian varieties. Only by understanding the history of American identity, he believes, can its future be safeguarded. An emigré in America during the Great Depression, Erikson also applied his understanding of the demands of economic justice to the national character as the United States accepted a new role in international affairs following the war. In order to do so, to achieve the range of *Childhood and Society,* Erikson depends on considerable historical generalization. While the synthetic quality of *Childhood and Society* is widely recognized as one of its virtues, it is also perhaps its chief defect. The very range of his judgments was probably what forced Erikson himself to recognize some obscurity in "Reflections on the American Identity." Ambitious, though perhaps somewhat impatient in his historical statements, Erikson sometimes seems determined to load his favorite images of national identity with enough ideas to make them more widely applicable than experience suggests. The behavioral polarities proposed by him and others are too inclusive, too easy to question if not refute with exceptions.

Similarly, Erikson's historical generalizations ignore the particulars that enable other accounts of national character, especially by historians, to minimize questions of identity and psychological development in favor of economics (or class) and politics. Sociologist and historian Ralf Dahrendorf, an admirer of Erikson, acknowledges in his own important study of the German character the arbitrariness of historical generalization on national identity and the need for a reliable theory. Until we have one, he admits, we will have to make do with several different "orientations" in order to "organize and relate the endless descriptive material about any society."[14] Erikson's is one such "orientation," as rich in historical suggestiveness as it is limited in the use of orthodox historical data. Always a reluctant user of the term "psychohistory," Erikson subscribes to the explanation of that method offered by his student Kenneth Keniston: "Psychohistory is more than anything else a series of questions that cannot be answered by psychoanalysis or history alone."[15]

Erikson's confidence in the basic argument of *Childhood and Society* lies in his understanding of the validity of certain kinds of evidence and inference. His firsthand studies of American Indians, of course, differ considerably from his "Reflections" on traits held in common by large classes of Americans, the meaning of Mom, John Henry, and allied myths and legends. To the first category of data he brought the tools of traditional psychoanalysis and ethnography: patient person-to-person inquiry into the motives, actions, ideas, and feelings of individuals, largely parents and children. Such clinical evidence is gathered within the four areas of psychoanalytical work he himself identified as crucial: intuition and objective data, a conceptual framework, and experience. While the clinical method and the evidence it yields has, as Erikson acknowledges, the appearance of "quicksand" to some, it actually depends on "a core of disciplined subjectivity in both patient and analyst, which it is neither desirable nor possible to replace altogether with seemingly more objective methods— methods which originate, as it were, in the machine tooling of other kinds of work."[16]

Even assuming the validity of such evidence, judgments made about the sickness or health of individuals are still difficult to prove conclusively. Proof lies, as Freud and his followers insisted, in the character and acts of those helped by psychoanalysis, the therapeutic results, and in the intellectual rigor and coherence of both clinical and therapeutic presentations to analysts and others. Nevertheless, whatever the inner logic and scholarly elegance of psychoanalytic generalization, acceptance still requires a leap of faith, belief in the unconscious and the relations of instincts and defenses identified by Freud as characteristic of mental and interpersonal behavior. The most convincing psychoanalytic evidence is still essentially inference, derived from assumptions and observations not available to the kind of testing associated with modern science. Psychoanalysis is empirical and poetic. And as Freud and others insist, as a mode of inquiry it is unique in the demands it puts on the observer to make himself or herself part of the inquiry. The data of *Childhood and Society,* including "Reflections on the American Identity," relies on this kind of psychoanalytic insight, responsible as it is to the rigors of clinical technique. Like many of the best scholars in other disciplines, Erikson recognizes the significance of his own stake in his subject. For "clinical evidence," he says, "will be decisively clarified but not changed in nature, by a sharpened awareness . . . of the psychotherapist's as well as the patient's position in society and history."[17]

There are, however, genuine differences among the data offered in *Childhood and Society*. The exactness of the opening chapters, devoted to several case histories of childhood disorders, reflects the clinical evidence Erikson compiled working in private practice and in research projects at Harvard, Yale and Berkeley. The Oglala Sioux and the Yurok were also the subjects of patient and orderly ethnographic investigation. With his theory of the eight stages of man, however, Erikson sought a more ambitious order of generalization, timeless in applicability while rich in suggestions for our time and place. The power of analysis of the eight stages carries over into the chapters that follow it, including "Reflections on the American Identity," while the historical evidence is largely inferential and even slight: the presumed origins of cultural sterotypes like Mom and the social meaning of myths and legends. The observations on adolescence are on somewhat firmer ground, based as they are on clinical work, but they are still mainly inferential. Yet inference in the building of theories of national identity is perhaps the only choice for Erikson and others. For the question is, what can be made of the limitless but obscure and often contradictory materials, and the near forbidding complexity of collective identities? Scholars of national character are among our most ambitious students of texts and events, devoted to their materials by the logic of evidence and the artistry of inference.

Erikson's determination to make American identity a subject of decisive psychological importance reflects also his belief that evidence and inference in psychology is the necessary counterpoint of the same two steps in historical inquiry. As he says in an important essay, "Psychological Reality and Historical Actuality," "Historians *and* psychoanalysts must learn to grasp fully the fact that while each individual life has its longitudinal logic, all lives lived interdependently within a given historical period share a kind of historical logic—and a-logic."[18] An integrative style of clinical and scholarly investigation (in the mind of one scholar or of several collaborating) into issues like national character is a fruitful way of weakening the borders between disciplines. Speaking of the role of anatomical evidence and neurological inference in Freud's early work, Erikson noted that "a transfer of concepts from one field to another has in other fields led to a revolutionary transcendence of the borrowed concepts by newer and more adequate ones."[19] The need to give free reign to new modes of thought must be balanced with care that inference reflects the traditions of, as well as the innovations in, technique. Erikson is himself a great innovator, but in his distinctive way of compiling evidence and his husbandry of inference he has avoided the estrangement of theory from clinical observation. National character study has benefited as has therapeutic technique.

Conclusion: The Future of a New Idea

Justifiably wary of forecasting, Erikson was nonetheless prophetic as he looked at the American character in an essay written during World War II:

> Historical change has reached a coercive universality and a global acceleration which is experienced as a threat to the emerging American identity. It seems to devaluate the vigorous conviction that this nation can afford mistakes; that this nation, by definition, is always so far ahead of the rest of the world in inexhaustible reserves, in vision of planning, in freedom of action, and in tempo of progress, that there is unlimited space and endless time in which to develop, to test, and complete her social experiments. The difficulties met in the attempt to integrate this old image of insulated spaciousness with the new image of explosive global closeness are deeply disquieting. They are characteristically met, at first, with the application of traditional methods to a new space-time; there is the missionary discovery of the "One World," aviation pioneering on a "Trans-World" basis, charity on a global scale, etc. Yet there also remains a deep consciousness of a lag in economic and political integration, and with it, in emotional and spiritual strength.[20]

Three decades before the "age of limits" was discovered by the press and politicians, and became a standard feature of even academic social analyses, Erikson suggested the political and psychological boundaries that are part of the American identity.[21]

In *Childhood and Society* he added another: the dangers associated with superorganization, whether a "total war machine" or its "facsimile" in peacetime. To secure an American style of identity formation Erikson first recalls the original mission of psychoanalysis. For Freud "knew that man, in building theories, patches up his world image in order to integrate what he knows with what he needs, and that he makes of it all (for he must live as he studies) a design for living" (*CS*, 412). Erikson asks, then, if the American design can originate not only in the desire to meliorate deviations from the norms of individual and social behavior but also in the recognition of fruitful variations. The ego, as the central principle of organization in thought, experience, and action, is the cornerstone of identity and as such should be the focus of clinical attention, domestic life, occupational choices, and social systems. Psychoanalysis, as a theory of ego development, can renew in America its own revolutionary impulse by supplying a workable if not infallible format. Practitioners of the discipline must also be responsible, as atomic scientists realized they must be attentive to the social and ethical implications of their work. For "we do not know in what way a new idea suddenly does the seemingly impossible and creates or maintains a variation of civilization in the midst of an apparent chaos of deviant contradictions" (*CS*, 415). Clinical knowledge, Erikson reminds us, is simply a tool dependent on the intentions and values of its users as they in turn are the unconscious and conscious instruments of national character.

America posed unique problems for Erikson as he was developing his developmental theory and as he continued in his clinical, historical, and biographical work at least through the publication of *Dimensions of a New Identity*.[22] He no doubt has shared at times the attitude of Saul Bellow's alter ego Charles Citrine in *Humboldt's Gift*. Bellow is another foreign born and astute observer of American life. Citrine is the author of *Some Americans: The Sense of Being in the USA* who wonders about America's need for the wisdom and joy supplied by "inner miracles" like art, humanistic learning, and psychological insight. "America . . . had so many outer ones. The USA was a big operation, very big. The more *it,* the less *we.*" Yet Erikson urges that the pace and scale of American life be adapted to the capabilities of its citizens. He even shows signs of a bit of native chauvinism. What is needed, he says, is a new kind of American, "one whose vision keeps up with his power of locomotion, and his action with his boundless thinking." To achieve this it will be necessary, as the conclusion of *Childhood and Society* states, to move beyond fear and anxiety to judgment and mastery. Such a transformation, Erikson believes, will depend on the amount of "judiciousness" available to sustain such initiatives in all stages of life. "Judiciousness in its widest sense is a frame of mind which is tolerant of differences, cautious and methodical in evaluation, just in judgment, circumspect in action, and—in spite of all this apparent relativism—capable of faith and indignation" (CS, 416).

Notes

1. Erik H. Erikson, *Insight and Responsibility: Lectures on the Ethical Implications of Psychoanalytic Insight* (New York: Norton, 1964), 86.
2. Erik H. Erikson, *Childhood and Society,* 2nd ed. (New York: Norton, 1963), 282. Subsequent references are incorporated into the text with the acronym *CS*.
3. See Robert Coles, *Erik H. Erikson: The Growth of His Work* (Boston: Little, Brown, 1970), 182–98 and Paul Roazen, *Erik H. Erikson: The Power and Limits of Vision* (New York: Free Press, 1976), 1–6.
4. Erikson, *Insight and Responsibility,* 90.
5. Erik H. Erikson, *Life History and the Historical Moment* (New York: Norton, 1975), 17–47.
6. Erikson, *Life History,* 44.
7. Erikson, *Life History,* 45. The lines that follow indicate Erikson's awareness of the internationalization of this theme: "The problems of identity become urgent wherever Americanization spreads, and . . . some of the young, especially in Americanized countries, begin to take seriously not only the stance of self-made men but also the question of adulthood, namely, how to *take care* of what is being appropriated in the establishment of an industrial identity."
8. See Thomas L. Hartshorne, *The Distorted Image: Changing Conceptions of the American Character Since Turner* (Cleveland: Western Reserve University Press, 1968) and Rupert Wilkinson, *The Pursuit of American Character* (New York: Harper and Row, 1988).
9. Richard I. Evans, *Dialogue with Erik Erikson* (New York: Dutton, 1967), 30.
10. Erik H. Erikson, *Identity and the Life Cycle* (New York: Norton, 1980), 50. This paper on "Ego Development and Historical Change" appeared originally in *The Psychoanalytic Study of the Child* 2 (1946).

11. See Hartshorne, *The Distorted Image,* chs. 3–5.
12. Coles, *Erik H. Erikson,* 156.
13. "Statement to the Committee on Privilege and Tenure of the University of California Concerning the Californian Loyalty Oath," *Psychiatry* 14 (May 1951): 245. Reprinted in Coles, *Erik H. Erikson,* 158.
14. Ralf Dahrendorf, *Society and Democracy in Germany* (New York: Doubleday, 1967), 30. An example, from among many, of an "orientation" to American identity that focuses on the period treated by Erikson, and that is convincing and largely free of psychoanalytic interpretation is Herbert G. Gutman, *Work, Culture and Society in Industrializing America* (New York: Knopf, 1976). Gutman and European historians like E. P. Thompson stress the functional role of systems of power and property relations rather than the adaptive methods of the mind. One weakness of *Childhood and Society* is that it does not demonstrate very much interest in the historical literature on national character, not to mention primary and secondary sources for particular events or issues. This is a flaw that Erikson himself apparently recognized, since both *Young Man Luther* (1958) and *Gandhi's Truth* (1969) include considerable attention to the scholarship in their respective subjects. On the virtues and limits of Erikson's method, and for a useful review of general sources, see Robert M. Crunden, "Freud, Erikson, and the Historian: A Bibliographical Survey," *Canadian Review of American Studies* IV (1973): 48–64 and Cushing Strout, "Uses and Abuses of Psychology in American History," *American Quarterly* 28 (1976): 324–42. An issue of the *Psychohistory Review* (December 1976) was entirely devoted to Erikson. Two highly regarded studies of the relations between psychoanalysis and history (though neither treats Erikson in any detail) are: Peter Loewenberg, *Decoding the Past: The Psychohistorical Approach* (Berkeley: University of California Press, 1985) and Peter Gay, *Freud for Historians* (New York: Oxford University Press, 1985). Useful selections of essays can be found in Geoffrey Cocks and Travis L. Crosby, eds., *Psychohistory: Readings in the Method of Psychology, Psychoanalysis and History* (New Haven: Yale University Press, 1987) and William M. Runyan, ed., *Psychology and Historical Interpretation* (New York: Oxford University Press, 1988).
15. Kenneth Keniston, "Psychological Development and Historical Change" in *Explorations in Psychohistory,* ed. Robert Jay Lifton (New York: Simon and Schuster, 1974), 150.
16. Erikson, *Insight and Responsibility,* 53.
17. Ibid.
18. Ibid., 207.
19. Ibid., 77. An important statement of the uses of such "transfers" is Clifford Geertz, "Blurred Genres: the Refiguration of Social

Thought," in *Local Knowledge: Further Essays in Interpretive Anthropology* (New York: Basic Books, 1983), 19–35.

20. Erikson, *Identity and the Life Cycle,* 44.
21. Some critics have found the political boundaries too narrowly drawn: see Paul Roazen, "Erik H. Erikson's America: The Political Implications of Ego Psychology," *Journal of the History of the Behavioral Sciences* 16 (1980): 333–41; Robert D. Holsworth, "The Politics of Development: The Social Psychology of Erik Erikson," *Georgia Review* 36 (1982): 385–403.
22. See my essay, "Jefferson and Erikson, Politics and the Life Cycle," *Biography* 9 (Fall 1986): 290–305.

4

Witness and Spokesman: Robert Coles in *Children of Crisis*

American psychiatry has been called by its leading historian an "ambivalent specialty," especially for its circumstances in the years after World War II when a sharply divided profession sought to reconcile habits of hospital-based practice with calls for the field's reorientation toward social activism.[1] Accordingly, American psychiatrists and psychoanalysts educated in the late 1950s and thereafter had less reason to be confident about the structure and uses of their training than did those who trained them. Both fields were highly regarded by the public and attracted sizeable numbers of recruits in the immediate postwar years, but by the early 1970s Robert Coles, speaking of the first decade or so of his own practice in a more skeptical atmosphere, wondered if "perhaps we should expect this ebb tide."[2] Coles himself of course was both a product of the changing reception for psychiatry and psychoanalysis and also one of those who deepened the internal and inevitably the external criticism of them. Well known now for his pathmaking series *Children of Crisis* and his simultaneous and continuing efforts to illuminate relations between medicine, the behavioral sciences, and the humanities (especially in his biographies and writing about literature), Coles has from the very beginning of his career also been a student of the "crisis" of his profession including its forms of expression.

When Coles decided to pursue a career in child psychoanalysis, after hearing a lecture in 1955 by Anna Freud, he entered a field that was barely three decades old. It had emerged from the

67

priority of childhood experience in Freudian thought, though in orthodox or adult psychoanalysis early experience appears only in memory and in the transference, that is, in the therapeutic relation with the analyst. When Freud acknowledged just after World War I the "widening scope" for psychoanalysis he had in mind the treatment of children and other socially meliorative activities for the still young and once despised profession. But Freud's own example suffered from the shortcoming of his having done himself very little work with children. Indeed, his famous case study of "Little Hans," still a cornerstone of psychoanalytic theory and training, is based on a secondhand account of the child.

Child psychoanalysis as we know it today began with the efforts of lesser-known analysts like Siegfried Bernfeld, August Aichorn, Lili Roubiczek among others, and of course Freud's daughter Anna, who nurtured the field in its early years by institutionalizing training in it at the Vienna Psychoanalytic Institute and in a network of Viennese schools and social institutions. The authority Anna Freud derived from her father was no doubt instrumental in the establishment of child analysis though her own theoretic, clinical, and discursive contributions are now plain, especially in the examples of her first trainees (like Erik H. Erikson) and later followers (like Coles). Behind the development of child psychoanalysis, she thought, was a problem in the psychoanalytic and psychiatric vocations as Coles too came to see them. Speaking of the training of child analysts she said there is "no guidance in such important matters as how to record their material, or sift and summarize it, or verify their findings, or pool them with others; how to trace the history of psychoanalytic concepts, or to inquire into their definitions, and to clarify and unify their technical terms; how to select specific areas for their research interests or to become alerted to the gaps in our knowledge."[3] Coles took up several of these themes as part of his pursuit of clinical work as a form of social activism and in light of his interest in redefining psychoanalytic and psychiatric traditions in the social sciences.

Child psychoanalysis arrived in the United States with orthodox analysis as part of the intellectual migration of the 1930s and early 1940s.[4] It proceeded as a specialty within the psychoanalytic tradition but with themes and problems of its own, especially the organization of developmental stages and the technique of direct observation for what it can reveal about play and symbolic functioning.[5] Still, like their counterparts in traditional psychoanalysis, and despite the uneven interest in children in the field's early years, specialists in children relied on the example of Freud. For Coles what matters most is the attention he gave to patients whose complaints were ignored or ridiculed by nineteenth-century physicians. Because he wanted to understand and to heal, Freud treated these people, says Coles, with a "revolutionary kind of respect." Freud's clinical habits represented his moral intentions: "He listened to [his patients]. He watched them. He held off judging them, or labeling them. . . . Eventually be began to feel that he had some idea what was going on in the minds of those 'outcasts' he was spending time with; and with that achievement secured, he could perhaps go on to do the most doctors can do—be of some limited help to them."[6] By describing Freud this way Coles also suggested his own intentions—as clinician, writer and advocate—on behalf of American children growing up in several kinds of social crises.

Inner and Outer Worlds

The five volumes of *Children of Crisis* are a landmark in the study of American children, for their documentary efforts on behalf of their mainly nonwhite and poor subjects, for their reflection of Coles' unusual psychiatric and psychoanalytic vocations, and for their rhetorical inventiveness.[7] The work that led to these books began in the late 1950s while Coles served as an army psychiatrist in Biloxi, Mississippi. While working and travelling in the Deep South he witnessed many civil rights demonstrations, including struggles over school desegregation, and was moved by the example of black children. Carrying the enormous burden of social change, they demonstrated to him unexpected courage, talent for adaptability, and power of expression. Thereafter, intimate knowledge of his subjects, based on fieldwork in several regions of the country, revealed them as healthy and even vigorous in a way largely unknown to social scientists favoring quantitative methods and handicapped by textbook theories of the culture of poverty. In the decade it took to complete *Children of Crisis* it became a record of the inner lives of children who had been largely hidden and ignored. Increasing public attention to their plight is partly due to Coles' work, its unusual format and powers of representation, and also its sense of personal mission. At the same time, the seeming intractability of the problems of the underclass reveals the limits of his style of witness and the difficulty of converting professional and scholarly innovations into social change. It may be said of *Children of Crisis* that it succeeded even if the "movement" of which it was a part—the progressive ethos of the 1960s and 1970s—has failed to institutionalize its point of view in social research and public affairs.

Coles' achievement on behalf of children is professional and scientific (on his terms), social, even rhetorical. He has enlarged the essential tasks of American child psychiatry by demonstrating the need for attention to the lives of children in their full social circumstances. He has given to these children a public voice, first in their own words, and then in his advocacy of their interests. And in *Children of Crisis* and in other work, he has demonstrated the contributions of the humanities, especially narrative literature, from regional American folktales to George Eliot's *Middlemarch* (high on his list of favorites), to social research.

Coles' unique combination of clinical interests, fieldwork, and habits of composition means that the results of his research are both psychological records and social documents. It is a style that depends in part on the examples of John Dollard, Erikson, and others who practice what the former called "life history" and the latter "psychohistory," though this second label is one with which Coles himself (and Erikson also) is uneasy. Speaking of adolescent ideological commitments he reminds us that "like adult sexuality, a political inclination has a developmental history,"[8] So too do the circumstances of this country's social and economic outcasts deserve fair-minded psychological attention. Still, the crises facing these children are not always dibilitating. Crises, social and psychological, can be the context for normal development, and it is the task of psychiatry and psychoanalysis to investigate the features of personality that originate in their relations. So too judgement must be suspended on the apparent psychopathologies that result from social crises and instead the habits of strength and survival that they also produce must be searched out.

In Coles' view Anna Freud corrected a critical lag in psychoanalytic thought between, as he puts it, "psychoanalytical *interest* in childhood and psychoanalytical *study* of childhood."[9] He recognizes in her work the central interest of his own: the power of ego psychology to explain childhood powers of adaptation to individual and social stress, and the legitimacy of studies of particular children in crisis. He admires, for instance, her comment on the young victims of World War II bombings:

> War acquires comparatively little significance for children so long as it only threatens their lives, disturbs their material comfort or cuts their food rations. It becomes enormously significant the moment it breaks up family life and uproots the first emotional attachments of the child within the family group. London children, therefore, were on the whole much less upset by bombing than by evacuation to the country as a protection against it.[10]

In the clinical culture of ego psychology, the English version under Ann Freud's leadership and the American one developed by Heinz Hartmann, Ernst Kris, and Erikson, adaptation became an inevitable and central virtue of normal development, a point of view whose implications have made it vulnerable to liberal criticism.[11] Coles' special interest is in adaptation as a response to large-scale social crises, hence the socialization of his subjects is a sign of triumph rather than, as Erikson's critics would have it in speaking for his identity-seeking subjects, a potential sign of defeat at the hands of social conformity.

"We May be Here for a Long Time"

The crises in Coles' title are many: school desegregation, unending poverty, urban migration, persistent racial and cultural discrimination, family dislocation, and the typical developmental crises of childhood and youth. The crises are specific and general, located in time and place, and also timeless and universal. They affect personality in many subtle ways beyond the reach of psychiatry, even when it is sympathetic to unusual external stresses on its subjects. That is, Coles would agree, as it should be, since psychiatric research in settings of social turmoil has more important goals than a complete psychological record. Its practitioners must listen and then try to understand in order to guide clinical work and—according to Coles' progressive professional stance—the meliorative intentions of society as a whole.

Considered as an elaborate documentary portrait of American children and their families, *Children and Crisis* will not, I think, yield all of its meanings to summary and sample. There are no really representative sections because in the vast scale of Coles' project there is no genuinely representative child. And according to Coles the meanings of the monologues are secondary to their interest as direct and accessible records. He rejects the necessity, in most research accounts of the poor, to convert all observation into theory, or to label observations as examples of any particular idea of the political, economic, or psychological state of American life. Coles himself is by no means free of judgments of this kind, but he recognizes another and equally important rationale for the study of children in crisis when he says that "surely at some level of theoretical elaboration it is possible for us to set aside the complexities of abstract thinking and our own intellectual self-esteem, and merely retain, intact, the reality of a child's experience as it can be observed or heard recounted."[12] Examples drawn from the sections on black, Appalachian, and Eskimo children suggest the character of Coles' work but not its scope or cumulative effect.

Orin is an eight-year-old black child whose family lived in a small North Carolina town before migrating to Boston. Coles is impressed by this child's sense of the relations between social, economic, and political issues. The following record of his thoughts is condensed, as are many of the recountings in *Children of Crisis,* from hours of conversation.

> If my daddy hadn't gone into the Army, he thinks he might still be back home, and we'd all be in bad trouble. He doesn't have the kind of job he wants, but he's on the way to getting one. He works in a factory; they make electrical equipment in it. They've promised that they'll keep on teaching him, and that he can be moved up and be over some of the other men one of these days. We're not rich, but we're not poor. My mother says that she'd like to get us out of here, into a better street. I like it here, but she says there are nicer places to live. The white people don't like us moving out to where they live, though; so we may be here for a long time. My dad says that even if

he'd gone to school a long time and had the best job he could ever want, we might not be able to live where we'd like. My mother says she can buy us the food we need, and the clothes; and that's more than she ever dreamed she'd be able to do when she was little. She says she likes to look at some of those dollar bills she has and smile and smile. She says when she was my age she'd never seen a dollar bill, never mind anything bigger. Dad gives her five ten-dollar bills every week to spend, and they have more; they're saving some money and they put away some for the rent. Dad says if he could only get some land he could build a house himself. But you can't just go and get land. Back in North Carolina there was plenty of land. The white people would have let us stay on theirs. They even offered to help fix up the place where my dad was born. But they didn't have money to give us, and that's why we're here. My dad says that when you weigh everything, we come out best right where we are—even if the building we live in is falling apart and you pay a fortune to stay in it.[13]

This mixture of curiosity, analysis, accommodation, and ambition is typical. The complex thoughts of children do indeed include an awareness of important political and social realities. And it is, Coles demonstrates, part of the child's development to seek to make sense of the "other" world and its connection to the experience of the child with parents, siblings, and friends.

Sally, who is ten and lives in Chicago, was born in Kentucky; her migrant family is one of thousands of poor ones that have moved to the north. At times she regrets the move but she is willing to learn to like the city. A sense of social injustice dominates her thoughts which are sober and undramatic in this otherwise playful child.

When I grow up I'd like to live in a nice, big home. I'd have a lot of food in the kitchen, and anyone who wanted food could just knock on the door, and I'd ask them to come in, and I'd tell them they should eat all they want, because it's no good to be hungry. I'd give people work to do. They could work on the house to make it look nice. My daddy had a job cleaning out a place; they had torn down a building, and they were going to build a new one. Daddy helped get all the wood and pipes and bricks into trucks. It's too bad they won't let him do work on the new building, then he'd make a lot of money, he says. He can build anything, I think. He says he can. But he's not in the union. All they let him do is clean up and load the trucks.

I don't think I'll ever live in a mansion, no. The teacher showed us some pictures of big homes, and she asked which we like best. I said I'd like to go and see them, and then I'd decide on my choice. The teacher said that was what she expected me to say. She said I was always wishing I'd get a peek at the rich people. I didn't answer her, but I was almost going to say that a peek would be all I'd ever get, I know for sure. Daddy said that's right, and so did my mother. It doesn't seem fair that only a few people have houses like that, big ones with a garden all around. If we had a garden, we could play on the grass. . . .

The saddest thing I see is when my mother has to go shopping, and she's afraid she hasn't the money she needs, and she starts crying. I try to make her stop. I come near and tell her something funny. If I can't make her smile, I keep on trying. I make up a new story, one she's never heard, and she pretends she's not listening, and her head is still down, and she's sniffing and wiping her eyes, but I know she's heard me. Yes sir, I know by the way she turns a little to me, and I can see her face, and there's a smile beginning on it. When I finish, she takes me round and says, 'God bless you,' and I can see she's more smiling than anything else. The tears are mostly gone.[14]

Such children are impressive for wisdom beyond their years, for their balance, and for their optimism. The structure of Cole's presentation and his sympathy for his subjects prompts his readers to take up their burdens even as they have little hope of abating. There is a tragic feel to these accounts, as there is also a sense of the child's resilience reflected in Coles' insistence on the remnant of optimism in all children. He is in his own profession also an outsider. Whatever the distance between their respective grievances the fact that they share in the disposition of someone struggling to be heard surely lends authority to these monologues. Crisis will no doubt continue in Sally's life, but Coles invites us to think that so too will her abilities to cope, to measure her prospects, and to add pleasure to other lives.

The portraits of children are often dramatized by their arrangement. Important differences in attitude and feeling are highlighted by contrasting the children as if they stood side by side in a dynamic group portrait. Two thirteen-year-old Eskimo cousins, for instance, think often about change in their culture. They live in a small remote village and acknowledge the influence of white settlers on critical features of native life; but they reveal different kinds of personal accommodations to it. One struggles for a position between the possibilities in change, even the attractions of life in the lower forty-eight, and the necessary limits on her family. She believes that there will be no transformation in the essential situation facing the Eskimos, but her words suggest only uncertain pleasure in that belief.

> Our people will not move to a big city; they will stay here and hope to get by the winter, and then the spring, and then the summer, and then it is winter again. My father says that the next season is as far ahead as he can look; he doesn't even like to think *that* much into the future. He is glad at the end of the day to see us eating supper and to know that there is food for breakfast—and that he has dried and put away plenty of salmon for the days to come. The minister tells us to think of many years ahead—to think of our lives after we die; and the teachers tell us to plan; and the government sends people to do tests on the ground, and to tell us the same thing—plan. But my father comes home and says he has been thinking and planning all day: will we all have a good supper? And he has known the answer: we will. That is good enough for him.[15]

Her cousin is equally suspicious of white influence, but certainly more resentful. He is devoted to the traditional tasks of his people, to old-fashioned village life and hence scornful of another young boy, the son of a well-paid state employee, who is "lazy" and "soft." His conversations with Coles, however, reveal his recognition of the ambiguous relations between tradition and change.

> My friends say they'd like to go hunting. They wish they knew how to live the way our ancestors did. But they don't. My mother is right: a lot of our ancestors died before they were as old as I am. But the ones who lived knew how to take care of themselves: My father says that when I'm his age, we'll all be sitting here in the village, eating frozen fish we've got from the store in the summer—through food stamps— and playing checkers during the winter and complaining that it's too hot in our houses. I woke up the other morning and it *was* too hot. My older brother Joe must have been smiling, and my grandfather, because they both had my name before me. My older brother used to tell my father that he wanted us to be able to get through a winter without buying food at the store, and without buying oil or kerosene either. My father would tell him that it's too late for us to live like that; we're different people than our ancestors were. But my brother said we could be the kind of people we want to be. He died before he could prove his point.[16]

Again, as he is represented by Coles, this child's insight is as strong as his gloom. We are asked to see him not as the passive victim of social forces, but as an articulate observer of their influence on and relation to his own life.

The Moral Compliance of Children

Coles is best known now for his presentation of the lives of such deprived children even as he stresses their lesser known virtues. But he concluded many years of research and writing on American children with a dramatic shift in subject. *Privileged Ones* is the last of the five volumes of *Children of Crisis*. Though it carries the subtitle "The Well-Off and Rich of America" it is mainly about the children of such people and it is based on the same premise as the earlier volumes, that the inner life of the child is a part of his or her outer life. "The 'tone' of a child's conscience," Coles notes, "is, to a large degree, a function of his or her family's psychological make-up, as well as its social and cultural character and its relationship to a certain region and to a historical era."[17] Though this ambitious plan for the book is not entirely fulfilled, the children of *Privileged Ones* reveal as much about their social, economic, and political circumstances as the poorer children of the earlier volumes. They do so in explaining their own view of the world, in seeking to understand and then accommodate their parents' ideas, and simply in the way they embody the expectations of wealth and privilege, their "entitlement."

Many of these privileged children have arrived at a view of the world that readers will expect. The young daughter of an Appalachian mine owner puts it this way: "Try to be nice to everyone, but look after yourself, because if you don't you'll have nothing to look after, and then you'll be in trouble" (*PO*, 501). In this vein, a twelve-year-old New Orleans boy suggests that there should be "special roads for people who have real good cars and really know how to drive and can afford to pay—first-class roads, they should be called, like the first class section of an airplane" (*PO*, 100). Few of these children, however, are so certain of the special needs of privilege. A ten-year-old girl in Boston speaks perhaps for most with this little composition on "My Parents":

My Daddy is going to be president of his company one of these days. I heard him tell my mother that. He said he had to work day and night, but in the end it would be worth it. My mother is not so sure. My brother and I are not so sure, either. My brother and I wish our father would be home with us, and not at the office or traveling all day and half the night. My mother wants him to keep his job, but she is afraid he could get sick. My grandfather has a farm, and many are the days when my brother and I say that it's too bad that Daddy doesn't own a farm, and then we'd see a lot more of him than we do. But we love our house here in Boston, and it is because he has such a good job that we can have all the toys and live where we do. You can't have everything. Our mother tells us that. I know what she means. (*PO*, 294)

This child, like the others, is of course only exploring meaning, constantly adjusting her views as she seeks to resolve the differences between her own understanding and the domestic and social imperatives that shape it.

According to Coles, the inherent contradictions central to any child's ethical struggles are in large measure a reflection of the child's judgment of his or her parents' social ideas. These children are not sure what to think of the parent who suggests the construction of a moat around the family house to keep out undesirables, or one who insists that migrant laborers have no claim on the fruit they harvest since they are "too ignorant" to know about the value of orange juice. In one of the best analytic passages in *Children of Crisis*, Coles explores the results of his subjects' recognition of these moral flaws.

The flaws discovered are not quite forgotten. The child who recalls a certain example knows that he or she had better explain to himself or herself why it has seemed best to be selective. It can take months, years, for those selective appropriations of parental words and deeds to be securely defended in a given child's mind. In fact, it can be argued that a considerable part of the childhood of certain children is spent on just such a psychological effort . . . they have learned how to reconcile apparent contradictions of intention or desire and are relieved as well as pleased at the reconciliation. The alternative, they know, is not a thorough, honest psychological scrutiny, but sadness and anxiety and a nagging sense of personal failure. (*PO*, 474)

This process is identified by Coles as "moral compliance" and it is a feature of child development common to rich and poor.

The chapter on "Entitlement," however, presents the distinctive situation of privileged children. "Entitlement" is the psychological common denominator, "an emotional expression," of the prerogatives of money and power. Psychoanalytic applications of the 1930s and 1940s, like John Dollard's *Caste and Class in a Southern Town* and his collaboration with Allison Davis in *Children of Bondage* (books to which Coles acknowledges his debts), stressed that culture and class do indeed help to structure the nature of a child's self-regard, and Coles confirms this view. Where ghetto children are often weak and vulnerable, privileged ones are confident and sheltered. Even among the latter, of course, there are variations. Coles believes that disturbed children of prosperous parents have expectations of themselves and make judgments about their environment that contrast strikingly with children from poor backgrounds.

No one of course would argue with the assertion that privileged children generally have high expectations of what life has to offer. Coles proposes, however, that a feeling of entitlement can and usually does develop without the parallel development of an excessively narcissistic tone. Children of wealthy families, he claims, have a realistic view of their lives as they exhibit predictable kinds of confidence. An eleven-year-old boy told Coles that "I don't think it's right to be easy on yourself. If you are, then you slip back and you don't get a lot of the rewards of life. If you really work for the rewards you'll get them" (*PO*, 405). This child displays exuberance that Coles admires as the natural expression of feeling entitled, and he is eager to act on it. The young boy says of his brother, whom he has watched climb a fence, "He got to the top, and then he just stood there and waved and shouted. No one was there. He was talking to himself. He was very happy. Then he would fall. He would be upset for a few seconds, but he would climb right back up again. Then he would be even happier! He was entitled to be happy. It is his fence, and he has learned to climb it, to stay up, and balance himself" (*PO*, 407). What is proprietary about this view is seemingly less important to Coles than what is adaptive or "balanced" in the mind of the child.

Privileged Ones also includes Coles' most direct comments on some central ideas in child psychiatry. His interest in ego psychology, for instance, appears this time in the form of a discussion of the need to balance psychoanalytic emphasis on the work of the superego, or the demands of conscience, with attention to the Freudian notion of the *ego-ideal.* The ego-ideal is the will to contemplate an adult life, the child's developing sense of what he or she would like to be and do. The chief privilege of well-to-do children is, again, an entitlement to such thoughts. And though he recognizes the social inequities that are often the source of privilege, Coles also admires the distinctive virtues of his privileged subjects. They are not, he says, spoiled simply by virtue of their social and economic background, just as children less privileged are not necessarily unspoiled.

Strong Sensible Words

Coles' observations of children have, of course, been observations of their families as well. *Children of Crisis* is also a record of American childrearing practices. It is not designed to suggest the correctness of certain styles, though Coles is often impressed with what must strike his readers as unorthodox kinds of parent-child relations. Again, the variety of his presentations makes sample risky, but the following passage is a good example of his comparative analyses and the virtues of his work beyond its observation of crisis.

> When white middle-class American parents tell their children the rights and wrongs of the world, or tell them how to do various tasks, they by and large assume themselves, as grownups, to be knowledgeable: mothers and fathers, hence the child's first teachers. When the child has trouble, the parent keeps trying, hopes the lesson will eventually get learned. If not, the boy or girl is judged slow, or declared in need of more time, or not quite "ready" or maybe, in possession of a "problem." Through discipline, through repetition, through persuasion, and by God, if necessary (at least in some homes), through "therapy" of one kind or another, the child will eventually learn. In contrast, Eskimo parents have quite a different manner of approach. They take small children with them, aim to teach them, of course, but put the burden on themselves rather than the children. The point is to *be* with the child, and try to *earn* the child's attention and responsibility. Children are rarely told they have failed and are rarely criticized directly or personally. And are rarely spanked, shouted at, called on the carpet, told to shape up or else. But they are not coddled, either—or endlessly "understood." In fact,

very little explicit instruction is given children by their parents
nor are there those "discussions" children elsewhere know as a daily,
maybe an hourly, experience. Instead, Eskimo boys and girls hear
memories, stories, reflections—narrative accounts by older people, in
front of younger ones, about what happened and why at certain times
and under certain circumstances. And those accounts are usually
given as the grown-ups and children work together on a particular
task.[18]

Observations of other children and their families throughout
Children of Crisis are equally informative about the relations
between inner and outer life, though they may be "progressive" as
part of Coles' political intentions as well as for clinically interpretive reasons. Crisis is indeed the major influence on the lives of
these children, but it is also, Coles is convinced, at least a partial
source of their strength and vitality. These children speak for
themselves as part of Coles' method for adapting child psychiatry
and psychoanalysis to the fields of social turmoil: one is quite
literally the natural setting for psychiatric and psychoanalytic
research, another is the discipline of child study constituted jointly
by these specialties, a field of inquiry suffering from its indoor
habits.

These methods have interested many of Coles' readers, though
he himself has often been puzzled by this because of what he takes
to be the essential simplicity of his approach. Each of the five
volumes of *Children of Crisis* has an introductory chapter on "The
Method," and each makes essentially the same points within
Coles' view of the clinical professions about the need for direct
observation and a simple apparatus and vocabulary. Yet its bold-
ness needs to be emphasized as do its ambiguities and its incom-
pleteness. Early in the first volume of *Children of Crisis* he
criticizes the limits of measurement-minded rigor in social science
research. Researchers, he claims, fail to understand the real
dynamics of social stress because all are "eager for the categorical
solution, afraid of the clumsy undefined, paradoxical flow of life
and its events which may, in fact, be the truth of it."[19] This kind of
truth, dependent on Coles' seemingly unmethodological methods,
is the goal of research true to its subjects as Coles would have
them understood. He is his subjects' spokesman as it were in the
professional debate over the kinds of data that will best represent
them. His views, as he well knows, carry the familiar burdens of

the ambiguous techniques of "participant observation," the form he recognizes he is working in but resists being bounded by.[20] Indeed, it is a form that developed, in examples like James Agee and Walker Evans' *Let Us Now Praise Famous Men* (another of Coles' favorites), side by side with the dedication of academic social research to quantitative studies rather than to narrative or to what might be called dialogic studies—an awkward but still suggestive name for the format of *Children of Crisis*.

This is an issue that Coles viewed with particular interest as a young American psychiatrist whose profession was, he felt, rapidly losing the unique advantages it had had for influential social research by being needlessly "scientific." Such a change was represented, as it is today in other disciplines, by a detached professional stance with a suitably scientific (or complicated) diction and syntax. Coles once asked if such a change was true to the traditions of psychiatry as he understood them and its potential for genuine utility. "The real test is whether we best understand by this strange proliferation of language the worries, fears, or loves in individual people. As the words grow longer and the concepts more intricate and tedious, human sorrows and temptations disappear, loves move away, envies and jealousies, revenge and terror dissolve. Gone are strong sensible words with good meaning and the flavor of the real."[21] Nothing could be more direct than the diction of Coles and his subjects, which is an important part of the contribution of *Children of Crisis*. Anna Freud insisted on its importance, and another of Coles' heroes in healing and literature, the pediatrician and poet William Carlos Williams, has a unique place in literary tradition for the simplicity and directness of his vocabulary.[22]

Still, plain speech is organized to serve complex thought and moral purpose. These are unusual works of child psychiatry and the fact that they carry headnotes from the Bible and contain many references to it should not be a surprise. *The South Goes North* concludes with a powerful account of religious faith among the urban poor after which Coles calls his own efforts at explanation merely the "distillation of one's confusions." *Children of Crisis* is a form of witness in the sense that it studies documents (the interviews) brought forth by important events—racial strife, rural and urban poverty, social isolation—and testifies to their origin, meaning, and significance. And Coles himself, of course, is very much the witness, the observer of the results of the events or crises in the lives of particular children, their families, and communities. For the headnote to *The South Goes North* he chose these words: "Doth not wisdom cry? and understanding put forth her voice? She standeth in the top of high places, by the way in the places of the paths. She crieth at the gates, at the entry of the city, at the coming in at the doors. Unto you, O men, I call; and my voice is to the sons of man" (Proverbs 8:1–4).

Coles is also, to use Robert Jay Lifton's phrase and to put the matter in secular and (ironically) scientific terms, "the person in the paradigm," whose own role is offered as an indispensable part of his documentary methods.[23] Coles insists on Freud's strong sense of advocacy as he defended the right of patients to treatment. And of course Freud's own life was itself the data for some of his most influential theoretical discoveries. Both aspects of his work abated as psychoanalysis moved closer to the clinical and even scientific respectability Freud craved. Nonetheless, Coles is justified, I think, to point out that the psychoanalytic process as it has come to be practiced in the American medical model—though training is centered in independent institutes—has been decidedly impersonal. Janet Malcolm's convincing portrait of one community of traditional analysts illustrates their fondness for the metaphor of surgery in the conduct of therapy.[24] Work with children, especially those facing developmental problems, has never been so purely scientific or detached in intention, but it has generally avoided the appearance of political partisanship on behalf of the professional ethos it shares with adult therapy.

Coles has never been diffident about the economic and social injustice he observed. In effect he took up the call for activism that for a time characterized the psychiatric community. As one controversial statement put it just a few years before Coles began his training: "We favor the application of psychiatric principles to all those problems which have to do with family welfare, childrearing, child and adult education, social and economic factors which influence the community status of individuals and families, intergroup tensions, civil rights and personal liberty."[25] He is, beyond even the reformist intentions of his profession's most eager activists, a spokesman for his subjects, though not merely in the sense that he speaks for them. He is also, and this is the point he would stress, the instrument of their own speech.

What he says in *his* voice, with a repetitiousness he acknowledges, and an insistence on a personal investigative style, is part of his argument for an intensely moral form of social inquiry. The post–World War II debate over value-free scholarship is now centered on expressions of epistemological skepticism and the social construction of meaning in the various "interpretive" schools of disciplinary inquiry.[26] Writing outside the vocabularies of this theme as they appear in philosophy and in literary and social theory, Coles has made himself a leading antagonist of clinical and scholarly neutrality and what he takes to be morally indifferent forms of social research. Edgar Friedenberg acknowledged what is obvious in *Children of Crisis* and also what lends it so much authority: "This is not ethical neutrality—But [Coles] keeps his cool in [these] desperate cases."[27] While repeatedly stating the case for more research shaped by personal values and moral purpose, Coles is indeed generous to styles unlike his own in the elaborate descriptive notes and bibliography for each volume of *Children of Crisis*. His scholarship is traditional—in its recognition of the continuity of inquiry and the fact of a community of scholars—and innovative at the same time, mainly in its argument for a sharp moral departure from professional habits in his own field at least.

Not surprisingly, Coles has been charged with being *too* committed to the objects of his research. Praised for his ability to recover real lives within the abstract problems of poverty and social alienation, and for the panoramic effects of his work, he has been found wanting in originality and in firmness. Though he has only rarely been reviewed in the academic journals, he has been unanimously praised in widely read organs of liberal opinion. In a front page review in the *New York Times Book Review* of the last two volumes of *Children of Crisis* (two previous volumes had also received such attention), sociologist Paul Starr proposed that "Coles is almost too gentle, too tentative, to give his analysis the necessary hard edges and firm conclusions."[28] Novelists Gore Vidal and Marge Piercy have praised Coles though the first confessed to being bored by his books because Coles' "heart is in all the right places" and the second found him also somewhat passive, unwilling to act, within his radical disposition. "He seems in an impasse," Piercy says, "addressing the liberal conscience when distant corporate and government decisions are cutting off the lifeblood of these people in poverty."[29]

And hardly anyone mentions Coles without remarking on his productivity. His writing comes almost too easily and it is often repetitious. Yet Coles, no doubt thinking of his subjects and not his attitudes toward them, sees his work as marked by considerable variety and, despite the hundreds of articles and dozens of books, considerable restraint. Its quantity is essentially a reflection of the scale and urgency of the social problems it addresses. *Children of Crisis* embodies the kind of intellectual flexibility that Coles' Harvard colleague David Riesman identified as the pursuit of "values in context." While Riesman believes of course that "men cannot live without values, without preferences and choices, without the vocabulary of motives that we partly learn and partly teach ourselves," he insists that social critics need to recognize the variety of contexts in which values are formed, maintained, even changed. Accurate and sympathetic scholarship requires a deliberate relativism. "There are issues," Riesman says, "on which I am an absolutist and those on which I am in doubt as to what I am or should be. Such moral experimentalism . . . is essential if we are to meet life flexibly, listening to the ancestor within and the friend without but not bound to obey either." And in his manifest idealism Coles also embodies what Riesman identified for himself as perhaps the most meaningful context, which includes "not only what is 'really' there, as our self-styled realist would see it, but as including what is potentially there, given what my intervention may invoke in others and theirs in me." To discover this potential, he adds, "one has to take risks and one may be disappointed."[30] For Coles the primary disappointments have been, perhaps, recognition of the limits of his influence, even as it is practiced in a deliberately unacademic style, and the slow pace of social change. But his patience is important as is his commitment to psychiatry as an instrument of public discourse on social issues.

The very public intentions displayed in *Children of Crisis* are no doubt one of the features that place the series in unusual relation with Freudian tradition. Philip Rieff, for example, states flatly in his justly influential *Freud: the Mind of the Moralist* that "psychoanalysis is the doctrine of the private man defending himself against public encroachment . . . it sponsors a rational alienation from public enthusiasm." Freud's legacy, he argues, includes "skepticism about all ideologies except those of the private life."[31] Coles' balanced view of political life—he manages to reveal the sources and integrity of both sides in local ideological debates over public policy matters like school busing, social welfare and labor laws—does not mean that he is unideological. No reader can miss his liberal sympathies. But he is especially ideological in his understanding of his own profession and its public responsibilities. For him psychiatry has powerful social meaning in its potential for very personal investigation of what appear to be impersonal social and economic forces. This means, in *Children of Crisis* and in several other works, the adaptation of clinical experience for forms of social documentary.[32]

Conclusion: The Sentiment of the Child Psychiatrist

Coles chose an unusual role in his research and writing early in his career. "In some way," he said, "we must manage to blend poetic insight with a craft and unite ultimately the rational and the intuitive, the aloof stance of the scholar with the passion and affection of the friend who cares and is moved."[33] Determined as he is to avoid the "solitary trek" of traditional psychiatry and psychoanalysis, he is still objective in significant ways, especially in balancing points of view from black and white parents on volatile social issues like busing, welfare, and claims of ethnic cultures to special treatment, but he is never disinterested. Coles recognizes the inevitability of his own participation in the lives of his young subjects, and he accepts it as a part of professional practice, at the same time adapting the popular surgical metaphor for his own purposes.

> Our feelings, our own disorders and early sorrows are for us in some fashion what the surgeon's skilled hands are for his work. His hands are the trained instruments of knowledge, lectures, traditions. Yet they are, even in surgery, responsive to the artistry, the creative and sensitive intuition of the surgeon as a man. The psychiatrist's hands are himself, his life. We are educated and prepared, able to see and interpret. But we see, talk, and listen through our minds, our memo-

ries, our persons. It is through our emotions that the hands of our healing flex and function, reach out, and finally touch."[34]

Few psychiatrists or psychoanalysts would make such a claim, and though it is not Coles' only virtue, it is surely the one that makes *Children of Crisis* the moral (even moving) experience that it is for the author and the audience.

There is indeed some truth in criticism of Coles that in the portraits of the poor there is a certain "ghetto romaticism." According to this view he has sentimentalized his subjects and overstressed—odd though this may sound—the benefits of their circumstances. *Children of Crisis,* therefore, is essentially a lesson in the uses of adversity. And for some of Coles' middle-class readers the volumes are perhaps an explanation of the natural limits of social programs. If such an impression is given it is certainly not Coles' intention that we admire his young subjects beyond the recognition of their ability to cope with social injustice. He cannot be charged with ignoring the real facts of poverty and alienation. The struggle of daily life for the children of the rural and urban poor is everywhere present in his accounts of the personal and social strategies devised to deal with it. Some distortion is perhaps inevitable given Coles' method and purposes and the expectations of his readers. The portraits are not written as true documentary accounts of the lives of his subjects but are presented as composite views of many children designed to highlight certain features of American social life neglected in other accounts of the poor. And if they are not true, neither are they false. In some respects—as his reviewers have acknowledged—they have the status of fiction based very firmly on the transcription of life. They examine the range of human possibility beyond category and social stereotype. Coles' optimism, like Dickens' and even Mark Twain's, is expressed as a form of sentiment. The facts of his subjects' lives are indisputable.

Public acclaim for *Children of Crisis* has not, of course, guaranteed that it will have an important impact on the lives of children in the sense at least that the crises to which they are subject are likely to be quickly resolved. In fact Coles himself, like Marge Piercy, has at times had some doubt about the efficacy of his books *because* they are books and not actions. Reassurance on that matter came from Dorothy Day, founder of the Catholic Worker movement, who once told him, "I have been reached so many times by certain writers. What is this distinction between writing and doing that some people make? Each is an act. Both can be a part of a person's *response,* an ethical response to the world."[35] Coles' own claim for *Children of Crisis* has always been modest. "Books like this one," he said of one volume, "can only be as successful as the questions they provoke, the second thoughts they encourage, the doubts they stir up, the formerly made-up minds they undo, jolt a little."[36]

Notes

1. Gerald N. Grob, "American Psychiatry: An Ambivalent Specialty," *Prospects: An Annual of American Cultural Studies* 12 (1987): 149–74. See also Grob, "Psychiatry and Social Activism: The Politics of a Specialty in Postwar America," *Bulletin of the History of Medicine* 60 (1986): 477–501.
2. Robert Coles, *The Mind's Fate: Ways of Seeing Psychiatry and Psychoanalysis* (Boston: Little, Brown, 1975), 6.
3. Anna Freud, "A Short History of Child Analysis." *The Writings of Anna Freud* (New York: International Universities Press, 1971), vol. 7, 57–8. See also Anna Freud's "Child Analysis as a Subspecialty of Psychoanalysis." vol. 7, 204–19. Anna Freud's role is of course a central subject in Elizabeth Young-Bruehl's biography *Anna Freud* (New York: Summit Books, 1988). The work of other child analysts can be observed in the annual *The Psychoanalytic Study of the Child.*
4. See Lewis A. Coser, *Refugee Scholars in America: Their Impact and their Experiences* (New Haven: Yale University Press, 1984) 19–82 and Nathan G. Hale, Jr., "From Berggasse XIX to Central Park West: The Americanization of Psychoanalysis, 1919–1940," *Journal of the History of the Behavioral Sciences* 14 (1978): 299–315.
5. See Anna Freud, "A Short History of Child Analysis," *Psychoanalytic Study of the Child* 21 (1966): 7–14; Marjorie Harley, "Child Analysis, 1947–1984: A Retrospective," *Psychoanalytic Study of the Child* 41 (1986): 129–53; E. James Anthony, "The Contributions of Child Psychoanalysis to Psychoanalysis," *Psychoanalytic Study of the Child* 41 (1986): 61–87.
6. Robert Coles, *The Mind's Fate,* 226.
7. *Children of Crisis: A Study of Courage and Fear* (Boston: Little, Brown, 1967); *Migrants, Sharecroppers, Mountaineers* (Boston: Little, Brown, 1971); *The South Goes North* (Boston: Little Brown,

1971); *Eskimos, Chicanos, Indians* (Boston: Little, Brown, 1977); *Privileged Ones* (Boston: Little, Brown, 1977).

8. Coles, *The Mind's Fate,* 271.
9. *Ibid.,* 118.
10. *Ibid.,* 115.
11. See Paul Roazen, "Erik H. Erikson's America: The Political Implications of Ego Psychology," *Journal of the History of the Behavioral Sciences* 16 (1980): 333–41.
12. Coles, *The Mind's Fate,* 240.
13. Coles, *The South Goes North,* 87.
14. *Ibid.,* 412–14.
15. Coles, *Eskimos, Chicanos, Indians,* 125–26.
16. Ibid., 141–42.
17. Coles, *Privileged Ones,* 461. Subsequent references to this volume are incorporated into the text with the acronym *PO.*
18. Coles, *Eskimos, Chicanos, Indians,* 224.
19. Coles, *Children of Crisis,* 13.
20. See especially the introductory section of the first volume in the series, *Children of Crisis: A Study of Courage and Fear,* which includes a chapter titled (perhaps coyly) "Observation and Participation." For a review of the epistemological and practical dimensions of this theme see Gary Schwartz and Don Merton, "Participant Observation and the Discovery of Meaning." *Philosophy of the Social Sciences* 1 (1971): 279–98.
21. Coles, *The Mind's Fate,* 9.
22. Coles, *William Carlos Williams: The Knack of Survival in America* (New Brunswick, NJ: Rutgers University Press, 1983).
23. Robert Jay Lifton, *The Life of the Self: Toward a New Psychology* (New York: Simon and Schuster, 1976), 151–71.
24. Janet Malcolm, *Psychoanalysis: The Impossible Profession* (New York: Knopf, 1981), 161–63.
25. Group for the Advancement of Psychiatry, "The Social Responsibility of Psychiatry," *GAP Report* no. 13 (July 1950), 5. Cited in Grob, "Psychiatry and Social Activism," 478.
26. See the essays in Paul Rabinow and William M. Sullivan, eds., *Interpretive Social Science: A Second Look* (Berkeley: University of California Press, 1987).
27. *New York Review of Books,* 28 September 1967: 29.
28. *New York Times Book Review,* 22 January 1978: 33.
29. Vidal's review of *Privileged Ones* appeared in the *New York Review of Books,* 9 February 1978. Piercy's review appeared in the *New York Times Book Review,* 13 February 1972.
30. David Riesman, "Values in Context," in *Individualism Reconsidered and Other Essays* (Glencoe, IL: The Free Press, 1954): 17–25. Coles cites Riesman's *The Lonely Crowd* (1950) as the most important book standing behind *Children of Crisis.* It "molded the thought

of a generation," and its author is one of America's most vital thinkers because "he has walked a certain middle path—between particularity and abstraction, between social criticism and ethical affirmation" (*Privileged Ones*, 568).

31. Phillip Rieff, *Freud: The Mind of the Moralist* (1959; reprint New York: Anchor Books, 1961), 278.
32. For a discussion of Coles' approach with regard to photography see my essay, "Prose for Pictures: Documentary Style and the Example of Robert Coles," *Kansas Quarterly* 11 (Fall 1979): 133–43.
33. Coles, *the Mind's Fate*, 10.
34. Ibid., 12.
35. Robert Coles and Jon Erikson, *A Spectacle Unto the World: The Catholic Worker Movement* (New York: Viking, 1973), xii.
36. Coles, *The South Goes North*, 41.

Part Two

ACADEMIC ATTITUDES

5

Social Science Toward Social Criticism: Some Vocations of David Riesman

Periodically a book based on scholarly research, if not typifying it, will capture public attention. Robert Bellah's *Habits of the Heart* (1985) is a recent example; Christopher Lasch's *The Culture of Narcissism* (1979) was the most notable one before that. Talk show hosts will vie with business consultants for the latest word on the American character until the next big idea comes along or until, as is more likely, the meanings of the text turn out to be more complex and indeterminate than the media allow. Not surprisingly, Bellah acknowledges the guidance of fellow sociologist David Riesman in making *Habits of the Heart* as effective as it is in revealing aspects of the "inner moral dialogue" in American life. For Riesman's *The Lonely Crowd* (1950) can be said to exemplify such works of social criticism and to have anticipated, allowing for changing times, their subjects and methods. Reviews of *Habits of the Heart* praised it with versions of "not since *The Lonely Crowd . . .*"

Riesman's book had an unexpectedly large sale in the early 1950s, and it has continued to claim an enthusiastic readership despite its author's insistence since 1960 (when he wrote a new preface) that many of its findings are dated and its methods sometimes uncertain. Moreover, he has never appeared on radio or television. Yet today, after the sale of over a million copies of *The Lonely Crowd,* Riesman's reputation as an all-purpose critic of social and cultural affairs, especially of the immediate postwar decades, stands undiminished. And such has been his authority since the 1960s as a critic of higher education, that campus reformers have been known to speak with anxiety about "what to do when David Riesman can't visit your campus."

Riesman did not plan for such a career, but in the decade before *The Lonely Crowd* he assembled the necessary tools: wide interests in law, history, politics, public affairs, economics, the arts, and education; curiosity about American lives of all kinds; and a fluid prose style reflecting great pleasure in reading and writing. Moreover, unlike today's academic specialists with accidental general audiences, Riesman during the 1940s was a man of several vocations, each with potential for satisfying his desire to write about American society and to influence it. By his own account, at least, he does not appear to have had to overcome a debilitating "crisis" in "becoming David Riesman" as today's popular form of intellectual life history, whatever its truth in other instances, might have it. Yet his experiments in vocation display the reasons he was capable of *The Lonely Crowd* and of an exceptionally durable style of cultural criticism that has been widely emulated but rarely matched. My title reflects, of course, Riesman's own habit in many essays of using the term *some* to signify the modesty of his intentions. It also reflects the emphasis in this essay on the early phases of his career.

Staying Put

Public recognition of Riesman's stature came quickly. Just after *The Lonely Crowd* he published detailed accounts of the interviews on which it was in part based *(Faces in the Crowd),* an authoritative study of Veblen, and in *Individualism Reconsidered* a collection of essays of astonishing diversity. Hence when *Time* magazine put Riesman on its cover in September 1954, it recognized his unexpected popularity as an academic author, the timeliness of his analysis of the American character, and the uses of his personal example as an intellectual at home in the culture at large as well as in the library and classroom. Compared to the politicians, diplomats, and businessmen *Time* favored, Riesman was an unlikely subject, devoted as he was to contemplative work with products of uncertain utility. So along with its enthusiasm for his taxonomy of character types *Time* accepted Riesman's claims for the "heuristic" goals of *The Lonely Crowd* and welcomed its effects on Riesman's professional colleagues. He counseled them, to *Time's* pleasure, "to pursue the truth as independent men, affecting society as models of autonomy, not as victors in this public issue or that." Of course Riesman himself was offered as the prototypical "autonomous man"—the one he had himself celebrated in the closing pages of *The Lonely Crowd*—capable of individuality and choice while loyal to social ideals.

Eager to claim discovery of the model American intellectual— few cultural critics have been so well received since—*Time* ignored Riesman's own cautions about the methodological limits of his books and essays. At the end of *The Lonely Crowd,* for example, he notes that study's margin for error due to "limitations of social class and region and of observational standpoint which frame the picture of America presented here."[1] Indeed, for *Time,* Riesman's "upper-class" Eastern background and comfortable Chicago home (with servants and a wine cellar) were points in his favor, at least insofar as they may have comforted *Time's* readers, given his otherwise discomforting message about the direction of American society.

Yet there was much in Riesman's upbringing that favored his intellectual development.[2] Riesman's father was a physician and writer on medical history who spoke five languages and would often send his children to the encyclopedia to clarify family discussions. His mother was an exceptionally cultivated woman, stymied in her professional ambitions by domestic and social conventions. Her circumstances, and especially her high intellectual standards, loom large in Riesman's memory.[3] Both parents were Jews, but he was raised in a home that fostered religious choice, including agnosticism. He became a Unitarian when he married. Later Riesman was able to move easily in learned circles, including the mainly Jewish "New York Intellectuals." His essays on anti-Semitism show no signs of his own religious background, not because he had any illusions about the value of strict objectivity in social analysis, but because his powers of understanding and sympathy did not depend, in this case or any other, on special forms of identification.

One consequence of his parents' intellectual sophistication was their advice that at Harvard Riesman major in science, a choice at odds with his emerging literary and historical interests. The idea was simple: capitalize when you can on opportunities to learn (well-equipped university laboratories in this case) not likely to be available in other settings. Riesman would make such intellectual opportunism a hallmark of his varied career. Yet after gaining his undergraduate degree in biochemical sciences he enrolled in Harvard Law School more by default than by design: "My primary purpose was to stay put." An academic career was out of the question, mainly for reasons he stated somewhat obscurely many years later: "Even if I had thought I had the capacity for the life of the scholar, I resembled my friends in not regarding our professors as leading lives we would want to follow." Indeed, Riesman had his mentors, chief among them the emigré political scientist Carl Friedrich. Though the atmosphere of the law school was "rapacious," Riesman led his class and joined the *Law Review.* He was independent and versatile and, with his appointment as a clerk to Supreme Court Justice Brandeis, seemed headed for a distinguished legal career. Allowing for the unorthodox uses Riesman later made of his professional education, that turned out to be true.

After his clerkship with Brandeis, Riesman worked for a short time as an attorney with a small Boston firm. He was prompted to take such a position because he felt himself to be ill prepared clinically for a legal career, his Harvard education having been "too bookish." Hence he found himself working as a trial lawyer, often in small suburban courts that could not have been further from the elevated discourse and solemn atmosphere of his clerkship. Yet Riesman found intellectual stimulation in other aspects of this position, especially in what he contributed to cases of corporate reorganization. Even more important, however, was his reentry into the Cambridge academic orbit where he participated in one of Friedrich's seminars and mingled with his graduate students and with the Harvard law faculty. It was against their advice that in 1936 Riesman accepted an offer from the new law school at the University of Buffalo.

At Buffalo Riesman took particular pleasure in his modestly prepared students, many of whom were the first in their family to attend college and professional school. He became active in civic affairs and taught evening classes in social science at the YWCA. Looking back on the interests of his Harvard professors Riesman notes their wish to categorize the law, to organize and explicate the precedent-setting decisions "for the benefit of the profession and the country." Moreover, like the other prestigious law schools, Harvard gave "house room" to scholars who taught legal history, foreign law, and other recondite subjects. In contrast, Riesman notes, he taught a seminar on the ordinances of the city of Buffalo.

It was in his modest classroom assignments that Riesman demonstrated his democratic educational goals but also found a lack of intellectual "nourishment" in legal work. Admirers of the law as a discipline rely mainly on the opinions of the "virtuosos of the literature" like Cardozo or Brandeis. Yet as most law professors know, the bulk of the literature of the law is the product of "journeymen" judges whose written work is uninspired, merely the case material for the rigorous classrooms of the major law schools. In comparison with the excitement Riesman found in the classic texts of history and social science—in Tocqueville and Weber for instance—"the regular gruel of the law appeared thin."

Riesman's own legal articles are carefully argued and dense with citations, but they also show signs of his impatience with the rhetorical routines of the law. His very first contribution is an unusually empirical examination of the laws of possession. It opens almost whimsically: "Once upon a time when there were no barbed wire fences, when wrecks at sea were frequent, and when money was hidden in the ground by citizens, instead of by government, problems of finding were of great concern to philosophers and lawyers." Then, after asserting the practical importance of the problem despite its neglect, Riesman adds, "In our metropolitan areas, harried, package-laden, rubber and hat clad losers raise questions that once carried a pastoral tang of straying sheep and cattle damage feasant."[4] Only the final technical term signifies this essay's intended audience, which was probably also surprised by its author's survey research (at Sears, Macy's, New York's Roxy Theater, and its equivalent in downtown Buffalo) into the actual behavior of finders.

Imagination versus Technique

Yet however parochial were his teaching assignments and empirical his research instincts, Riesman also employed the forum of legal discourse to propose nascent relations between public opinion and public policy. An essay on restricting foreign enlistment cited as the timeliest of precedents the American volunteers to the Loyalist cause in the civil war in Spain. "Public opinion," Riesman says, "should be weighted by intensity as well as numbers—a factor apt to be overlooked by followers of the Gallup or *Fortune* polls. Men who will freely die for a cause deserve the full persuasiveness of their courage." To apply legal restrictions to such efforts would be to violate the "true though not the judicially enforceable liberties of a free constitution."[5]

On other themes Riesman abandoned legal discourse entirely. Essays on education and persecution are noteworthy for their confidence in the public power of ideas and the effectiveness of intellectuals. There is little sign in these pieces of their author's legal background, Riesman's apparent assumption being that it could simply provide the appropriate analytic tools without the self-conscious professional authority. In one essay Riesman asks that the federal government itself organize and support programs of public education in the virtues of the American system. The goal is not just patriotism but participation: "What is vital is that the inarticulate, nonparticipating enclaves be brought to democratic life." His naive optimism—"once democratic spirits have been excavated by criticism of anti-democratic ways, the meetings can serve the two-way need of give-and-take between the government and the community"—can perhaps be explained as a refuge from the rigor and realism of the law.[6] Friedrich's own *The New Belief of the Common Man* (1942) is no less hopeful and pietistic. And this theme was salvaged, with great insight, in the section of *The Lonely Crowd* devoted to politics.

Certainly when he turned to the question of persecution of the Jews (the essay appears to have been written just prior to public knowledge of their mass murder in concentration camps) Riesman had no illusions about how difficult the problem was. Yet the solution is still what he calls, with unfortunate Orwellian overtones, "attitude or opinion re-education." We must turn to "large scale utilization of the newer techniques for making people conscious that they hold definite opinions on many subjects which they have acquired by mental osmosis, not by investigation of the problem. . . . And then education must go on to show on what inherited or manipulated grounds they have become anti-Semitic, and to mobilize those elements in the personality which can appreciate the equal dignity of all men and women."[7] For reasons that are plain, there is more conviction in this second essay but, like its predecessor, it leaves unexplained how exactly the gap is to be closed between what ordinary citizens think and what they need to know. To do so would require convincing the public and the intellectuals alike that freedom of thought had narrowed but that resources remained to open channels of independence and insight.

As these essays and others show, even as he was entering the legal profession Riesman was rethinking its tasks and goals. And it did not take long for him to find that one important limit was its ambivalence about, if not antipathy to, other disciplines, especially the social sciences. Moreover, the case method of legal instruction was too particular, almost anti-intellectual in its isolation of experience from general or historical ideas: it "drowns imagination in technique." The real issue is not simply technical preparation for legal careers but the way that lawyers construct intellectual and social roles for themselves, defining their vocation along the lines of the narrow applications to be derived from the case method.

With his brief but still diverse experience of the law, Riesman found the chief public task to be the organization of social forces, or planning. He identified "draftsmanship" as the necessary but underutilized tool. Lawyers were trained and rewarded on the basis of their analytical skills in inductive reasoning, the manifest goal of the case method being extrapolation of cases to account for the hypothetical situations of the law classroom. What worked as a system of training, however, fell short as a framework for practice of the law as a form of inquiry into social practices and policies.

"The draftsman's job," Riesman said in 1941 in welcoming a new textbook on criminal law, "is imaginative and synthetic. He must envisage the controversies of the future, and organize opposed social forces into harmony for the resolution of these controversies. . . . The case system's feeling for words is semantic, but the draftsman needs another feeling, creative as well as critical. Planning the future with words, he must compromise divergences with them; he must educate or manipulate congresses and courts and publics."[8] Riesman's choice of "manipulate" here is disappointing in light of his distaste for intellectual cynicism. But in exploring, in the urgent circumstances of the early war years, potential roles for himself in organizational and public life he was also defining his political views. Hence he termed himself a "reluctant liberal" when he proposed government planning in education and the realm of ideas. For he had "come to believe that the ideological order is almost as unfree as the economic and that in both conjointly the government must plan for freedom."[9]

Mindful that programs designed on behalf of particular principles might later be used against them, and diffident about government service, Riesman was also reluctant to lend more than rhetorical enthusiasm to his ideas. It turned out that his chief contribution to education was within formats provided by elite research universities. And it was through inventive forms of scholarship that he pursued his public responsibilities by supplying a vocabulary and conceptual framework for thinking about the national character.

Career Drama

Riesman spent the 1941–1942 academic year at Columbia Law School where, without teaching assignments, he produced an extensive study of the laws of defamation. This elaborate work (it was published in three installments) was both the culmination of Riesman's career as a law professor and a valedictory to it. And in its major themes and method it anticipated his work as an academic sociologist later in the decade. What drew him to the study of defamation laws was what they revealed about a "community's cultural level and democratic quality." Controversy over group libel, he found, was an index of social relations, the matter of "honor" being a sign of the need to "safeguard" myriad forms of group identification. "In the political as in the economic struggle, modern democracy operates through the interplay of group activities, and it is through participation in groups that persons contribute to the social welfare and develop their individual capacities."[10] With a subject as ambitious as this Riesman's attention to method is not surprising. He was aiming in these essays at establishing the relations between historical legal doctrine and general systems of social cause and effect.

Riesman's second thoughts about a career as a law professor, therefore, reflected his recognition that his methods did not fit the routines of legal scholarship. In another long study, this one of civil liberties, he declared his interest in making use of cases like a social historian, searching for clues to the "temper" of a country or a region or an epoch.[11] His goal was to introduce more "empirical grounding" into such work as well as to demonstrate the intrinsic interest of vexing and perhaps fundamentally unresolvable matters in the law. Yet, among the law professors he knew, Riesman admits, "few were perplexed about anything, except the implementation of their own clear ideas."

Equally important at the time of his move to New York were opportunities to expand his interests via relations with a diverse group of friends and colleagues that included Margaret Mead, Ruth Benedict, Lionel Trilling, and Robert Lynd. Each contributed to Riesman's intellectual development, but Lynd especially might be said to have had a role in the direction of his career. Lynd's *Knowledge for What?* (1940) was a forceful statement of the need for reform of the social sciences. He was particularly dismayed (if that is a strong enough word), just as many of today's critics of higher education are, by the isolation of the disciplines from each other and the social consequences of excessive specialization. For Lynd the narrow research of many scholars was good only to stock "the ditty bag of an idiot." The new kind of academic social scientists Lynd called for would be capable of multidisciplinary work, empirically minded, attracted by major social problems, and eager to contribute to change through research. Lynd's book included its own taxonomy of the essential elements of human nature needing attention from scholars. Hence Lynd can be said to have provided a blueprint for *The Lonely Crowd* and the career of its author who, as a great admirer of the *Middletown* series, could not have ignored *its* authors' account of what was needed to advance the academic professions. One of the few disappointments of Riesman's career was Lynd's failure to offer him a chance to give up his legal career to work on a new community study.

In any case, although his Columbia colleagues included legal scholars with genuine cultural interests, Riesman decided that a career as a law professor was not likely to satisfy him. Returning to Buffalo would have been impossible anyway—the law school closed while Riesman was in New York—but he turned down offers to join the law faculties of several large state universities. Friedrich proposed that he take a Ph.D. in government, but Riesman thought that field would offer little by way of empirical or ethnographic research experience.

A chance meeting with a Harvard classmate led, in 1943, to a position in the office of the New York District Attorney, where Riesman wrote appeal briefs or, as he remembers, overwrote them to satisfy the perfectionist habits of a bureau head legendary for his erudition and scrupulousness. The caseload, however, turned out to be without much variety and, having already mastered the habits of research and writing, Riesman spent only a few months with the D.A. before "casting about" for another position. He wound up, again part by chance and part by choice, at the Sperry Gyroscope Company where he spent the next two and half years as contracts termination manager.

Riesman took much more from his experience with Sperry than the gyroscope as one of the central metaphors of *The Lonely Crowd* (it helps the "inner-directed" type find his way). For he welcomed the opportunity to work with the military; having been denied a commission, his work in industry would have to count as his contribution to the war effort. Ten years later Riesman would note, in a slight but suggestive essay on the psychology of careers, that the key variable was the historical developments that coincided with any particular life cycle.[12] Like countless others of his generation he experienced the moral turmoil of the war as something of a "career drama." Always inclined to see himself as a student, Riesman was also pleased to learn something about business and industry. "I worked hard under great pressure," he recalls, "with a kind of stubborn rationality." He was, to the potential dismay of some colleagues, an exceptionally candid negotiator with the military, earnestly trying to serve at once the national interest and the company.

Not surprisingly, Riesman wrote little during this period; 1945 and 1946 are the only years in a long and unusually prolific career showing no publications; his work required practical and strategic judgments and, he recalls, had little "intellectual substance." He was, in fact, surprised at being so intensely involved. One reason may have been that at Sperry he could safely ignore one of the burdens of the socially oriented intellectual of the 1940s. According to Riesman's sometime colleague C. Wright Mills, "The writer tends to believe that problems are *really* going to be solved in *his* medium, that of the word."[13] Faced with business and labor problems awaiting organizational and fiscal solutions, Riesman could still rely on his collaborative and persuasive powers (hallmarks of his scholarship) with the advantage of more readily observable results.

Never as angry as Mills about the impact of organizations (and for that matter universities) on intellectual life, Riesman's business experience helped him to speak more comfortably, and with more authority, about and to character types he would otherwise have known only second hand. He used his experience without glamorizing it. For he did indeed suffer some ideological discomfort at Sperry, having to work with enthusiasts for private enterprise in a company completely dependent on government contracts. This hardly mattered when he kept to managing material resources, but he admits now that "when I faced hostility there, it was not from people within my own intellectual and moral universe."

This may be as close as Riesman came to a career "crisis." His efforts to take stock of his situation when the war ended certainly appear, from his written account at least, to be measured. One reason, of course, is that he had attractive possibilities. He was offered the presidencies of two fine liberal arts colleges, Sarah Lawrence and Reed, where one might suppose the circumstances would be just right for someone seeking to combine scholarly, educational, and managerial talents. Yet Riesman declined both offers, thinking himself lacking the necessary patience and allegiance to the "semi-participatory milieu" of small college life.

"While I liked the idea of influence on college affairs, I would have preferred to seek it in ideas."

There is, I think, less grandiosity in Riesman's decision than this remark suggests. Compared to the circumstances in which he set aside legal practice and happened on the position at Sperry, Riesman now knew more about himself and, unlike the sheltered scholars of succeeding generations, he knew more of the culture he intended to study. He had learned from courtroom and classroom, library and corporation. And he had the advantage of several years of psychoanalysis with Erich Fromm. This aspect of Riesman's personal life and career is, for obvious reasons, scarcely documented. He reports that he entered into analysis, at the behest of his mother, sometime after he moved to Buffalo. She asked that he do so not because of any apparent clinical problem but because she was herself in analysis with Fromm's colleague Karen Horney and wished for someone to talk to about it.

Fromm accepted Riesman as patient and as colleague, even asking his help with a chapter of *Man for Himself* (Fromm never used the revision). By attending training sessions for psychoanalysts conducted by Fromm and Harry Stack Sullivan, Riesman perhaps satisfied his curiosity about yet another vocation, just as he was later to inquire into the intellectual and rhetorical foundations of psychoanalysis in a series of essays about Freud.[14] In his relations with Fromm, of course, Riesman fortified his growing interest in "social character" and the potential for classifying its forms as they finally appeared in *The Lonely Crowd.* And Riesman could hardly have resisted Fromm's enthusiasm for the "productive orientation" in living and working, partly because he spoke with the authority of an analyst, and partly because such a view was compatible with Riesman's own energetic style. He was the kind of liberal rationalist Fromm had in mind when he exhorted his readers to improve themselves and society with determined and benevolent self-development. "There is no meaning to life except the meaning man gives his life by the unfolding of his powers, by living productively."[15]

For more particular career advice Fromm first proposed that social criticism could only reflect modern man's contradictory circumstances. We are, Fromm argued, shaped by the pressure put on the timeless needs of individuals by our history as a society. For scholars with Riesman's putative ambitions, Fromm set this standard: "It is the obligation of the student of the science of man not to seek for 'harmonious' solutions, glossing over this contradiction, but to see it sharply. It is the task of the ethical thinker to sustain and strengthen the voice of human conscience, to recognize what is good or bad for society at a special period of its evolution."[16]

But Riesman was not starting from scratch. His background in law, business, and scholarship meant that he might employ powers of exposition and argument on behalf of conciliation as well as conflict. He was, after all, a "reluctant liberal," eager to improve society but skeptical about the need for "freedom" from history and uncertain about the meliorative capacities of modern industrial democracies. Accordingly, his two collections of essays were titled *Individualism Reconsidered* (1954) and *Abundance for What?* (1964). As troubled as Fromm by increasing social conformity and as utopian in his hopes for change, Riesman nonetheless could eschew exhortation in proportion to his presentation, in *The Lonely Crowd,* of the diversity of American life, and thereby locate resources for renewal even as he explored the past.

Conclusion: from Apprenticeship to Autonomy

When, in 1946, Riesman completed a decade of experiments in vocation by joining the faculty of the University of Chicago as an assistant professor, he showed great professional humility. He was "intensely eager," he recalls, to embark on a teaching and scholarly career, including the study of higher education itself, with which he is now identified. His position on the staff of the undergraduate sequence in the social sciences, with its combination of pedagogic innovation and textual tradition, allowed him to pursue historical and conceptual themes across the disciplines. He also gained the colleagueship in intellectual work he had hoped for. Riesman read widely and rapidly to prepare. And he happily attended colleagues' lectures and audited graduate courses, beginning with those of Everett C. Hughes, the influential sociologist of the professions, who became Riesman's closest friend. It was Hughes who once noted that "although a man's work may indeed be a good clue to his personal and social fate, it is a clue that leads us—and the individual himself—not by a clear and single track to a known goal, but into a maze full of dead-ends and of unexpected adventures."[17]

At Chicago, Riesman could also capitalize on the renowned multidisciplinary committees initiated by the legendary innovator Robert Maynard Hutchins. The groups working on social thought and on human development were especially attractive, and so too were the activities of the University's National Opinion Research Center, which was perhaps too empirical for Hutchins's educational idealism but ideal for Riesman's growing interest in survey research. Driven largely by his responsibilities as a teacher, Riesman was also further equipping himself as a social critic. Unhampered by formal preparation for an academic career, he came to one with his usual high-minded opportunism, zest for reading, writing, and observation, and his "productive orientation." He recognized that many people are aware of the "danger that they will not become what in character they might be." Still, there was no false (autobiographical) modesty in his judgment that "to become and remain autonomous is never easy."[18]

Whatever his previous accomplishments, Riesman called his first years at Chicago an "apprenticeship," a term whose modesty belies the fact that *The Lonely Crowd* was in large part a product of this period. It was actually written at Yale, where Riesman spent the greater part of 1948–1949 doing research on public opinion, mass communications, and popular culture under the auspices of the Committee on National Policy. Oddly enough, Riesman found the integrative ambitions of the Chicago curriculum an obstacle to his complementary taste for greater specialization in sociology and emerging sub-disciplines. Finding little interest at Yale in his project, he made of his novel interests, in relation to traditional sociology at least, a book that literary critic Lionel Trilling was to call one of the most interesting he had ever read.

Insisting that Riesman showed great literary as well as sociological gifts in his presentation of American manners and morals, Trilling found in Riesman the reasons that social science could now claim as one of its tasks the kind of cultural criticism often associated with literary studies. Trilling confessed some envy (given the direction of his own career) but also gratitude to

Riesman for suggesting through his "strong sense of social actuality . . . that there are new and wonderfully arable social fields to till."[19] *Individualism Reconsidered* prompted even greater enthusiasm from the American scholar who himself became an example in cultural criticism.[20]

Not everyone in the (mainly New York) community of literary and cultural critics was so sanguine about such a transformation or about Riesman's role in it. Writing just a few weeks before the *Time* cover story Elizabeth Hardwick said this:

> It is hard to know how to judge a thinker whose intellectual positions are so profoundly modified by "psychology," who treats his own opinions as if they were those of a character in a novel he was writing. Or again, standing in the center of the stage, watching the audience assemble, he waits for the feel of the thing and then chooses his rubbery mask, comic one way, tragic upside down. Solid success, effective therapy, animated delivery—all of this is achieved, but frequently at the expense of the brilliance that undoubtedly might be there otherwise. Riesman has genuine vitality and, of course, remarkable gifts. But if you make yourself honey the flies will eat you.[21]

Riesman had his own ideals, of course, but he was proud of his pluralism, and he felt that both needed to be held in balance in order that his program of "Values of Context" be maintained. In his essay by that name he preached the "heresy" of "intransigent" relativism. "All my adult life," he said, "I have been besieged by people who wanted to convert me to their loyalty and thought me cowardly for refusing to join."[22] Riesman has now, however, justifiably been enlisted in the struggles of the "liberal mind" during the postwar years.[23] In his own view at the time his habit of refusal meant that he had to be unusually self-conscious in his work if only to avoid the "terrible moral pitfalls of convenient uncommitment." To put the matter paradoxically, in the manner of the phrase "the Lonely Crowd," becoming a social critic meant welcoming only enough socialization (academic, political, or institutional) to fortify his individualism.

Never wholly sympathetic to the "adversary culture" of the 1960s and 1970s, as Trilling named it, Riesman is unlikely to be an ally of neo-conservative critics of the impulse toward skepticism and relativism in liberal intellectual life. It was, he said as he undertook his academic career, the "nerve of failure" that animated the best work in social science, and it was pragmatism and humility that was necessary in transforming social science into social criticism. "Moral experimentation," Riesman believed, "is essential if we want to meet life flexibly, listening to the ancestor within and friends without, but not bound to obey either."[24]

Notes

1. David Riesman (in collaboration with Reuel Denney and Nathan Glazer), *The Lonely Crowd: A Study of the Changing American Character* (New Haven: Yale University Press), 373.
2. The biographical information and quotations in the following pages are contained in two unpublished essays kindly furnished to me by David Riesman: "Becoming an Academic Man" and "My Education in 'Soc 2' and My Efforts to Adapt It in the Harvard Setting."
3. See David Riesman, "Two Generations," *Daedalus* 93 (1964): 72–97.
4. David Riesman, "Possession and the Law of Finders," *Harvard Law Review* 52 (1939): 1105.
5. David Riesman, "Legislative Restrictions on Foreign Enlistment and Travel," *Columbia Law Review* 40 (1940): 834.
6. David Riesman, "Government Education for Democracy," *Public Opinion Quarterly* 5 (1941): 205, 208.
7. David Riesman, "The Politics of Persecution," *Public Opinion Quarterly* 6 (1942): 56.
8. David Riesman, "Law and Social Science: A Report on Michael and Wechsler's Classbook on Criminal Law and Administration," *Yale Law Review* 50 (1941): 638–9.
9. Riesman, "Education for Democracy," 209.
10. David Riesman, "Democracy and Defamation: Control of Group Libel," *Columbia Law Review* 42 (1942): 731. See also "Democracy and Defamation: Fair Game and Fair Comment I," *Columbia Law Review* 42 (1942): 1085–1123 and "Democracy and Defamation: Fair Game and Fair Comment II," *Columbia Law Review* 42 (1942): 1282–1318.
11. David Riesman, "Civil Liberties in a Period of Transition," *Public Policy* 3 (1942): 33–96.
12. David Riesman, "A Career Drama in a Middle-Aged Farmer," *Bulletin of the Menninger Clinic* 19 (1955): 1–8.
13. C. Wright Mills, *Power, Politics and People: The Collected Essays of C. Wright Mills,* ed. Irving Louis Horowitz (New York: Oxford University Press, 1967), 304.
14. See my essay "David Riesman's Freud," *Transaction/Society* 26 (May/June 1989): 73–7.

15. Erich Fromm, *Man For Himself: An Inquiry Into the Psychology of Ethics* (1947; reprint New York: Holt, Rinehart and Winston, 1976), 45.
16. Fromm, *Man for Himself,* 244.
17. C. Everett Hughes, *Men and their Work* (Glencoe, IL: The Free Press, 1958), 8.
18. Riesman, *The Lonely Crowd,* 356.
19. Lionel Trilling, *A Gathering of Fugitives* (Boston: Beacon Press, 1956), 86.
20. See Mark Krupnick, *Lionel Trilling and the Fate of Cultural Criticism* (Evanston, IL: Northwestern University Press, 1986).
21. Elizabeth Hardwick, "Riesman Considered," *Partisan Review* 21 (1954): 549.
22. David Riesman, *Individualism Reconsidered* (Glencoe, IL: The Free Press, 1954), 22.
23. See Richard Pells, *The Liberal Mind in a Conservative Age: American Intellectuals in the 1940s and 1950s* (New York: Harper and Row, 1985).
24. Riesman, *Individualism Reconsidered,* 23.

6

C. Wright Mills's Great File: Sociology and History, Ideology and Imagination

As the founder of a discipline that is now an important element in interdisciplinary studies, Freud himself was enviably cautious about the results of such efforts. He acknowledged, in his contribution to anthropology, for instance, that "such writings can only be in the nature of an instigation: they put before the specialist certain suggestions for him to take into account in his own work."[1] We are often less modest now and hardly a statement on higher education in the past two decades has failed to endorse interdisciplinary courses and programs. There is much educational sloganeering in this enthusiasm but even so scholars have rightly been urged to cross disciplinary boundaries in recognition of the general direction of intellectual life. As anthropologist Clifford Geertz put it in his now widely cited essay on "Blurred Genres," scholarship is being transformed, and "something is happening in the way we think about the way we think."[2]

Metaphors and Morals

According to Geertz interdisciplinary work has little to do with the design of a curriculum (for now at least) and everything to do with the rapid transfer of ideas, images, and metaphors between the humanities and the social sciences. We face, he says with pride in the new styles, "a situation at once fluid, plural, uncentered and ineradicably untidy" (*LK,* 21). He has in mind applications in the social sciences of timeless ways of representing human experience: the game, the drama, and the text. They liberate their users (and those employing other analogies and strategies) by enabling them to stay close to their materials instead of merely to the traditions or habits of their own disciplines. "Individuals thinking of themselves as social (or behavioral or human or cultural) scientists have become free to shape their work in terms of its necessities rather than received ideas as to what they ought not to be doing" (*LK,* 210). As the materials for study increase, diversify, and intersect across disciplines, scholarly identities are muddled. What is needed according to Geertz are not curricular pieties but awareness of the new and potential intellectual relations. In fact Geertz uses the term "interdisciplinary" but once, and in a way that indicates his belief in its limits. "It is not interdisciplinary brotherhood that is needed, nor even less highbrow eclecticism. It is recognition on all sides that the lines grouping scholars together into intellectual communities, or (what is the same thing) sorting them out into different ones, are these days running at some highly eccentric angles"(*LK,* 23–4).

Future work in the relations of the humanities with the social sciences might well begin with Geertz's analysis and his own estimable scholarly productions. Geertz shares with many of today's most influential critical theorists the capacity to grasp many different interpretive styles and to make evocative applications. So too does he think that a traditional figure like Lionel Trilling represents the same intention. Trilling's goal, as he put it in a statement of his reliance on philosophic and social ideas, was "to see literary situations as cultural situations, and cultural situations as great elaborate flights about moral issues, and moral issues as having something to do with gratuitously chosen images of personal being, and images of personal being as having something to do with literary style."[3] Trilling's "hip bone connected to the thigh bone" declaration does not actually match Geertz's command of scholarship in several fields. But Geertz, who is a great admirer of Trilling's ability to capture "the social history of the moral imagination" (so he titled a 1977 essay in Trilling's memory), closes his statement on our changing genres by indirectly at least acknowledging that the moral point of view is in considerable jeopardy. He terms some implications of the newer styles of interdisciplinary thinking "disequilibrating" because they suggest that there will not be a place for Trilling's moralism, for traditional humanistic concern with the uses of teaching and scholarship in the study (not to mention promotion) of spiritual values and virtues of the examined life. In the emerging "eccentricities" of thought, Geertz says, "The specialist without spirit dispensing policy nostrums goes, but the lectern sage dispensing approved judgments goes as well. The relation between thought and action in social life can no more be conceived of in terms of wisdom than it can be in terms of expertise" (*LK*, 35). In this light Geertz's subtitle for his essay—"The Reconfiguration of Social Thought"—is not a mere elaboration of the suggestive title. It is more like a warning (or note of alarm given Geertz's own disposition and preferences) that in the new inter-relations among the disciplines some highly valued assumptions and ideas may not be simply changed but altogether lost.

Trilling's habit of seeing literary questions also as moral and social ones is typical of many scholars and intellectuals who practice what has come to be called "cultural criticism."[4] Today's forms are often more theoretically oriented, and obscurely presented, than those that Trilling and his contemporaries favored, and accordingly they have prompted the charge that an important cultural tradition is in danger.[5] Even in stating his own interests, therefore, Geertz is cautious. "How the games, dramas, or texts which we do not just invent or witness but live, have the consequences they do remains very far from clear. It will take the wariest of wary reasonings on all sides of all divides to get it clearer" (*LK*, 35). We need in other words to move backwards and forwards at the same time, to look at the scholar's vocation as itself full of meanings to be supplied by historical resources and examples as well as by conceptual innovations.

Distortions and Promises

Few American scholars have thought more about the nature and uses of scholarship in its ideological and interdisciplinary aspects or expressed themselves more forcefully about them than C. Wright Mills, who was Trilling's colleague at Columbia during the 1940s and 1950s. In fact, Mills's major statement on the subject, *The Sociological Imagination* (1959) was inspired in more than its title by Trilling's influential *The Liberal Imagination* (1950).[6] A scholar less congenial than Mills to the interdisciplinary avant-garde cited by Geertz (though not uniformly admired by him) could hardly be imagined. Except for Max Weber, Mills largely eschewed twentieth-century European thought, and despite his enthusiastic defense of breaking down the boundaries separating the disciplines of the social sciences and the humanities, he did very little lasting work in anything but sociology.

Mills's contribution in *The Sociological Imagination* and in many of the essays collected in *Power, Politics, and People* (1963) is durable because it dramatizes the circumstances of work in the social sciences and the humanities as do few other methodological studies. Mills scorned excessive professional (usually professorial and hence even more distasteful to him) interest in methodology as a sign of indifference to social problems which were in his view the real subject of social inquiry. His own work on method, therefore, exhibits a certain unintended irony as he struggles to reveal the "why" and "for what" in social science. Moreover, he not only recognized the personal element in scholarship but celebrated it. He showed how protective approaches to the styles and findings of individual disciplines stood in the way of knowledge and of satisfying and productive careers pursuing it. Mills never achieved a model sociology, but he was in many ways a model sociologist because of his zest for inquiry and because of his determination to demonstrate in his own career the complex relations in intellectual work among personal motives, historical themes and events, disciplinary perspectives, and interdisciplinary potentials.

In *The Sociological Imagination* Mills presents social science's "habitual distortions" and its "promises." Chief among the first he terms "Grand Theory" and "Abstract Empiricism." In chapters devoted to each he seeks to illustrate some failures of social science in research and social problem solving. For Mills the weaknesses in Grand Theory are revealed in the social detachment and rhetorical obscurity of Talcott Parsons. He discusses several long passages from Parson's influential *The Social System* (1951) as representative pieces of "irrelevant ponderosity." Parsons, in Mills's view, "abdicated" plain description of human conduct and society and is typical of grand theorists who are "so rigidly confined to such high levels of abstraction that the 'typologies' they make up—and the work they do to make them up—seem more often an arid game of Concepts than an effort to define systematically—which is to say in a clear and orderly way—the problems at hand, and to guide our efforts to solve them."[7] The result of such work according to Mills is the tacit endorsement of society's symbols of legitimation and hence indifference to the practical problems of real people and to social change. Put another way, the grand fault of the grand theorists in individual disciplines of the social sciences is their indifference to history and to the need for a philosophy of history to complement other theoretical efforts. "What is systematic about [Parson's] grand theory is the way it outruns any specific and empirical problem. It is not used to state more precisely or more adequately any new problem of recognizable significance. It has not been developed out of any need to fly high for a little while in order to see something in the social world more clearly, to solve some problem that can be stated in terms of the historical reality in which men and institutions have their concrete being" (*SI*, 48). The ideal scholar in Mill's view joins general conceptions and historical exposition. In fact, "the productions of historians may be thought of as a great file indispensable to all social science" (*SI*, 145).

The second important distortion in social science according to Mills is a tendency toward the accumulation of detail without context or purpose. Like Grand Theory, Abstracted Empiricism "seizes upon one juncture in the process of work and allows it to dominate the mind" (*SI*, 50). He rejects the idea that data collection is a central function of sociology since in his view that is most often done, like in grand theorizing, as a deliberate withdrawal from integrative ideals. To make his point Mills cites the ideas of another distinguished sociologist,

Paul Lazarsfeld, who claimed with enthusiasm a role for sociologists as "toolmakers" for the other social sciences. While it is true that Lazarsfeld saw also an interpretive function for sociology, that is not good enough for Mills since it is too scientific in intention, too ready to limit interpretation (and hence "social theory") to the systematic collection of conceptions verifiable by empirical research, in Mills's words, "of variables useful in interpretations of statistical findings" (*SI*, 63). Mills risks banality by pointing out the emptiness of data without theory, and the reverse, because he is wary of syntheses which are not fully realized, that is, ones that are inattentive to substantive social problems and the uses of several disciplines working together in understanding and solving them. The development of social science is not like making a quilt from miscellaneous designs, for the "little pieces, no matter how precisely defined, are not to be so mechanically and so externally linked" (*SI*, 68). He grants the formal ingenuity of much empirical work but laments its hold on many of the disciplines. "Those in the grip of the methodological inhibition often refuse to say anything about modern society unless it has been through the fine little mill of the Statistical Ritual" (*SI*, 71–2). What concerns Mills is the use of a particular method to limit the kinds of problems deemed proper for study. It is the elevation of a method, empiricism, into a philosophy, and for some practitioners into an epistemological dogma.

Mills acknowledges that nothing is in fact immune to measurement and that empiricism is a suitable and convenient approach to many problems. Nor does he oppose the specialization of tasks that empiricism serves and fortifies. The question for responsible scholarship is, in his view, what then? "If it is claimed that these [empirical] studies are parts of some division of labor which as a whole constitutes the social science endeavor, where are the other divisions of which these studies are parts? And where is the 'division' wherein just such studies as these are put into some larger picture?" (*SI*, 74) Abstracted from social problems and thus from adjacent and allied disciplines, eager empiricists cannot help but overestimate the "truth" in their work. Excessive attention to precision as a criterion for social research will not guarantee truth because it is often found in problems invisible to scholars by virtue of their trained incapacity. "The most interesting and difficult issues of method," Mills notes, "usually begin where established techniques do not apply" (SI, 72). He names the practice of these techniques in the university and the institution and agencies it serves "the bureaucratic ethos." In this domain research technicians practice a morally antiseptic method in which the autonomy (and imagination) of individual scholars becomes less important than the institutional interests they serve.

Mills finds his colleagues to be "managerial" and "manipulative," shaped by bureaucratic routines that have standardized scholarship and accommodated it to clients in business and government. In Mills's view academic sociology suffers from theoretical pretensions, quantitative bias, and detached empirical methods. Its products are poor because sociology and allied disciplines do not properly understand their tasks and the ideologies related to them. "No problem," Mills says, "can be adequately formulated unless the values involved and the apparent threat to them are stated" (SI, 129). Scornful of "scientific method" and "value free" teaching and scholarship as unifying rationales in the social sciences (the principle "distortions"), Mills proposes that the disciplines be "opened up" and encouraged to explore their "cumulative" capacities. "Objectivity in the work of social science requires the continuous attempt to become explicitly aware of all that is involved in the enterprise; it requires wide and critical interchange of such attempts" (SI, 130).

When he turns from distortions to promises, Mills relies on a simple definition: "What social science is properly about is the human variety, which consists of all the social worlds in which men have lived, are living, and might live" (SI, 132). He asks for "viewpoints" in the disciplines working singly and collaboratively that will yield work that is both understandable and comprehensive. These viewpoints must have, Mills insists, the orienting conception of social science as the study of biography, of history, and of their intersection within social structure. To achieve this we will need individual teachers and scholars who see that it is through their affiliations with allied disciplines that they can best pose problems worth studying. Mills anticipated a pluralistic but collaborative social science unified not by a comprehensive theory but by a new academic disposition.

> It is now entirely possible for the individual practitioner to ignore the "accidental" developments of departments, and to choose and shape his own specialty without much hindrance of a departmental sort. As he comes to have a genuine sense of significant problems and to be passionately concerned with solving them, he is often forced to master ideas and methods that happen to have arisen within one or another of these several disciplines. To him no social science specialty will seem in any intellectually significant sense a closed world. He also comes to realize that he is in fact practicing social science, rather than any one of the social sciences, and that this is so no matter what particular area of social life he is most interested in studying (*SI*, 141–2).

Such a scholar would be devoted to the uses of history as outlined by Mills. History is "the great file" because it is the primary resource for scholarship in all disciplines. It does not actually contain them as some claim but supplies materials and, more important, a way of framing questions, especially social and psychological ones. In fact, as Mills's argument unfolds, psychology replaces biography as one third of his interdisciplinary triad. Yet Mills is aware of the practical limits of abstraction even for his own preferred method. There is always a need to argue from cases. "The relevance of history [to psychology and sociology] is itself subject to the principle of historical specificity" (*SI*, 156). Even when proposing the promise of a fully historical and psychological sociology, Mills cannot resist suggesting that the interdisciplinary model organized around the discovery of psychological and behavioral essentials is misguided, another "distortion."

> Anything that can be asserted about man apart from what is inherent in the social-historical realities of human life will refer merely to the wide biological limits and potentialities of the human species. But within these limits and rising out of these potentialities, a panorama of human types confronts us. To attempt to explain it in terms of a theory of "basic human nature" is to confine human history itself in

some arid little cage of Concepts about "human nature—as often as not constructed from some precise and irrelevant trivialities about mice in a maze. (*SI*, 164)

The gifts of history and psychology to sociology will yield material too specific to be forgotten in grand theorizing and too generic and suggestive to be hidden in statistical or empirical studies. The material will represent the sociological imagination at work.

It is of course the capacity for integrative scholarship in the social sciences that constitutes its greatest promise. The sociological imagination will bind the disciplines as they discover common problems and goals. Moreover, the personal motives and interests of individual scholars, their "ideologies," will be properly realized, and the relation between academic scholarship and the social sciences confirmed. All of these attributes are made plain in the opening pages of *The Sociological Imagination*, as Mills defines his subject with rapidly increasing scope.

It is the quality of mind essential to grasp the interplay of man and society, of biography and history, of self and world. (*SI*, 4)

It is a quality of mind that will help [men] to use information and to develop reason in order to achieve lucid summations of what is going on in the world and of what may be happening within themselves. (*SI*, 5)

The sociological imagination enables its possessor to understand the larger historical scene in terms of its meaning for the inner life and the external career of a variety of individuals. It enables him to take into account how individuals, in the welter of their daily experience, often become falsely conscious of their social positions. Within that welter, the framework of modern society is sought, and within that framework the psychologies of a variety of men and women are formulated. By such means the personal uneasiness of individuals is focused upon explicit troubles and the indifference of publics is transformed into involvement with public issues. (*SI*, 5)

Variations and additions appear throughout the book but the main point remains: sociology and allied disciplines need a new and sympathetic motive to enable each to achieve its promise, and more important, to collaborate in a new set of grand goals for scholarship. Those who possess the sociological imagination instinctively relate one discipline to another because they are quite deliberately comparative and historical. In an outburst of optimism Mills sees the total transformation of scholars and scholarship in the practice of the sociological imagination.

> By its use men whose mentalities have swept only a series of limited orbits often come to feel as if suddenly awakened in a house with which they had only supposed themselves to be familiar. Correctly or incorrectly, they often come to feel that they can now provide themselves with adequate summations, cohesive assessments, comprehensive orientations. Older decisions that once appeared sound now seem to them products of a mind unaccountably dense. Their capacity for astonishment is made lively again. They acquire a new way of thinking, they experience a transvaluation of values: in a word, by their reflection and by their sensibility, they realize the cultural meaning of the social sciences. (*SI*, 8)

Mills's own discipline is not the only one that would benefit. All of what he calls the "human disciplines" would exist in a near utopia of insight and progressive social reform.

Mills's version of critical sociology will be familiar to many because he anticipated, some would say helped to inspire, social activism and related efforts at curricular reform in the 1960s and 1970s. The trend toward interdisciplinary studies, it can be argued, emerged from a liberal, melioristic, even transformational ideology. Mills celebrated the interdisciplinary instincts of individual practitioners but hedged somewhat in predicting that the academic and intellectual division of labor would be quickly replaced by a "very active fusion" of the disciplines. Institutional habits and the limits of textbooks, for instance, stood in the way, as did the dependence of the disciplines on abstractions. "The idea of distinct fields is based less on iron problem areas than on tin-foil Concepts. These Concepts are, nevertheless, difficult to overcome, and I do not know whether they will be. But there is just a chance, I feel, that within the society of academic disciplines certain structural trends will in due course overcome those who—often entrenched and obstinate—are still trapped in their specialized milieux" (*SI*, 141). Whether Mills had any more basis to believe in the triumph of these trends than his own optimistic belief in their history is not clear. In any case, he was left with relying on pioneering individuals to carry out new interdisciplinary initiatives.

Politics and/or Craftsmanship

From the point of view of those interested in curriculum reform and stylistic innovation Mills's program was timely and even perhaps influential. In fact, enough of his argument has been incorporated into teaching and scholarship in the social sciences and the humanities that it may be said that *The Sociological Imagination* no longer has quite the polemical force it did when it appeared and throughout the 1960s. As a writer on the sociology of knowledge Mills's limits are acknowledged even among partisans of his point of view who note that he dealt with the subject "in an expositional manner and without contributing to its theoretical development."[8] Mills himself appears to have realized this, at least in the sense that *The Sociological Imagination* was aimed at several different audiences. His capacity for advancing theory aside, Mills's talent for communicating the importance of the sociology of knowledge to workers in other disciplines is plain.[9] Mills's insistence on an inclusive and imaginative sociology is a rationale for interdisciplinary studies only partially directed at his colleagues. He risked repetition and some naive enthusiasm on behalf of attempting to unify the work of humanists and social scientists. This ambition is forcefully presented in the book's final chapter and in its novel appendix, which suggest that at times Mills was as uncertain of the need for ideological fervor as he was certain of the need for interdisciplinary scholars to be conscious of their ideology.

In "On Politics," which closes the formal part of his book, Mills resumes his analysis of the curriculum and the likely results of new interest in teaching and scholarship at the borders of the traditional disciplines. Those who work there, he repeats, will inevitably and constructively realize the political and social meanings of their work. "No one is 'outside society'; the question is where each stands within it" (*SI*, 184). But the social role of the intellectual also entails public responsibilities.

He must first translate the problems of individuals into social problems for analysis and solution. Second, he must help to create an audience beyond the classroom. A truly democratized curriculum would yield able citizens as well as students. "What he ought to do for the society is to combat all those forces that are destroying genuine publics and creating a mass society—or put as a positive goal, his aim is to help build and to strengthen self-cultivating publics" (*SI*, 186). These Jeffersonian ideals could hardly be criticized if Mills did not mix them with what appears to be a strong measure of liberal activism. Behind his hopes for a "democratic polity" is his interest in social injustice, and it is not always clear how far the sociological imagination will take its practitioners in the direction of converting scholarship into a vehicle for advocating social change. In his polity scholars would apparently speak for and against particular movements and interests.

Mills welcomes ideology in the lives of scholars as citizens. He abides by its definition as a system of ideas appropriate to a class, occupation, or other interest group that uses it in relation to struggles with competing interests. Ideologies are personal motives in the context of history. Hence the relationship of scholarship to ideology is twofold. As citizens, scholars have an intellectual role in rebuilding or replacing the classical ideologies—liberalism and socialism—which in Mills's view had virtually collapsed by the mid-twentieth century. As scholars and citizens of a professional community, sociologists and other intellectuals also have a role in shaping the ideology behind their academic activities. According to Mills what is needed is greater consciousness of the inevitability of these roles and their transformation into timely teaching and scholarship. "Where is the intelligentsia," he asks, "that is carrying on the big discourse of the western world *and* whose work as intellectuals is influential among parties and publics and relevant to the great decisions of our time?" (*SI*, 183). Mills appears to assume that to ask large questions is ipso facto to move in the ideological direction he prefers. Robert Nisbet has argued that the historical study of sociology proves just the opposite, that the great moral thinkers in the field have been conservatives and that the narrowness of contemporary sociology is a function of its "modernism," that is, its political liberalism. Ironically, he too favors more imagination and interdisciplinary work in sociology, confident that it will lead to a conservative revival.[10]

Unimpressed by Mills's program for pursuing large ideas, antagonists in the complicated scholarly debate about the relation of ideology to objectivity—the issue is usually the possibility and desirability of "value-free" research—often have Mills in mind as an example. The ideologies of these scholars are apparent from their use of Mills: liberals are sympathetic and see in him an invaluable model of intellectual responsibility; conservatives are hostile and see him as an unappealing model of intellectual recklessness.[11] What Mills himself never makes quite clear is whether ideology is only an aspect of the imagination he invokes or whether imagination, the active use of the perspectives of multiple disciplines, is essentially the best vehicle for ideology because it is the most historical. Mills in his late work appears to have begun with ideology (and in effect to have abandoned sociology). *The Sociological Imagination* seeks to convince us that we should begin with imagination or at least cultivate it side by side with ideological sophistication.

Mills's critics are prone to see him always at the barricades of struggles in sociology and in society. He was committed (the favorite adjective of his supporters) to both but was also more realistic than is sometimes acknowledged. In his view the newly interdisciplinary character of their work would enable imaginative scholars to range widely in ideologically self-conscious criticism of issues and in their special form of academic or scholarly advocacy. It is special to Mills at least because it does not entail what might normally be called action on behalf of ideology and particular causes.

> The role of reason I have been outlining neither means nor requires that one hit the pavement, take the next plane to the scene of the current crisis, run for Congress, buy a newspaper plant, go among the poor, set up a soap box. Such actions are often admirable, and I can readily imagine occasions when I should personally find it impossible not to want to do them myself. But for the social scientist to take them to be his normal activities is merely to abdicate his role, and to display by his action a disbelief in the promise of social science and in the role of reason in human affairs. This role requires only that the social

scientist get on with the work of social science and that he avoid furthering the bureaucratization of reason and of discourse. (*SI*, 192)

Sensitive to the charge that he is seeking to convert scholarship into an effort to "save the world" Mills sounds after all rather traditional—like his colleague Trilling—in his defense of research and reason. "It is on the level of human awareness that virtually all solutions to the great problems must now lie" (*SI*, 193). The values and interests of scholars, and the institutions and agencies they serve, are still decisive, but their efforts can actually lead to the revitalization through imagination of scholarship and to the improvement of society. Mills would only have social scientists and humanists confront their "major moral dilemma—the difference between what men are interested in and what is in men's interest" as a means of achieving the sociological imagination (*SI*, 193).

The surprisingly ambivalent or realistic note in Mills's view of the politicization of learning is revealed in his understanding of what is the essential heritage of the social sciences. In the closing sentence of "On Politics" its "classic values" are said once again to be in the potential for creating a democracy of reason by formulating personal troubles and social issues as scholarly and practical problems. In the very first sentence of the next section Mills asserts that "to the individual social scientist who feels himself a part of the classic tradition, social science is the practice of a craft" (*SI*, 195). It is the internal interests and activities of the disciplines that are the subject of "On Intellectual Craftsmanship," an appendix to *The Sociological Imagination* longer than any of the book's chapters.

In its candor about Mills's working methods (sociologist Lewis Feuer called it a statement of "workology") and insistence upon the role of personal experience in any intellectual work, this essay is a logical extension of the goals of *The Sociological Imagination*.[12] "Scholarship," Mills affirms, "is a choice of how to live as well as a choice of a career" (*SI*, 196). A career in systematic reflection on the meaning of history and the organization of society, however, entails gaining some control over personal experience. For this Mills recommends keeping a file. Less directly metaphoric than his earlier designation of history, the file of the individual scholar is nevertheless a sign of his need to be self-reflective and his instinct (often stifled as a member of a department and discipline) toward inclusiveness. "You learn how to keep you inner world awake" (*SI,* 197) and to cultivate a kind of deliberate intellectual restlessness. "Any working social scientist," Mills says, "who is well on his way ought at times to have so many plans, which is to say ideas, that the question is always, which of them am I, ought I to work on next?" (*SI,* 198). The file is the symbol (and tangible record) of a process that has a momentum of its own when it joins issues of substance and the life of the scholar. "You do not really have to *study* a topic you are working on . . . once you are into it, it is everywhere. You are sensible to its themes; you see and hear them everywhere in your experience, especially . . . in apparently unrelated areas. Even the mass media, especially bad movies and cheap novels and picture magazines and night radio, are disclosed in fresh importance to you" (*SI,* 211).

Mills describes his "workology" by reviewing a section from his file for *The Power Elite* (1956). Its orderliness belies the spontaneity of *The Sociological Imagination.* The key, however, is not simply careful notetaking and determined cross-classification. It is multiple perspectives. Ask yourself, Mills advises sociologists and others, how a political scientist, or historian, or a psychologist would look at the text, data, or problems at hand. The goal, he says in words similar to Geertz's, is to "let your mind become a moving prism catching light from as many angles as possible" (*SI,* 214). Keep your mind, he continues, on the images of man and of history and resist pressures to give up your ideological autonomy. The sociological imagination will emerge from two principles of the scholarly craft. They are cited separately in Mills's text but are for obvious reasons closely related. First, "Thinking is a struggle for order and at the same time for comprehensiveness" (*SI,* 223), and second, "Never write more than three pages without at least having in mind a solid example" (*SI,* 224).

Ironically, the part of *The Sociological Imagination* that is most about methodology and least concerned with ideology proves to be one of its more durable contributions. Even Mills's critics, like Feuer, praised its usefulness.[13] Writing about his own work no doubt made Mills's generalizations and advice more reliable. For while many of Mills's colleagues greeted *The Sociological Imagination* with enthusiasm as a salutary effort at stimulating the profession, they also regretted Mills's lack of restraint in judging by a single standard the ultimate worth of a diverse endeavor. Lewis Coser, for instance, grants Mills his gripes but complains about his habit of denigrating the efforts of those who work "in a different analytic vein." He cites the example of the history of science as evidence that important intellectual breakthroughs are "often achieved in seemingly remote areas, in the explanation of what appeared at first peripheral phenomena." Coser is also uneasy about Mills's demands for moving among several disciplines in search of imagination. Speaking of Mills's work in general, Coser says that he "always thinks on the skin of things. He is too much in a hurry, too eager to get at 'the big problems' to afford the patience for the painful compilation of detailed knowledge which is one of the marks of the major scholar."[14] Mills's Columbia colleague and methodological foe Robert Merton dealt with Mills's argument in a different way altogether. It was, he claims, dated when it appeared. Speaking in 1959 at an international sociological congress he refers in passing to Mills's "recent little book" and proposes that its program is already a part of mainstream sociology and that it will further institutionalize itself only if critics like Mills desist from exacerbating internal disputes.

> Each of the various patterns of interdisciplinary collaboration has its intellectual rationale. They are not merely the outcomes of social forces. However, these rationales are apt to be more convincing . . . to sociologists who find their discipline is no longer on trial. It has become sufficiently legitimized that they no longer need to maintain a defensive posture of isolation. Under these social circumstances, interdisciplinary work becomes a self-evident value and may even be exaggerated into a cultish requirement.[15]

Merton's view suggests the volatile professional environment in which *The Sociological Imagination* appeared. It reflected controversy as much as it stimulated it.

Conclusion: Finding Out

Mills was sure of an audience for *The Sociological Imagination* in and out of sociology. For despite Coser's doubts and Merton's dismissal, he was responding to criticism of his discipline as it was typified by political and social historian George Lichtheim who proposed that the future of the field required "some leading sociologist to get up in public and announce in plain terms that there is no such thing as statistical phlogiston."[16] Mills did this and more. Intellectual achievement, especially work that illustrates the binding of the disciplines in studies of social importance, was in Mills's view a matter of ideological commitment and scholarly craft. His own career is ample testimony of the pressure of one on the other. *The Sociological Imagination* seeks to translate the problem into a matter of intentions, to make, as Nisbet would say, a "creative paradox" of the occupational dilemma of the sociologist.

There was more to Mills's analysis than academic militancy. The issue of institutional reform was only an aspect of the problem. Like Geertz he saw in the historical development of the social sciences and the humanities—the building of his Great File—the beneficial results of the diffusion of methods, subjects, and styles.

> Intellectually, the central fact today is an increasing fluidity of boundary lines; conceptions move with increasing ease from one discipline to another. There are several notable cases of careers based rather exclusively on the mastery of the vocabulary of one field and its adroit use in the traditional area of another. Specialization there is and there will be, but in ought not to be in terms of the more or less accidentally built disciplines as we know them. It should occur along the lines of problems the solution of which requires intellectual equipment traditionally belonging to these several disciplines. Increasingly similar conceptions and methods are used by all social scientists. (*SI*, 140)

Unlike Geertz, Mills was primarily interested in the reorganization of the disciplines according to "problems," which he sometimes defined as both the subjects and themes of inquiry and the practical difficulties of individuals and groups in society.[17]

For Mills, scholars could no more escape ideology then they could history, or department meetings and professional associations, or the politics of their neighborhoods and cities. In fact it was part of his purpose to demonstrate their relations. *The Sociological Imagination* gives us reasons to do so but not the means. A better guide, once again, would be Geertz, whose essay on "Ideology as a Cultural System" presents the subject in a fresh way. He grants the power of "interest theory" as a key element in the analysis of ideology (and the role of Mills) but proposes that it has reached its limits. As a theory, and we can suppose also as a plan for problem solving, it has "turned out to be too rudimentary to cope with the complexity of the interaction among social, psychological and cultural factors it itself uncovered."[18] Geertz proposes instead the incorporation of ideology into interdisciplinary scholarship through the study of rhetoric, figurative language, and symbolic action. The models for this work are in literary criticism but of the kind practiced by critics like Kenneth Burke and not Trilling, whose interest in ideology, though strong, did not yield a comprehensive theory of its expression and meanings.

The Sociological Imagination is a work of debunking and advising but mainly of exhortation. It retains its importance because it stands for an ideal of scholarship even if it does not entirely demonstrate it. That is why Mills has been celebrated as an influence on the academic generation that succeeded his even if it has not lived up to his putative standards. Hence, today's "radical sociologists may dream of revolution, but they bank on their profession. Professionalization also spells privatization, a withdrawal from a larger public universe. Mills was a scrappy public thinker, who was also a professor; today radical sociologists are first professors and rarely, if ever, public intellectuals."[19]

Mills was describing himself in a passage about his hopes for younger scholars to escape the Bureaucratic Ethos. He asks for "passionate curiosity about a great problem," the sort that "compels the mind to travel anywhere and by any means, to re-make itself if necessary, in order to *find out*" (*SI*, 105). To this ambition must be added Mills's equally zealous moralism, which reflects Trilling's approach to literature. As Richard

Hofstadter, who though a friend of Mills by no means shared his social views, said: "His work was undertaken as a kind of devotional exercise, a personal discipline, and to think of it in this fashion was possible because it was more than merely workmanlike and professional: it was work at thinking, work done supposedly in the service of truth. The intellectual life here has taken on a kind of primary moral significance."[20] If as Geertz suggests the future of "wisdom" as a function of academic work in the social sciences and humanities is endangered, then it will need to be served by example as well as by argument.

Notes

1. Sigmund Freud, *Totem and Taboo,* trans. and ed. James Strachey, *Standard Edition of the Complete Psychological Works* (London: Hogarth Press, 1953–1975), XIII, 75.
2. Clifford Geertz, *Local Knowledge: Further Essays in Interpretive Anthropology* (New York: Basic Books), 20. Future references appear in the text with the acronym *LK.*
3. Lionel Trilling, *Beyond Culture: Essays on Literature and Learning* (New York: Harcourt Brace Jovanovich, 1979), 12.
4. See Giles Gunn, *The Culture of Criticism and the Criticism of Culture* (New York: Oxford University Press, 1987).
5. See Russell Jacoby, *The Last Intellectuals: American Culture in the Age of Academe* (New York: Basic Books, 1987).
6. Midway between the publication of the two books their authors became estranged. They debated the postwar transformations of intellectual life which in Mills's view compromised certain ideals of independent criticism. See Irving Louis Horowitz, *C. Wright Mills: An American Utopian* (New York: The Free Press, 1983): 84–7. Horowitz notes also the more palpable influence on Mills of Robert Lynd's *Knowledge for What?* (1940). Even so, their relations (Lynd was aloof to the younger man) reflected a clash of personalities and ideas (88–93).
7. C. Wright Mills, *The Sociological Imagination* (New York: Oxford University Press, 1959), 34. Future references appear in the text with the acronym *SI.*
8. Peter Berger and Thomas Luckmann, *The Social Construction of Reality: A Treatise in the Sociology of Knowledge* (New York: Anchor Books, 1967), 12.
9. The lesson has been summarized this way: "Sociologists attracted to research . . . are subject to strong organizational pressures. They

confuse metaphysics with morality; in rejecting (rightly) any realm of a priori judgments in their work they also assume (wrongly) that research must be free of the tasks of addressing the meaning of moral action and the place of knowledge" (Horowitz, *C. Wright Mills,* 158).

10. Robert Nisbet, *The Sociological Tradition* (New York: Basic Books, 1966) and *Sociology as an Art Form* (New York: Oxford University Press, 1976).

11. See Irving Lewis Horowitz, ed., *The New Sociology: Essays in Social Science and Social Theory in Honor of C. Wright Mills* (New York: Oxford University Press, 1964) and Maurice Stein and Arthur Vidich, eds., *Sociology on Trial* (Englewood Cliffs, NJ: Prentice-Hall, 1963). An enthusiastic account of Mills in relation to work in other fields can be found in Richard H. Pells, *The Liberal Mind in a Conservative Age: American Intellectuals in the 1940s and 1950s* (New York: Harper and Row, 1985), 249–61. For Russell Jacoby, Mills is an intellectual model for his accessibility and his interest in reaching a general audience (like Trilling and Mills's other Columbia colleague, Richard Hofstadter) but also for his resistance to the academic ethos (*The Last Intellectuals,* 78–85).

12. "On Intellectual Craftsmanship" was actually begun before *The Sociological Imagination.* A 1952 draft appeared in *Society* (January/February 1980) with a previously unpublished tribute by Mills's mentor Hans Gerth.

13. Lewis Feuer, "A Neo-Marxist Conception of Social Science," *Ethics* 70 (1960): 237–40.

14. Lewis Coser, "The Uses of Sociology," *Partisan Review* 27 (1960): 170.

15. Robert Merton, "Social Conflict over Styles of Sociological Work," in Larry T. Reynolds and Janice M. Reynolds, eds., *The Sociology of Sociology: Analyses and Criticism of the Thought, Research and Ethical Folkways of Sociology and Its Practitioners* (New York: David McKay, 1970), 179. Merton's remarks may be behind this comment from Norman Birnbaum: "Specific studies of groups of sociologists and their work have been very rare. C. Wright Mills, to be sure, did attempt such a study for contemporary American sociology in his recent *The Sociological Imagination;* the reception accorded his work will not encourage many to follow him. His book has simply not been followed by the serious discussion of its merits" (*Toward a Critical Sociology* [New York: Oxford University Press, 1971], 39).

16. George Lichtheim, "Is There a Sociologist in the House?" *Partisan Review 27 (1960): 310.*

17. Mills's focus on the latter is the reason he is still part of the debate over the intellectual vocations (see Jacoby, *The Last Intellectuals* and Pells, *The Liberal Mind in a Conservative Age*) but absent from

influential work on the transformations of scholarship (e.g. Paul Rabinow and William Sullivan, eds., *Interpretive Social Science: A Second Look* [Berkeley: University of California Press, 1987]).

18. Clifford Geertz, *The Interpretation of Cultures* (New York: Basic Books, 1973), 202.

19. Jacoby, *The Last Intellectuals,* 118. Irving Louis Horowitz, in a revealing "Postscript" to his authoritative biography of Mills, concurs on the matter of Mills's interest in a public audience, but he offers some reasons to be skeptical about him as a model for progressive social views, especially with regard to minorities and women. See Horowitz, *Persuasions and Prejudices: An Informal Compendium of Modern Social Science 1953–1988* (New Brunswick, NJ: Transaction, 1989), 438–52.

20. Hofstadter's statement appears in his influential *Anti-Intellectualism in American Life* (1963) and is cited in a perceptive essay by Richard Gillam: "Richard Hofstadter, C. Wright Mills and 'The Critical Ideal,'" *The American Scholar 47 (Winter 1977/78): 69–85.*

7

Teachers, Truants, and the Humanities:
Lionel Trilling Among "People Like Us"

Shortly before he died in 1975, Lionel Trilling recalled with
some amusement a problem he had recently faced in offering a
course on Jane Austen. Many more students had enrolled than
could be accepted, and when he decided to admit only a modest
number he found a "bizarre show of almost hysterical moral
urgency" among those denied. Thinking about this "uncanny
episode" Trilling contemplated a psychological explanation: by
reading Jane Austen the student enthusiasts believed they
could "in some way transcend our sad contemporary existence,
that, from the world of our present weariness and desiccation,
they might reach back to a world which, as it appears to the
mind's eye, is so much more abundantly provided with trees
than with people, a world in whose green shade life for a
moment might be a green thought." At the same time Trilling
realized that this reason might be termed social or even political. He noted that during the 1960s many students found in
William Blake a literary figure relevant to their individualistic
and sometimes rebellious aspirations. Blake and Jane Austen,
Trilling suggested, offered students "a position from which to
scrutinize modern life with adverse intention." Both writers
can be said to have contributed to what Trilling had once
termed the "adversary culture," a style of thought generally
hostile to prevailing social values. Trilling also observed the
oddness of associating Jane Austen with Blake as an inspirational figure, though he explained it by noting that the climate

133

of critical and cultural opinion changes so rapidly. "The style phases of our culture are notoriously short; it was not to be thought anomalous that at one moment disgust with modern life should be expressed through devotion to a figure proposing impulse, excess, and the annihilation of authority, and then a scant five years later through devotion to the presiding genius of measure, decorum, and irony."[1]

Less temperate and certainly less generous than Trilling, more recent observers of scholarly and intellectual life suggest that the thesis and antithesis interpretation of cultural trends is insufficiently rigorous. Sociologist Robert Nisbet termed the last few decades the "Age of Vandalism" in the arts and humanities, a point of view widely publicized by Allan Bloom in his bestselling attack on the contemporary university, *The Closing of the American Mind.* In 1982 in a similar vein, art critic Hilton Kramer inaugurated his journal, *The New Criterion,* with an assault on other critics and scholars. In his self-proclaimed "disinterested" view, their work is dominated by "dishonesties, hypocrisies, and disfiguring ideologies," and hence presents an obstacle to the identification and maintenance of "standards of quality" in the creative and critical disciplines. He and his journal, Kramer asserts in his first editorial, will speak for the "values of high arts," for "informed intelligence," and for the "criterion of truth" in criticism. His tone and the tasks he assigned to himself and other contributors indicate just how contentious the cultural environment became in the 1970s and 1980s.

The political division among liberals and conservatives has had its counterpart in scholarly affairs, and in a cultural politics even more divisive in some ways than the 1960s version. It poses a threat to scholarship and intellectual life more important than the widely publicized "crisis" in the humanities, which often amounts to laments about lack of public regard and the decline in the popularity of the liberal arts curriculum. There is a crisis *within* the arts and humanities reflecting competing ideals of achievement and utility and their relation to the meaning of recent American history and the future of our culture. A point of view which only simmered in Trilling's late work has now boiled over in the jeremiads of neoconservative cultural critics whose devotion to "standards" is offered as the way to reclaim the hegemony of "high" cultural ideals in the arts and in scholarship.[2]

Politics, Pedagogy, and People Like Us

Long before the educational and intellectual dispute became an item in newspaper editorials and popular magazines, critics had noted a decline in the status of scholarly achievement. Trilling himself, speaking in 1972 as the National Endowment for the Humanities' first Jefferson lecturer, outlined the crisis without mentioning the humanities at all. He described the fate of "Mind in the Modern World." In Trilling's view many American intellectuals, and a good part of the general public, had lost confidence in "mind" or the power of thinking and were unsure of their relation to history. We face as a culture, therefore, a self-imposed crisis in authority, as the ideology of experimentation, immediacy, and rapid change has captured our educational institutions and the learned disciplines, especially literature. "Resentment of the authority of mind," Trilling says, "has grown to the point of becoming a virtually political emotion." What have been lost are the long admired attributes of mind, "its energy, its intentionality, its impulse toward inclusiveness and completeness, its search for coherence with due regard for the integrity of the elements which it brings into relation with each other, its power of looking before and after."[3] Restoring these virtues or making a new case for traditional humanistic study, Trilling argued, is actually a matter of resistance to aspects of the "adversary culture" and of will in defining and promoting the uses of mind.

Like other scholars of his time, Trilling was concerned but confident, since one characteristic of mind is "its wish to be conscious of itself, with what this implies of its ability to examine a course it has taken and to correct it." As the nation's most eminent literary critic as well as a partisan in the educational and ideological debates of the period, Trilling also used the NEH pulpit to assail the federal affirmative-action program as an example of public misunderstanding of the philosophical and historical meaning of equality. In doing so he illustrated how the pressure of politics can influence thinking about scholarship and intellectual life and how the humanities are inevitably instruments for thinking about public policy. Trilling's high-mindedness and his topicality mixed well and anticipated the intellectual debates of the 1980s, shaped as they were by the relations of educational philosophy and public affairs.

As Trilling often acknowledged, however, the roots of scholarly pride in the capacities of the humanities lie in the traditions of advanced learning and in their twentieth-century uses in classroom teaching. For instance, sociologist Lewis Feuer remembers his teacher, the great philosopher Arthur Lovejoy, as a man of "searching vision" and inspiring pedagogy. He "conveyed the sense of the collective human mind, struggling with certain basic axioms to which it tried to accommodate all it experienced, and with expressing its gropings consecutively in poetry, romances, philosophies, political ideologies, and scientific ideas. He conveyed it not vaguely but with clarity and an overwhelming documentation."[4] Feuer's tribute is one in a gallery of portraits of well-known scholars. All were written for *The American Scholar*—most during the 1970s—at the invitation of its editor Joseph Epstein, who notes that "teaching like opera is a performing art," and who was determined to preserve accounts of some of the best performers. The portraits of teachers like Lovejoy, I. A. Richards, and Hannah Arendt—written by students who themselves have become distinguished scholars—illustrate how the pleasure and wisdom derived from the humanities are usually products of passionate and expert pedagogy. These masters were all moralists, but they generally eschewed "humanistic" piety in favor of close attention to ideas, events, and texts. For Epstein, who largely shares Bloom's view of the contemporary university, the great teachers and scholars were "deadly serious" about the need to carry the imperatives of the distinctive methods and powerful texts of their disciplines into their teaching.

Yet Epstein's confidence in the techniques and achievements of great teachers masks somewhat the ambivalence of academic intellectuals. Like Bloom, Kramer, and others, Epstein rejects many of today's leading scholars as ideologically motivated. *Masters* conceals the deep divisions within the teaching profession as they appeared during the recent tumultuous period of academic experimentation and change. There is no sign among Epstein's model scholars, for the record at least, of the uncertain will among American academics in the postwar decades. In Trilling's novel *The Middle of the Journey* (1947), a disaffected literary intellectual contemplates the ironies of the popular child's tale of Ferdinand the bull, who was enchanted by flowers away from the violence of the ring. "I wonder," he says, "if we're not developing a strange ambivalent kind of culture, people like us. I wonder if we don't rather like the idea of safety—a loss of bullhood. A kind of Kingdom-come by emasculation." Trilling saw how the responsibilities of teaching and scholarship, especially the rigorous questioning of social values, would inevitably conflict with the attractions of a society willing to accept if not celebrate its best thinkers, and frequently to domesticate them, so to speak, in academic departments.[5]

The seemingly harmless ambivalence identified or perhaps even satirized by Trilling, however, has also inspired professional controversy. Indeed, a convenient way of measuring the divisions among teachers, and the distance between the attitudes and methods of Epstein's masters and those of the pedagogic activists who succeeded them in the classroom, is to look at another influential collection of essays on teaching. In *The Politics of Literature: Dissenting Essays on the Teaching of English,* young teachers and accomplished scholars explore the social and political meanings of the English curriculum, critical theory, and the organization and goals of the academic profession. Their premise is that educational problems are rooted in politics, economics, and the historic class struggle. They find traditional forms of literary theory, pedagogic style, and professional activity indifferent to politics and the need for social change. Feuer praised Lovejoy because he was impervious to ideology, "his critical spirit, elevated by his historical researches, seemed to dwell in a transtemporal realm." For the radical critics of the late 1960s and since, effective pedagogy requires ideological commitment.

To appreciate the difference between the classroom results sought by the pedagogic dissenters and the habits of teachers like Lovejoy, Richards, and Arendt, it is necessary only to observe one of the educational "sanctuaries" organized in 1970 at MIT. As described by a participant, this two-week-long "learning community" shared lodging, meals, subjects, and fatigue. In a single large room a class in one corner discussed Proust, another corner housed a discussion about symbolic logic, a third had as its subject community organizing. "In another [corner] people might just be sacked out." The value of such a community, it is proposed, is that it is the "absolute negation" of ordinary academic life in which teaching is hopelessly compartmentalized. The "sanctuary" was intended to make learning accessible and to symbolize through its physical intimacy the actual relationships between subjects and disciplines. Discussions of Proust, for example, were available to "anyone passing by."[6]

Students and teachers found the greatest satisfaction, however, in the group's desire to integrate intellectual and social interest. "There was . . . the immediate sense," we are told, "that one's deepest feelings, as one listened to the testimony of the GI who had left the army, were similar to those one sometimes had when studying Proust, cell biology, English social history; that one carried on all aspects of one's life within the clear, full light of political purpose."[7] Contempt for the traditional classroom (and the scholarly professions it represented) along with idealization of experimental ones were hallmarks of the period. Teaching the humanities was assumed by many to have become a mere elitist exercise, confirming the sterility of bourgeois life under capitalism. As another radical scholar put it, "To remold our ideas so that we can join the people and serve them, it is necessary to find out how we got to be what we are. We must practice self-criticism, and we must do this on the basis of objective analysis and a clear identification with the oppressed classes."[8] Such sentiments were probably no more or less typical in the sixties and seventies than the achievements of Epstein's masters in the preceding decades, but they suggest the ethos of academic life as it was experienced by many scholars in the humanities and social sciences, and the tangle of intellectual, instructional, and social motives with which we still live.

Explaining the relations between those motives is one of the daunting if appealing scholarly tasks of our time. It prompted Bloom's angry attack on his colleagues.[9] Yet books like Daniel Bell's *The Cultural Contradictions of Capitalism* (1976), Richard Sennett's *The Fall of Public Man* (1977), Christopher Lasch's *The Culture of Narcissism* (1979), and Robert Bellah's *Habits of the Heart* (1985) expertly mingle intellectual and social themes. They derive in part from a great tradition of social criticism originating in English writers of the nineteenth century, including Carlyle, Mill, Ruskin, and of course Matthew Arnold. Trilling himself, a proponent of Arnold's ideas, contributed to the synthesis of motives in all of his work, from *The Liberal Imagination* (1950) to *Sincerity and Authenticity* (1972). In fact, in the former he stated a program for a synthetic style: "It is no longer possible," he says, "to think of politics except as the politics of culture, the organization of human life toward some end or other, toward modification of . . . the quality of human life."[10] The modification that first dominated this critical tradition was the fortification of private and public life against the harmful effects of industrialization, technology, and mass communications. But another modification, favored by contributors to *The Politics of Literature,* is the enlargement of opportunities for the poor and minorities. A third, favored by those now called neoconservatives, is the rescue of modern society from the excesses of the welfare state and bureaucracy, and from the decline of authority in politics, the arts, and education. While many teachers and scholars see themselves only marginally related to these tasks, those who have accepted Trilling's program eagerly incorporate into their work wide-ranging interests. For some, however, the only responsible approach is the direct application of their disciplines to ideological issues.

During the period of academic turmoil, critics of depth and deserved influence insisted on the assimilation of social ideals into teaching and scholarship. Richard Ohmann's essay in *The Politics of Literature,* for instance, includes a careful, detailed analysis of the dominant style of literary criticism. He argues that in their wish to convey the autonomy of literature many influential scholars and teachers (like Richards, in Ohmann's view) deliberately ignored its potential as a format for ideological debate and as a resource for social change. "They see art," he says, "as freeing man *from* politics by putting him above his circumstances, giving him inner control, affording a means of salvation, placing him beyond culture."[11] Ohmann acknowledges, as many other partisans of the period did not, that teaching and scholarship in the humanities have relied less on intrinsic class bias (or unconscious sympathy with cultural elitism and therefore also with social and economic oppression) than on the simple or simple-minded wish of most academics to be free of politics. Timidity, he claims, together with social and professional aspirations and the wish for security, made them this way—not just the promulgation of a particular literary theory. The remoteness of most literary theorizing is just another symptom and not the cause of the aridity of most teaching.

In Ohmann's analysis, the real crisis in the humanities has its origins in their deliberate isolation from politics and social action and hence their collaboration in the transformation of the university into a place where "the administrative class learns to think, where the scientific foundations of technology are laid, and where ideology is built to sanction the distribution of power and wealth in capitalist society."[12] The issue for Ohmann, then, is what will animate responsible teaching in the future. He offers the goals of Marxist criticism and pedagogy: rebuilding the whole person by connecting literature and social ideals, and exploring the relation between elite culture and the lives of ordinary people. Writing in 1970, Ohmann attaches great urgency to the fulfillment of these goals. Though he begins his essay by citing Trilling's genteel despair, Ohmann closes with the radical alarm of British Marxist Christopher Caudwell who predicted in the mid-1930s, shortly before he was killed fighting with the Loyalists in the Spanish Civil War, that "Humanism, the creation of bourgeois culture, finally separates from it . . . [and] must either pass into the ranks of the proletariat or, going quietly into a corner, cut its throat."[13]

According to standards defined by Ohmann and his radical colleagues, the great teachers of Epstein's *Masters* contributed to a scholarly and pedagogic style that isolated the humanities from politics and advocacy of social change. The exceptions, like Arendt and F. O. Mathiessen, were more inclined to explore political theory or abstract social ideas than to organize their classes according to explicit political goals. The counterpoint to *Masters* offered by the radical critics, however, has now a seemingly permanent place in our expectations for scholarship and intellectual life. It is one reason why Ann Douglas, in her portrait of the influential literary critic and colonialist Perry Miller, terms deplorable his merely minor interest in the meaning of social class and the political process. And it accounts for William Barrett's decision to devote much of his important memoir, *The Truants,* to the impact of radical politics on the renowned New York intellectuals. Politics, in short, is not to be excluded from discussions of intellectual life, and *Masters* will be judged by some as utopian.

It is the "grip of orthodoxy" among writers influenced by Marxism that interests Barrett. For Douglas, an historian with strong social interests, it is the possibility of influence without ideology that counts. She sees more in Miller than his elitist views. He deserved but did not get a place in *Masters,* she suggests, because he embodied—as great teachers must—"the romance of the mind, the hubris of striving for perfect intellectual command." Miller was intense and ambitious. His dignity and influence derived from his inspirational pedagogy. He invited students to "read and think and write as if they were the burning business of life." In her explanation of what motivated Miller, Douglas provides a timely rationale for scholarship: "To Miller, ideas were only trivial when, as they usually are, they are incomplete, borrowed or unthought, and books are only unimportant to those who cannot read."[14] Through his erudition and gift for re-creating the making of great works of literature, Miller made the classroom into an arena that did not exclude politics but, according to Douglas, subsumed it into a more primary enterprise. As surely as we need political ideals and heroic examples like Malcolm X, she claims, we need Miller's "sheer commitment to thought." Unwilling to accept the assumption that the classroom is a natural refuge from politics, Douglas shows how an academic career can express both intellectual and social ideals. She agrees, therefore, with the portrait artists of *Masters* who are witnesses to the building of a pedagogic tradition, the chief flaw of which perhaps is not indifference to politics but the tradition's potential for housing "people like us," stalled in ambivalence, who neither emulate the great teachers nor contribute to social change.

Truants and Partisans

Despite his coy subtitle, *Adventures among the Intellectuals,* Barrett hopes in *The Truants* to explain the major trends in post–World War II American culture. While the mixture of personal and intellectual relationships associated with the influential *Partisan Review* is the chief theme of this memoir, he claims that its "fugitive" theme is actually "the mind of our century." He shares the view of other critics of the period that our best minds tried to combine Marxist political beliefs with a taste for modern literature and art. Yet the inaccessibility (to ordinary readers) of writers like Eliot, Yeats, and Joyce, their conservative political ideas, and the totalitarianism characteristic of most modern socialist states made the combination difficult to sustain. The *Partisan Review* intellectuals sought a purer Marxism than the Soviet Union's and a modified modernism in literature which sometimes sidestepped the political interests of the great modern writers in favor of their technical innovations and relation to tradition. Barrett's firsthand account of the making of this compromise and its costs is his intended gift to today's teachers and scholars in the humanities. In his view, the fate of academic liberalism is inevitably its awakening to the real dangers of international communism and the reshaping of scholarly interests and pedagogic styles around nationalistic and religious ideals.

Barrett accepts the idea that the study of culture *is* the study of politics, that the interpretation of books and events as well as disputes over the curriculum and the tasks of scholarship are often a format for the emergence of new political ideas or for the reemergence (or modification) of old ones. Hence Barrett's personal history of the *Partisan Review* and its circle of editors and contributors is offered as a paradigm for the study of the relations between literary and political ideas. In defense of the autobiographical style of scholarship, he proposes that many of the social effects of intellectual work are discernible from the perspective of personal memory in addition to formal history. The importance of *his* portraits, he claims, is in the indirect but still powerful influence his subjects have had on today's ideas and attitudes.

> Intellectuals are less disconnected from the social body than they like to imagine. As their attitudes shift, some cultural middlemen will always be around to transmit the tremors of change to society at large. The shift may not be noticeable at once, and may seem an entirely small-scale and private affair; and usually the rate of transmission requires a decade or so to be effective. But follow the zigs and zags of any given intellectual and you may turn out to be reading the fever chart of the next generation.[15]

Barrett is not above playing middleman himself as he explores how a group of celebrated humanists (they would have resisted being called that), many of whom worked outside the academy, carried out a loosely organized but influential program of literary, social, and political criticism. Those he favors anticipated, he claims, the neoconservative views now popular; those he rejects, forerunners of Ohmann, were in his view permanently misled by Marxism, truants from the realities of American life. Some of his friends and colleagues wavered or changed their views and are hence difficult to classify, but the lesson of Barrett's scholarly and journalistic adventures is that in the politics of culture the right ideas about communism and capitalism are at least as important as good taste in the arts and a sophisticated historical sensibility.

The Truants has its own candidates for the title of master. Chief among them is Trilling, whose portrait is framed by Barrett's memories of life among other New York intellectuals following World War II. He offers, for instance, a glimpse of Hannah Arendt with a different emphasis than that provided in *Masters* by her former students. When seen among her peers, and at an earlier stage in her career, Arendt is more than an exemplary teacher. According to Barrett she served as the "Good European" during the immediate postwar period, the interpreter to New York intellectuals of European tendencies toward violence and totalitarianism. At the same time she also became an interpreter and advocate of the major existentialist philosophers. Her occasional arrogance and sense of superiority to things American were tolerated because they were grounded in her relation to the central social and philosophical movements of this century. There was, therefore, a paradox implicit in her reputation as essentially a political thinker. For though she "had little taste or feeling for the humdrum and gritty actualities of American politics" she overcame this short-coming by her powers of theoretical argument. In fact she was, and still is, idealized by many as a prototypical intellectual and humanist precisely because of her indifference to practical politics and to popular culture generally. "She was always conscious of coming from elsewhere—of speaking from something older and deeper that she understood as European culture, something she guarded at her center" (99). For some of Barrett's truants, American life was too young and shallow to be of real interest. Others felt responsibility for instructing Americans in advanced forms of intellectual cosmopolitanism.

According to Barrett, many of the teachers, scholars, and poets who for a time following World War II dominated New York intellectual life deserve to be called truants. One of them, in fact, supplied the term. Literary critic and *Partisan Review* editor Philip Rahv had planned to use it as the title for a novel (never written) which was to have as its main characters intellectuals from many fields who played truant at the magazine, "escaping for a while," in Barrett's words, "from the harshness of whatever practical reality would claim them again." Barrett sees further meanings in the epithet; for Rahv apparently also had in mind the man or woman who escapes from an unpleasant (usually bourgeois) background or job by assuming a Bohemian lifestyle and writing novels or poems. Barrett claims that the professional intellectual, usually a political liberal, is often a truant in a different, perhaps subtler way. "He has only to turn his mind in a certain direction and some unpleasant realities can disappear. He goes in search of original and sweeping ideas, and in the process may conveniently forget the humbling conditions of his own existence"(13).

As his memoir unfolds, Barrett offers new definitions of intellectual truancy. For instance, in a chapter on the "Painters

Club"—Barrett's name for the informal gatherings of painters and art critics he attended—he re-creates a conversation with Clement Greenberg, who describes Barrett's intellectual heroes as "negative in their thinking [without] the possibility of any infectious enthusiasm unless it be calculated and measured beforehand" (139). In retrospect, Barrett sees this trait as common among scholars and teachers and asks, "What was it that was 'negative' or nihilistic about modern intellectuals as a class?" He offers these explanations: the marginal social and economic position of American intellectuals, the influence of European philosophical movements, especially existentialism, and eventual disillusionment with Soviet communism. The popularity of existentialism, of course, could be called a symptom rather than a cause and a sign of cynicism about religious belief. So too with communism which, according to Barrett, tempted his learned colleagues as a self-conscious complement to aestheticism. Those "who had seemed secure and at ease within their own secular mind may be suddenly driven to find substitutes for religion in political causes and crusades, and to carry utopian hankerings into the field of politics" (183). Indeed, Barrett's sympathy for some of the truants he knew is limited or even canceled by his disdain for their devotion to Marxism.

Barrett clearly relishes the chance to review the "love affair" between liberal American intellectuals and the Soviet Union. It is a sign to him of another way in which humanists are tempted to play truant, "to cultivate politics as if it were a purely aesthetic discipline" (93). He finds the critical capacities of many—like Rahv and Greenberg—harmed by ideology which "is a cruel taskmaster and may require of us the sacrifice of our best perceptions." But he adds that "the thirst for an ideology is also one of our modern addictions" (151). However advanced as intellectuals, Barrett's truants were in his view also victims of modernism, especially the tendency to join retreat from society with the wish for its radical transformation. Many sought to avoid direct political interpretations in literary criticism and other disciplines but were politically radical at the same time. The moral inadequacy of this strategy is Ohmann's theme. Its practical failure, because it has relied too heavily on the tactics of the Left, is Barrett's. Seen from the Left and the

Right, then, many of our great humanists and teachers have failed to find a scholarly and pedagogic format for the integration of liberal learning and liberal politics faithful to the two meanings of the term *liberal*. Curiously enough, Ohmann and his radical colleagues writing in the late 1960s found literary academics too timid in their politics. Barrett, looking at the type a decade later and from a very different point of view, finds them too aggressive. To be sure, they are not describing the same people and critical theories, but they are both interested in the same intellectual ethos, one easily recognizable to teachers, scholars, and students who worked in it. Ohmann's armchair radicals are Barrett's truants.

The intersection of political views is also apparent in Trilling's legacy. Ohmann found in him a useful index to the professional self-doubt and malaise characteristic of literary intellectuals in the 1960s. Trilling was among the first, Ohmann acknowledges, to recognize how complex social and educational developments had produced by the mid-twentieth century a large and active "adversary culture." Again, the roots of this culture—its opposition to middle-class or bourgeois values—can be found in the nineteenth century. Its interests and purposes were codified, of course, by Trilling's early idol, Matthew Arnold. A century after Arnold, however, parts of the middle class itself had absorbed and even learned to advocate the cultural ideals proposed by him (its one-time adversary) and his twentieth-century interpreters like Trilling and thousands of humanities professors scattered across the country. The expansion of higher education, especially the teaching of the humanities from within the historical and ideological spirit of the adversary culture, was perhaps the crucial factor in the prosperity of opposition to the nation's prevailing values. The irony of such a success and the baleful influence of the adversary culture on artistic and scholarly standards is now frequently asserted by patriotic intellectuals like the neoconservatives.

Mindful perhaps of Trilling's liberal political beliefs, Ohmann characterizes his view of the adversary culture as "equivocal." Other radical critics have not been so kind. They have charged Trilling, Arnold, and their followers with actually promoting elitist conceptions of culture that exclude popular and proletarian forms of expression in favor of their own interpretations of literary culture—in Arnold's words, "the best that has been thought and said in the world." Exclusivity, or elitism, has been battling egalitarianism as competing educational and cultural ideals since the 1960s.[16] Teachers and scholars on both sides have claimed Trilling, some on the Left for his effort to combine liberal politics and high critical standards, the Arnoldian heritage, others on the Right for his labeling of the adversary culture as a threat to high standards and social stability.

The latter is Barrett's Trilling, who is the subject of an extended tribute in *The Truants* titled "The Beginnings of Conservative Thought." Barrett calls him "the most intelligent man of his generation" and "the best example of the civilized humanist our period had to offer" (186). Trilling is justifiably admired by humanists in many disciplines, according to Barrett, because he was a moral, virtuous man with a subtle and complex intelligence. He was cool, cautious, and balanced in his critical and cultural views, and he was magnanimous toward friends and colleagues. Nevertheless, Barrett's esteem for Trilling is accompanied by some reservations about the implications of his thought. He presents his criticism indirectly. Like Rahv, whose enthusiasm for Trilling's contributions to the *Partisan Review* waned, Barrett uses poet Delmore Schwartz as a vehicle for questioning Trilling's ideas. Rahv commissioned Schwartz's essay "The Duchess's Red Shoes" as a critique of Trilling, and in commenting on it Barrett capitalizes on the same opportunity. His criticism of Trilling—via Schwartz—is based on two issues. First, Trilling is found to be, in his devotion to nineteenth-century writers (especially the English), insufficiently appreciative of modern ones. His taste for Jane Austen, for instance, is somewhat old-fashioned. As Barrett puts it (again paraphrasing Schwartz's charges): "Trilling was a reincarnation of the Genteel Tradition, for whom modern literature was still too destructive and shocking to be accepted" (179). At the heart of Trilling's views, of course, was his restatement of Arnold's principle of literary criticism, especially the idea that literature and criticism are moral activities that deliberately express social meanings. Barrett proposes that had Trilling more fully appreciated a writer like Flaubert, the purity of his detachment and technical achievements in the novel, he would have discovered the virtues of the great twentieth-century writers.

Trilling's second major fault, paradoxically enough considering his traditional tastes, was his thoroughly modern secularism. His apparent indifference to religious experience, Barrett asserts, was a result of his devotion to Freud, his lifelong affiliation with Columbia University (where, according to Barrett, Deweyan naturalism was the orthodoxy), and his wish to join with other Jewish intellectuals seeking assimilation into the American mainstream.

It is, he claims, his respect for Trilling that inspires Barrett to raise these "unpleasant thoughts." For Trilling is worthy of "the most searching questions we can ask [and] in pressing these questions, we place ourselves and our whole culture in question along with him" (186). Trilling's most recent biographers have also asserted as much.[17] And as a self-proclaimed cultural middleman, Barrett relishes the use of others' ideas in shaping his own views. His debt to Trilling is plainest when he proposes a new interpretation of "Manners, Morals, and the Novel." Trilling had sought in that influential essay (included in *The Liberal Imagination*) to explain the relation of novels to the social habits and codes prevailing at the time of their composition. The manners and morals of subsequent readers, of course, were also critical in the interpretation of novels. In proposing the links between the dynamics of social class— including exploitative class distinctions and discrimination— and literature, Trilling was explaining creative and critical techniques. He also *preferred* novels of manners and morals like those of Jane Austen and E. M. Forster. Such preferences were another reason Trilling was dismissed by many literary radicals and revered by traditionalists (although some like Barrett regretted his ambivalence about modernist literature).

Barrett finds in Trilling's essay, however, another and more timely reason to advance him as a forerunner of the neoconservatives. Barrett hopes that Trilling was actually an admirer of the social systems that produced his favorite books. "Might it not be that the conditions which led to a more interesting literature also produced a more satisfying life within society itself? If in the literature of the past we observe human personality developing its varied riches within the framework of class distinctions, might it not be that those distinctions permitted, and in their own way even promoted, the well-being of society?" (171). Even to propose such an idea, given Trilling's liberal reputation, is to "think the unthinkable thought." Yet Barrett is sure that Trilling was hinting as much, that his thought certainly "could lead one in that way" and hence toward a cluster of neoconservative social, political, and economic views. But Barrett, who is determined to find model partisans, can only assimilate Trilling into neoconservative thought through hints and hopes. Trilling is an exemplary humanist not because he avoided intellectual truancy nor because he anticipated currently fashionable ideas.[18] His good sense and generosity as a critic, his synthesis of literary and social ideas and ideals, and his consistently liberal if not intensely ideological views won him a deservedly wide and loyal following.

Conclusion: The Adversary Culture and its Adversaries

The politics of scholarship and intellectual life means much more than the intra- and interdepartmental struggles on college campuses and the jockeying for status in professional associations. Neoconservative scholars like Barrett and Bloom invoke the adversary culture (and its liberal teachers) as a specter haunting American society. The ironies in its development, as noted above, may be amusing but its social effects, they claim, are serious indeed, a threat to the university, to society, and to the responsible practice of the humanities. To be sure, the "adversary culture"—as defined by Trilling, who invented the phrase—embodies the spirit of social change by detaching its devotee from "the habits of thought and feeling that the larger culture imposes, [and] giving him a ground and vantage point from which to judge and condemn, and perhaps revise, the culture that produced him."[19] Unimpressed by the cautious "perhaps," critics of the "adversary culture" have stressed its destabilizing social program, blaming it for the student revolts of the sixties and seventies; the development of a large bureaucratic new class of advocates for ambitious tax-supported health, education, and welfare initiatives; and the demand for programs in the arts and humanities that stress popular or egalitarian interests at the alleged expense of excellence. In short, the original revolt against the bourgeois has now itself been institutionalized. Neoconservative critics reject the adversary culture as a vulgar form of cultural modernism based on the application of utopian romanticism to the arts, humanities, and all levels of education. Postmodernism, where thought itself is taken to be merely contingent and all language and forms of writing "deconstructable," is an even less appealing trend, though some liberal critics of postmodernism—like the philosopher Jürgen Habermas—find in it forms of conservatism.[20] Ironies abound in the world of cultural politics. The political meaning of the achievements of the great teachers of *Masters* is clear, as is their charm. They taught great books and ideas but not social revolt. Come to class and complete your assignments, they said to their students; leave social change to others. Ohmann and his colleagues said no—if not perhaps as students, then as teachers themselves. They encouraged their students to say no to traditional pedagogy and to many American values, especially those associated with capitalism. In their view, the humanities are indeed a criticism of life, as Arnold and Trilling would have it, but they are also, then, a profound and potentially disruptive criticism of society.

Critics and advocates of the adversary culture agree about the powers of scholarship. As political philosopher and advocate Sheldon Wolin says, looking back at the post–World War II decades in higher education: "In a social and economic system based on technical functions the humanities can appear useless and powerless. [They] did not make sense in an input-output model of the knowledge-power relationship but they spoke instead of how a person should live by himself and with others. And because they spoke to persons rather than things, they formed a critical presence of unincorporable power in a world where increasingly the line between treating persons and handling things was becoming obliterated." The key issue in higher education, and in other more public uses of the humanities, according to Wolin, is whether the humanities will be assimilated into the technocratic culture as aesthetic ornaments, as neutralized nonideological "perspectives," as applied systems of ethics and values sympathetic to capitalism, or whether the humanities will be cultivated for their critical and meliorative capacities. As Wolin adds, "Contrary to the conventional wisdom of many social scientists, the trouble with the historical understanding is not that it has proven too little but that it knows too much."[21] Yet what history and the other disciplines of the humanities know is just what is disputed. Wolin believes it is that Western industrial capitalism sustains economic injustice as well as personal, communal, and social inequality. The humanities, therefore, are instruments of discovery and melioration, and inevitably radical politics. The opposing view, typified by Barrett and Bloom but advanced by many others, is that history contains the cumulative evidence for the legitimacy of traditional economic, social, and communal institutions.[22] They undergird the moral authority necessary to political order. The humanities, in this view, are instruments of reflection and affirmation, even patriotism. Like Ohmann, Wolin urges humanists to admit that "there are political stakes and determinants in matters of knowledge." Neoconservative opponents of the adversary culture share this idea. The real crisis in the humanities and in scholarship generally is in the possibility that liberal and conservative views may not be reconcilable and that a new and timely synthesis may not emerge before the two sides move even farther apart. The solution may also be, as Gerald Graff suggests, in finding ways for the university to "dramatize its conflicts" more openly (or educationally) for students and faculty alike.[23]

Barrett's portrait of Trilling is only one reason, therefore, why *The Truants* deserves attention as a resource for observing the humanities. Like the radical critics of traditional humanistic teaching, Barrett begins where *Masters* ends, by proposing that politics is at the heart of the enterprise. His memoir, *because* it is partisan, illustrates why we need to know more about the influence of ideology on literary criticism and other disciplines as scholarly fields and as professions; the process by which the ideas of intellectuals (teachers, truants, and others) enter or elude the general culture; and the origins, role, and influence of journals cum institutions like the *Partisan Review,* Kristol's *The Public Interest,* Wolin's (short-lived) *democracy,* and *The New Criterion.* Pietistic defenses of the humanities are unsatisfactory because of their banality and inability to reflect the complex inner and public life of the scholarly disciplines. Close observation of teachers, truants, and other intellectuals, by contrast, tells us what a career with texts and students is really like and what the humanities have to offer in scholarship, pedagogy, and social criticism.

But neoconservatism in politics has its pieties also. Eager to demonstrate that liberal academics have been wrong all along—and that he and like-minded critics have known why— Barrett lacks generosity despite his wish to memorialize Rahv and Schwartz as idiosyncratic intellectual liberals. Determined to be a hardheaded realist in political and cultural matters, Barrett—like the other neoconservatives—dismisses today's liberals as sentimentalists foolishly indifferent to the lessons to be learned from the history of the post–World War II American Left. Had he seen beyond his own experience (that is, taken his fugitive theme more seriously), he might perhaps have achieved Richard Hofstadter's view in the closing paragraph of *Anti-Intellectualism in American Life* where he identified a major virtue of American liberalism to be "the openness and generosity needed to comprehend the varieties of excellence that could be found even in a single and rather parochial society."[24] Some of our best teachers and scholars have in fact been truants in the sense defined by Barrett. But the beliefs of all partisans come closer to being dogmas than they may realize or admit, even those of former liberals who have seen the neoconservative light.

While he noted in his Jefferson lecture the capacity of mind to "examine its course and correct it," Trilling had no illusions about the objectivity of intellectuals. He pointed out later that however disinterested they claim to be they are not "innocent." Ideology will not disappear at Bloom's or Kramer's request, nor will detached teaching and scholarship at Ohmann's nor truancy at Barrett's. The humanities, in fact, can be said to be

the sum of their and others' partisan ideas, provided that
teachers insist on realizing from them a format for teaching,
scholarship, and criticism appropriate to a time when neither
Blake nor Jane Austen appears able to fill the classroom.

Notes

1. Lionel Trilling, *The Last Decade* (New York: Harcourt Brace Jovanovich, 1981), 209-10.
2. For a literary counterpart to Bloom, whose field is philosophy, see
   Peter Shaw, *The War against Intellect: Episodes in the Decline of
   Discourse* (Iowa City: University of Iowa Press, 1989).
3. Trilling, *The Last Decade,* 120, 126.
4. Lewis Feuer, "Arthur O. Lovejoy," in *Masters: Portraits of Great
   Teachers,* ed. Joseph Epstein (New York: Basic Books, 1981),
   126–27.
5. In this Trilling anticipates Russell Jacoby, *The Last Intellectuals:
   American Culture in the Age of Academe* (New York: Basic Books,
   1987).
6. Ellen Cantarow, "Why Teach Literature? An Account of How I
   Came to Ask That Question," in *The Politics of Literature: Dissenting Essays on the Teaching of English,* ed. Louis Kampf and Paul
   Lauter (New York: Vintage Books, 1973), 74.
7. Ibid.
8. Bruce Franklin, "The Teaching of Literature in the Highest Acade-
   mies of the Empire," *The Politics of Literature,* 107.
9. Though I find Bloom's book often mean spirited I recognize the
   truth in parts of its argument. See my essay "My Allan Bloom
   Problem—And Ours," *Iowa Review* 19 (1989): 142–53. On the
   matter of tone in a work like Bloom's see note 18 below.
10. Trilling, *The Liberal Imagination: Essays on Literature and Society*
    (New York: Anchor Books, 1953), ix.
11. Richard Ohmann, "Teaching and Studying Literature at the End of
    Ideology," *The Politics of Literature,* 142. "Beyond Culture," of
    course, is a phrase Trilling also used—in the title of an essay on
    Freud and for the collection of essays (1965) in which it was
    reprinted. In the preface he acknowledges that the phrase "can be
    said to make nonsense . . . it is not possible to conceive of a person
    standing beyond his culture." Yet Trilling also states that "the belief
    that it is possible to stand beyond the culture in some decisive way is
    commonly and easily held. In the modern world it is perhaps a
    necessary belief." *Beyond Culture: Essays on Literature and Learn-
    ing* (New York: Harcourt Brace Jovanovich, 1965), iv. Trilling tried
    to resolve the paradox in his conception of the "adversary culture."

12. Ohmann, "Teaching and Studying Literature at the End of Ideology," 153.

13. Christopher Caudwell, *Further Studies in a Dying Culture* (London: John Lane, 1949), 72.

14. Ann Douglas, "The Mind of Perry Miller," *The New Republic* 3 February 1982, 26–7.

15. William Barrett, *The Truants: Adventures Among the Intellectuals* (New York: Anchor Press, 1981), 193. Page numbers (with no acronym) of future references appear in the text.

16. Kathleen Ellis declares Arnold an apologist for elite culture and the inspiration behind the habit of modern teachers and scholars to separate culture and politics. See "Arnold's Other Axiom" in *The Politics of Literature,* 160–73. In his widely cited essay "The Scandal of Literary Scholarship," Louis Kampf refers to "Arnold's once cogent argument for the usefulness of academics . . . now burdened with the pathos of its irrelevance." *The Dissenting Academy,* ed. Theodore Roszak (New York: Vintage Books, 1968), 43. Joseph Epstein speaks for the Arnold who is, predictably, also Trilling's (the subject of his first book): "Matthew Arnold and the Resistance," *Commentary* (April 1982): 53–60.

17. See Mark Krupnick, *Lional Trilling and the Fate of Cultural Criticism* (Evanston, IL: Northwestern University Press, 1986) and Daniel T. O'Hara, *Lionel Trilling and the Work of Liberation* (Madison: University of Wisconsin Press, 1988). These books also reflect the uses of Trilling to his critics and followers, the measured prose of Krupnick contrasting quite vividly with the postmodern vocabulary of O'Hara. So too in a matter of cultural iconography do the dust jackets of the books reflect the theme. The first carries Jill Krementz's well-known portrait of Trilling as a weathered but genial (older but wiser) academic. The second displays a grainy photo of a haunted Trilling half covered in shadows.

18. Trilling did anticipate aspects of the point of view of neoconservatism. In notes prepared in 1971 for an autobiographical lecture, he described his relationship to intellectuals who accepted Stalinism: "The task, as I saw it, was that of *unmasking.* Not merely of saying what lay behind the false representations, but of discovering and disclosing what was really being served in the liberal ideas. The undertaking was the more complex because the people I had in mind thought of themselves as devoted precisely to the work of *unmasking*—of disclosing the falsehood of the established order. To unmask the unmaskers—to show that the very ideals they were committed to were betrayed to very death by their way of dealing with ideas: as if they were totems, in the way of piety" (*The Last Decade,* 240). Trilling avoided, however, what Peter Steinfels identifies as the "combative" and "assertive" style of neoconservatives and their "knowing attitude" (*The Neo-Conservatives: The Men Who Are*

Changing American Politics [New York: Simon and Schuster, 1980], 73–4). See also, on this important point, Sanford Pinsker's two essays, "Revisionism with Rancor: The Threat of the Neoconservative Critics," *Georgia Review* 39 (1984): 243–61 and "Bashing the Liberals: How Neoconservative Essayists Make Their Point," *Virginia Quarterly Review* 63 (1987): 377–92.

19. Trilling, *Beyond Culture,* iv.
20. See Jurgen Habermas, "Modernity Versus Postmodernity," *New German Critique* 22 (1981): 3–15.
21. Sheldon Wolin, "Higher Education and the Politics of Knowledge," *democracy* (April 1981): 51–2. Ohmann offers an extended version of similar arguments in *English in America: A Radical View of the Profession* (New York: Oxford University Press, 1976).
22. See, for example, Irving Kristol, "The Adversary Culture of Intellectuals," in *The Third Century: America as a Post-Industrial Society,* Seymour Martin Lipset, ed. (Chicago: University of Chicago Press, 1979), 327–44. Kristol claims that the circumstances of the United States in the past few decades—"a civilization whose culture was at odds with the values and ideals of that civilization itself"—are historically unique. Robert Nisbet makes an allied argument in *The Twilight of Authority* (New York: Oxford University Press, 1971): "It is both good and necessary that culture should be feudal. . . . The contemporary intellectual . . . is likely to assault the coercions, disciplines, and careers of traditional culture, combining an equalitarianism of political mind with devotion to subjectionist retreat from culture and assault upon its constraints" (120). A good counter argument and useful supplement to *The Truants* is Irving Howe's long essay "The New York Intellectuals" in *Commentary* (September 1968; reprinted in *The Decline of the New* [New York: Horizon, 1975]) and Howe's own autobiography, *A Margin of Hope* (New York: Harcourt Brace Jovanovich, 1982).
23. Gerald Graff, "The University and the Prevention of Culture," in *Criticism in the University,* Graff and Reginald Gibbons, eds. (Evanston, IL: Northwestern University Press, 1985), 62–82. Richard Rorty urges the same in "Education Without Dogma: Truth, Freedom and our Universities," *Dissent* 36 (1989): 198–204.
24. Richard Hofstadter, *Anti-Intellectualism in American Life* (New York: Vintage Books, 1963), 432.

8

Richard Hofstadter
and the Anti-Intellectuals

When Frederick Bancroft asked in 1900 why "none of our schools of history has ever produced a historian of special merit as both scholar and writer" he spoke as one of the last popular historians then being displaced by academic professionals largely devoted to the new scientific styles of scholarship. When Richard Hofstadter quoted this remark in 1968, prospects for the historical vocation as defined by Bancroft were still uncertain, as Hofstadter's own career revealed.[1] And so too did he carry a burden typical of his own time: "As one who matured in the 1930s," he said in 1960, "my interest has centered mainly on politics"[2] In the tumultuous 1960s Hofstadter sought to reconcile modern aspects of the scholarly vocation with the moral intentions he had nurtured. The academic attitude he represented appeared most notably in *Anti-intellectualism in American Life* where he explored its antecedents and antagonists and codified the ideals for which he is now admired. Hofstadter appears to be the most written about historian of his generation, hence the book in which he spoke so personally (if often indirectly) about the intellectual vocations will be durable beyond even the intentions of its author.[3]

No Place to Go

No less than other young intellectuals, Hofstadter confronted the ideological turmoil of the depression and the post-

World War II years with an acute sense of the mingling of historical and personal motives. Hofstadter's scholarly vocation was made in the immigrant family in which he grew up in Buffalo, his marriage into a family very much more politically self-conscious than his own, and in the fragile affiliations he had with left-wing politics as a student at the University of Buffalo. Shortly after the signing of the nonaggression pact between Hitler and Stalin in 1939, Hofstadter wrote to his brother-in-law, the leftist writer Harvey Swados, of their shared disillusionment: "We are not the beneficiaries of capitalism, but we will not be the beneficiaries of the socialism of the 20th century. . . . We are the people with no place to go. . . . Comes the revolution—which we both agree is far off, thank God—and then what? So where are we and what do we stand for?"[4]

The next year Hofstadter wrote to Swados, "We aren't tough enuf" to be part of the working-class political movement. By this time, of course, Hofstadter had abandoned his half-hearted plans to study law and was an ambitious graduate student in history at Columbia. But he was also struggling to find a place for the vestiges of his radical instincts amidst the conventions of an academic career. Toward the end of World War II, while teaching at the University of Maryland, Hofstadter wrote to a colleague:

> As for me, for what reasons, I can't say just now, I am by temperament . . . conservative and timid and acquiescent. I suppose that at bottom I am a radical only because I can't function intellectually any other way, but not because I have the true flame. You can set this down to true opportunism if you choose. I think you would be mistaken. It is due among other things to a pervasive inner despair which I doubt that you can very well understand.[5]

There were distinctly personal reasons for Hofstadter's frame of mind at the time—his wife's fatal illness especially—but there were professional ones also.

Having completed his first book, *Social Darwinism in American Thought* (published in 1945), and established himself as a teacher, Hofstadter made a part of his work the resolution of a familiar postwar intellectual dilemma. He had rejected the political logic that had led him into the Communist party for a brief period without at the same time reaffirming American values. Far from ever resolving his problem, Hofstadter came to show how it might be variably represented in works of historical scholarship. And it is perhaps why he noted near his death at age fifty-four, thinking of his relations to scholarly tradition, "the mind of the modern American intellectual is nothing if not self-doubting and self-critical."[6]

Hofstadter's generation also experienced of course the personal consequences of ideological disputes. The publication in the past few years of autobiographies by influential intellectuals has taught us—if we did not know it already—that love of learning does not preclude personal malice. It must, therefore, have surprised many readers of Irving Howe's autobiography that he praised Hofstadter as "a model of what the scholar intellectual ought to be." The key to their relationship, which was not intimate but still quite personal since it was based on a "shared affection for the life of the mind," was Hofstadter's modesty, his reluctance to impose his ideas on others, and most of all, considering the tendencies of American intellectual life between 1930 and 1970, his freedom from obsessions. "He had no interest," Howe says in mingled envy and admiration, "in casting himself in the historical roles that stirred the fantasies of intellectuals . . . [and] had no taste for an identity that comes out of the drama of reenactment." *The American Scholar's* Joseph Epstein has called intellectuals "the verbal class," so it is a measure of Hofstadter's power that Howe says of him "there was profit even in his silence."[7]

In *Anti-intellectualism in American Life,* however, Hofstadter had rebuked Howe for his delusive political and scholarly utopianism, especially his forlorn devotion to "bohemianism" and his role in the "cult of alienation" on the intellectual Left. Despite his erudition and vigor, Howe represented a threat to American life from within, a danger that added some poignancy to Hofstadter's interpretation of American history as a decline into philistinism. The differences between Hofstadter and Howe, and their eventual resolution (as Howe now sees it), form a suggestive episode in the history of American intellectuals. Hofstadter's understanding of the origins and consequences of their differences gave *Anti-intellectualism in American Life* its sense of urgency and ideological significance. And in the possibilities Hofstadter saw for their resolution in the early 1960s we can find the principles that animated his text and career.

Engaging the Present

After he joined the faculty at Columbia in 1946 Hofstadter embarked on a series of attempts to synthesize past and present and to forge a scholarly identity in which his skepticism about American values might coexist with his belief in the historical durability of the culture. Never quite a "cold-war liberal," as the forerunners of today's neoconservatives were called in the late 1940s and 1950s, Hofstadter was too troubled by popular forms of anticommunism to risk the skepticism he felt to be essential to intellect. But as a scholar he subordinated his early Marxism to less deterministic explanations of the past, those that were more responsive to the peculiarities of American culture.

In the famous introduction he wrote for *The American Political Tradition* (1948), where some critics have located the origins of the "consensus theory" of American history, the faults of American society are said to be part of its success and the role of intellectual critics like Hofstadter uncertain. Mindful of American material power and productivity, he nonetheless noted, "Societies that are in such good working order have a kind of mute organic consistency. They do not foster ideas that are hostile to their fundamental working arrangements. Such ideas may appear, but they are slowly and persistently insulated, as an oyster deposits nacre around an irritant."[8]

Even the popular success of *The American Political Tradition* did not mean for him a breakthrough of the sort that put the moral meanings of the "good working order" in question. Instead the book was celebrated for its accessibility and for its proposal that a "common climate" rather than ideological divisions dominates American political history. And consequently Hofstadter was himself found complacent, resistant not to tradition but to change.

By the time of *The Age of Reform* (1955) Hofstadter was inclined to blame academic intellectuals themselves for problems in the advancement of progressive political goals. Their naive populist sympathies, moreover, removed them from history—Hofstadter's disillusioned liberal version, that is—and blinded them to what might still be claimed for intellect on behalf of democratic if not populist ideals. Their isolation from society prompts liberal intellectuals to sentimentalize the "folk" and to construct images of popular revolts conforming to their own rebellious desires. Hence "they choose to ignore not only elements of illiberalism that frequently seem to be an indissoluble part of popular movements but also the very complexity of the historical process itself."[9]

While he was certainly no more liberal than other American academic intellectuals in the postwar years, Hofstadter thought more intensely and more candidly than most about the relation of scholarship to politics and of both to the institution of American higher education. "I know it is risky," he said shortly before *Anti-intellectualism in American Life* was published, "but I still write history out of engagement with the present."[10] Even as he made his reputation Hofstadter recognized in his own strong sense of vocation the ideology of scholarship, including romanticizing the opposition.

Hofstadter thus joined scholars in several fields eager to find a format for the participation of intellectuals in politics, one that would incorporate both the actual lessons of history and the rhetorical strengths of historical scholarship. If it turned out, as Howe proposed, that Hofstadter was more successful in devising models of inquiry than of action, that is because he was himself a victim of the very process he set out to explore: the marginalization of intellectuals in public life, even as the stature and influence of the universities that sustained them increased. That is what makes his work as timely now as when it appeared.

For the years during which *Anti-intellectualism in American Life* was planned and written were also those in which "consensus history" had its initial impact as a historical method and, as John Higham and others have noted, a cultural program. In his first attack on the "cult of consensus" Higham charged that

"current scholarship is carrying out a massive grading operation to smooth over America's social convulsions." He found in
The Age of Reform and other influential revisionist books a
taste for continuity and for a largely unified national character
drained of the conflicts that had given it the dynamic shape
favored by the progressive historians. The new history, having
neutralized the moral fervor of the previous generation, is
pragmatic and bland. "Classes have turned into myths,"
Higham said ruefully, "sections have lost their solidarity, ideologies have vaporized into climates of opinion."[11]

The solution proposed by Higham a few years later was not a
return to partisanship and the polarization of issues and groups,
but a new form of history as moral criticism. "Professional
historians," he reminded us, "have hardly begun to consider
moral insight as something they can gain by skilled and patient
historical study. . . . To write as a critic is to assume active
responsibility both to a phase of the past and to a contemporary
public and to engage one with the other." Moral historians
would be active in their texts by displaying, in Higham's phrase,
"complex awareness" of change and choice, and of the pressure
that the present puts on history, not only as a form of explanation but as a source of ideals.[12]

Seeing Things in Degrees

As *Anti-intellectualism in American Life* demonstrates, this
was hardly a lesson in methods that Hofstadter needed. He had
begun work on it before the publication of *The Age of Reform,*
and its decade-long gestation and relation to his own life and
work made it perhaps the central text in his career. Looking at
American society from its "nether end," Hofstadter admitted
at the outset of the book that its development was "impulsive"
and its details dominated by his own views. Begun in the early
1950s, it was prompted as much as anything else by McCarthy-
ism and its "atmosphere of fervent malice and humorless imbe-
cility."[13]

Anti-intellectualism in American Life is actually a tale told four
times of the displacement—in religion, politics, business, and
education—of intellectual values by pragmatic and philistine

ones. The tale was already something of a liberal piety when Hofstadter retold it. In 1922, for example, Dewey termed the "net result" of American history "social and political liberalism combined with intellectual illiberality." He was not the first or last to wonder if the Founding Fathers, sharing as they did the legacy of the intellectual enlightenment of the eighteenth century, could as free thinkers and political leaders have been elected town officials in the generation following their own. The occasion for Dewey's review of American political history as the fixing of limits to thought was the campaign of William Jennings Bryan against evolutionary science. In searching for what was truly progressive in populism, Dewey, like Hofstadter, identified Bryan as a symbol of attachment to stability, homogeneity, and finally the anti-intellectualism that results from fear of inquiry and criticism.

Bryan is one in a gallery of demons who populate *Anti-intellectualism in American Life*. It includes famous and obscure preachers, businessmen, and educators and, perhaps not surprisingly, Dewey himself. For in Dewey Hofstadter found not only often hazy prose but the philosophic rationale for romantic primitivism in modern American schooling. In the failure of this implied syllogism—Dewey dislikes Bryan: Hofstadter dislikes Bryan: therefore Hofstadter admires Dewey—can be found much of what makes Hofstadter important to us as a historian and exemplary intellectual. He pursued some of the most compelling paradoxes in American history: regressive elements in progressivism, antidemocratic tendencies in populism, conventionality in political radicalism. Hofstadter was essentially an oppositional historian who was skeptical of political and historiographic traditions and who resisted some of the major myths of American history. He also understood the pressure that oppositional scholarship puts on the self when it cannot act in society.

The very subject of *Anti-intellectualism in American Life* suggests an unusual degree of intimacy and coherence between an author and audience for a scholarly work in history. Though Hofstadter says early in the book that "no one who lives among intellectuals is likely to idealize them unduly" (20), he is fiercely loyal to intellect itself, defined as the "critical, creative and contemplative side of mind" (25). Moreover, even Hofstadter's contempt for the "vigilante mind" was muted, like Dewey's, by respect for some of its motives, especially its passion for equality. "As far as possible," he said, "our anti-intellectualism must be excised from the benevolent impulses upon which it lives by constant and delicate acts of intellectual surgery which spare the impulses themselves" (23). Enough irony and humility are distributed through the text to demonstrate interest in reaching an audience not made up exclusively of scholars but of what he called "thinking people," those devoted to intellect if not to all of its institutional products.

Yet Hofstadter's rhetorical gifts were also underlined by his dislike of particular kinds of anti-intellectuals, especially public-school administrators devoted to "life adjustment" in teaching, and corporate executives who saw themselves as losers to intellectuals in the status politics of postwar American life. Ironically, Hofstadter noted, the prestige of the businessman was largely destroyed by his own achievements, especially the giant impersonal corporation. Moreover, "it was his own incessant propaganda about the American Way of Life and Free Enterprise that made these spongy abstractions into public generalities which soak up and assimilate the reputations of individual enterprisers. Once great men created fortunes; today a great system creates fortunate men" (235-6). Religion was another target. Hofstadter denounced the "punitive capacity" and absolutism of evangelical and secular fundamentalism in contrast to the "civic force" of liberalism.

When he turned to the development of domestic policies to fight the cold war, Hofstadter offered his own form of moral pragmatism as an alternative to the "clash of faiths" favored by the Right. As a form of "political intelligence," intellect

> accepts conflict as a central and enduring reality and understands human society as a form of equivocation based upon the continuing process of compromise. It shuns ultimate show-downs and looks upon the ideal partisan victory as unattainable, as merely another variety of threat to the kind of balance with which it is familiar. It is sensitive to nuances and sees things in degrees. It is essentially relativist and skeptical but at the same time circumspect and humane. (134-5)

Both religious anti-intellectuals and cold war hard-liners are dangerous, therefore, because they dislike debate and "tolerate no ambiguities, no equivocations, no reservations and no criticism." To be committed is to be tough and fearless, in no need of observation and argument. "The issues of the actual world are hence transformed into a spiritual Armageddon, an ultimate reality, in which any reference to day-to-day actualities has the character of allegorical illustration, and not of empirical evidence that ordinary men offer for ordinary conclusions" (136).

Accordingly, an important feature of anti-intellectualism is its rhetorical rigidity. It appears as forms of thought and action that are insufficiently dialectical and skeptical. They fail even when they are not punitive, as in the case of progressive education reform of the twentieth century, which was, in Hofstadter's view, "presented to the world not simply as an instrumentality but as a creed, which went beyond the hope of this or that strictly educational result to promise some kind of ultimate salvation for individuals or for the race" (367). Such rhetorical innocence, Hofstadter thought, derived from misplaced optimism and uncritical belief in progress. In other words, Hofstadter preferred Freud to Dewey, whose good intentions do not survive his faith in the future.

Dewey is not Bryan, but he appears in *Anti-intellectualism in American Life* as the culmination of a tradition that, sometimes intentionally and sometimes not, made history into a mere subject. Hofstadter found one source of Dewey's program and influence in this remark from *Democracy and Education:* "The present is not just something which comes after the past. . . . It is what life is in leaving the past behind it" (388). For Dewey, history and hence many of the activities of the modern disciplines threaten his utopian methods, his search for a "higher synthesis" that would overcome the polarities of intellect.

Hofstadter's frustration with Dewey no doubt inspired the forceful essay that closes *Anti-intellectualism in American Life.* This effort to restore conflict to American history ends with a review of the struggle of intellectuals to settle what he called their "grievances" as American citizens, their unsatisfactory relation to political power. "It appears then," Hofstadter said, "to be the fate of intellectuals either to berate their exclusion from wealth, success and reputation, or to be seized by guilt when they overcome [it]. . . . The intellectual is either shut out or sold out" (417). But within this historical predicament—one that had special meaning during the early months of the Kennedy administration, when the last part of *Anti-intellectualism in American Life* was being written—Hofstadter identified a grievance of his own. It is the conversion of independent, diverse forms of critical inquiry or dissent into programs of mere negation and rebellion, a "conformity of alienation" in the hands of critics like Howe, Norman Mailer, and others. He offered a number of reasons: resentment of administration intellectuals; a compliant, uncritical middle-class audience for assertions of romantic individualism; and glorification in our therapeutic environment of neurosis as a source of creativity and intellectual achievement.

Hofstadter offered these explanations without quite endorsing them, for he himself spoke out of the experience of scholarship and its obscure relation to solidarity. "Facing the world together," he said, "is a tactic of politics, but facing it alone seems to be the characteristic creative stance" (426). This dilemma turns out to be the chief consequence for intellectuals of his history of anti-intellectualism. That is, now duly marginalized, American scholars have polarized their own interests according to nearly irreconcilable ideologies of authority and alienation.

As Russell Jacoby argues in his account of today's intellectual culture, very few American academics have been able to overcome their institutional habits, chiefly social isolation and academic specialization, on behalf of the inclusive and accessible social criticism the culture needs and in fact had in the pre–World War II years and even for a time after them. Standing between his Columbia colleagues Lionel Trilling and C. Wright Mills, Hofstadter was not nearly so traditional as the former or so disruptive as the latter. His "critical liberalism that looked both ways" gains Jacoby's admiration even though it could hardly, like Mills's example, mobilize intellectual radicals or, like Trilling's, justify completely the scholarly and institutional styles of conventionally liberal academics.[14]

Caught in the middle of this conflict in the scholarly vocations, Hofstadter displayed the paradoxical quality of forceful moderation for which he was later celebrated by Howe. So that at the end of *Anti-intellectualism in American Life* he collapsed the ideological divisions and their competing moral claims in the possibilities for conscience to be derived from intellectual conviviality. "One of the major virtues of liberal society in the past was that it made possible such a variety of styles of intellectual life—one can find men notable for being passionate and rebellious, others for being elegant and sumptuous, or spare and astringent, clever and complex, patient and wise, and some equipped mainly to observe and endure. What matters is the openness and generosity needed to comprehend the varieties of excellence that could be found in a single and rather parochial society" (432).

Conclusion: The Native Skeptic

Yet Hofstadter's optimism belied his fear that no model of conciliation could survive the 1960s and their campus and cultural upheavals. Near the beginning of *Anti-intellectualism in American Life* he endorsed Dewey's characterization of the "subversive" meanings of inquiry. "If we once start thinking," Dewey had said in 1929 (in *Characters and Events*), "no one can guarantee what will be the outcome, except that many objects, ends and institutions will be surely doomed. Every thinker puts some portion of an apparently stable world in peril" (45). The writing of *Anti-intellectualism in American Life* was intended as something of a stay against alienated and even apocalyptic styles of American intellectualism. Writing from deep within his own experience of history and the historical vocation, Hofstadter hoped to recruit his academic colleagues to a form of intellectual liberalism commensurate with what he took to be the promise of the new political generation.

Just a few years later, however, he appeared to have much less faith in such a project. Hofstadter had accepted Trilling's epithet "the adversary culture" for nonconformist intellectuals of the 1960s. Writing in a neoconservative journal in 1967 he acknowledged, "Perhaps we are really confronted with two cultures (not Snow's), whose spheres are increasingly independent and more likely to be conflicting than to be benignly convergent: a massive adversary culture on one side, and the realm of socially responsible criticism on the other."[15]

In momentarily abandoning the generosity that had made his scholarship so distinctive, Hofstadter revealed just how difficult it had been in the years since *Anti-intellectualism in American Life* to maintain the values it described and represented. Being adversarial, he knew, does not always preclude being responsible, although, as Jacoby shows, the shelter of the university has made it harder to discover the relations between the two. In his June 1968 commencement address at protest-torn Columbia, Hofstadter defended traditional academic culture even as he called for institutional reforms. It was, however, the attitude toward inquiry shared by scholars and students that mattered most: "The very possibility of civilized discourse rests upon the willingness of people to consider that they may be mistaken."[16]

Some of today's cultural conservatives would like to claim Hofstadter, as they have Trilling, as a partisan. But Hofstadter's native skepticism included even his talent for history. As a graduate student at Columbia Hofstadter had told his friend Alfred Kazin, then working as an independent scholar on his pathfinding literary study *On Native Grounds,* "Don't class me with the genus historicus. . . . I am really a suppressed litterateur who couldn't make the grade just writing good prose and had to go into history."[17] Kazin himself remarked many years later that Hofstadter "cared as much about literature as any writer I have ever known, knew it intimately and lovingly, and he responded to other people's writings with the same feeling for literary effect that he had sought in his own."[18]

Most of those who have written about Hofstadter have acknowledged his stylistic ambitions though not everyone has granted him a "literary effect" for the complex *Anti-intellectualism in American Life.* Arthur Schlesinger called it "confusingly organized" but still rich in its interpretations.[19]

For Hofstadter, I think, the latter was actually inseparable from the rhetorical innovations he made in his book, ones he identified as part of the "new historical genre" emerging in his time: "part narrative, part personal essay, part systematic empirical inquiry, part speculative philosophy."[20] Hofstadter's interest in the rhetoric of history was of course much less theoretical than the kind favored by many of his academic successors. Still, it represents a point of contact, and perhaps even continuity, between traditional academic discourse and the several innovations—in historiography and in history writing itself—deriving from critical theory and postmodernism.

Hofstadter's lifelong modesty could not conceal his gift, the one identified by literary critic Wayne Booth as typical of great rhetoric in history and other disciplines: it "presents us with the spectacle of a man passionately involved in thinking an important question through in the company of an audience."[21] For those with "grievances" and those without, Hofstadter is himself good company in the searching out of the resources—personal, historical, rhetorical—demanded by academic and intellectual life today.

Notes

1. Richard Hofstadter, *The Progressive Historians* (1968; reprint, Chicago: University of Chicago Press, 1979), 36.
2. David Hawke, "Interview: Richard Hofstadter," *History* 3 (1960): 136.
3. On Hofstadter's interest to other historians the most recent account (it includes the comment on Hofstadter being the most written about) is Robert M. Collins, "The Originality Trap: Richard Hofstadter on Populism," *Journal of American History* 76 (1989): 151–67. Other useful general accounts (apart from the controversies over particular books) include: Arthur M. Schlesinger, Jr., "Richard Hofstadter," in *Pastmasters: Some Essays on American Historians,* ed. Marcus Cunliffe and Robin Winks (New York: Harper and Row, 1969), 278–315; Daniel Walker Howe and Peter Elliott Finn, "Richard Hofstadter: The Ironies of an American Historian," *Pacific Historical Review* 43 (1974): 1–23; Stanley Elkins and Eric McKittrick, "Richard Hofstadter: A Progress," in *The Hofstadter Aegis: A Memorial,* ed. Stanley Elkins and Eric McKittrick (New York: Knopf, 1974), 300–67; Daniel Joseph Singal, "Beyond Consensus: Richard Hofstadter and American Historiography, *American Historical Review* 89 (1984): 976–1004.

4. Cited in Susan Stout Baker, *Radical Beginnings: Richard Hofstadter and the 1930s* (Westport, CT: Greenwood, 1985), 151.
5. Ibid., 180–1.
6. Hofstadter, *The Progressive Historians,* 150.
7. Irving Howe, *A Margin of Hope* (1982; reprint, New York: Harcourt Brace Jovanovich/Harvest, 1984), 322–23.
8. Richard Hofstadter, *The American Political Tradition and the Men Who Made It* (1948; reprint, New York: Vintage Books, 1974), xxxviii.
9. Richard Hofstadter, *The Age of Reform* (New York: Vintage, 1955), 19.
10. Hawke, "Interview: Richard Hofstadter," 136.
11. John Higham, "The Cult of the 'American Consensus': Homogenizing our History," *Commentary* 27 (February 1959): 95.
12. John Higham, *Writing American History: Essays on Modern Scholarship* (Bloomington: Indiana University Press, 1970), 151.
13. Richard Hofstadter, *Anti-intellectualism in American Life* (New York: Vintage, 1963), 3. Future references appear in the text.
14. Russell Jacoby, *The Last Intellectuals: American Culture in the Age of Academe* (New York: Basic Books, 1987), 78–85. Mills's relations with Hofstadter (and Trilling) foundered in the mid-1950s (see Irving Louis Horowitz, *C. Wright Mills: An American Utopian* [New York: The Free Press, 1983], 250–52). Still, later in his career Hofstadter acknowledged an important debt to Mills that was to have considerable meaning for the rhetorical innovations of *Anti-intellectualism in American Life.* Speaking of the differences between history and sociology and the habit in the first of writing in a personal voice Hofstadter said: "The misunderstandings that have hitherto separated the disciplines can be overcome not by flouting this profoundly ingrained feeling of historians but rather by showing them that there is a possible historical genre in which the personal voice still remains and for which the sociological imagination is of the highest value ("History and Sociology in the United States," in *Sociology and History: Methods,* ed. Seymour Martin Lipset and Richard Hofstadter [New York: Basic Books, 1968], 12).
15. Richard Hofstadter, "Two Cultures: Adversary and/or Responsible," *The Public Interest* 6 (1967): 74.
16. Richard Hofstadter, "The 214th Columbia University Commencement Address," *American Scholar* 37 (1968): 584.
17. Baker, *Radical Beginnings,* 249.
18. Alfred Kazin, "Richard Hofstadter, 1916–1970," *American Scholar* 40 (1971): 399.
19. Schlesinger, "Richard Hofstadter," 298.
20. Hofstadter, "History and Sociology," 18.
21. Wayne Booth, *Now Don't Try to Reason with Me* (Chicago: University of Chicago Press, 1970), 32.

Part Three

WAYS WITH WORDS

9

The Making of a Method:
Margaret Mead in Her Letters

When A. C. Haddon, a pioneer in British anthropology, dismissed Margaret Mead as a "lady novelist" he could not have anticipated a time when her putative creative talents would come to be seen as essential to ethnography.[1] So Clifford Geertz proposes in his authoritative account of ethnographic writing, where he designates as a scholar's "signature" the product of the construction of a "writerly identity." He asserts the importance of this aspect of the anthropological vocation in relation to the traditional priority given to fieldwork and then to "discourse" or the pattern of scholarly arguments.

> . . . no matter how delicate a matter facing the other might be it is not the same sort of thing as facing the page. The difficulty is that the oddity of constructing texts ostensibly scientific out of experiences broadly biographical, which is after all what ethnographers do, is thoroughly obscured. The signature issue . . . demands both the Olympianism of the authorial physicist and the sovereign consciousness of the hyperauthorial novelist, while not in fact permitting either.

Being an anthropologist means being a writer, a part of the vocation seemingly unrelated to its scientific ambitions. As Geertz says. "Finding somewhere to stand in a text that is supposed to be at one and the same time an intimate view and a cool assessment is almost as much of a challenge as gaining the view and making the assessment in the first place."[2]

In the theory-laden atmosphere of today's anthropology hardly any practitioner would be unaware of this problem.[3] Pioneers in the field, as Geertz's most recent work is meant to show, had their own ways of balancing science and "signature." Speaking as a specialist in the study of Bali he says of Margaret Mead—author with Gregory Bateson of *Balinese Character* (1942)—that the "passé" quality of her speculations on culture and personality "doesn't seem to detract very much from the cogency of her observations, unmatched by any of the rest of us."[4]

Mead was an observer in a variety of prose forms: books and essays for professional journals of course, but also many contributions to popular magazines and newspapers where her "signature" came to be well known (often to the dismay of academic colleagues). She wrote fiction as an undergraduate at Barnard and then as a graduate student at Columbia but gave it up after she began fieldwork. Critical admirers and opponents have agreed on the vividness of her prose, its capacity to suggest the workings of the imagination even as it strives for documentary authenticity. The very opening of *Coming of Age in Samoa,* with its well wrought landscape, and the book's closing exhortations on behalf of reform in education, show how Mead "oscillated" (as Geertz says most ethnographers do) between rhetorical intentions.

As a child and eager public speaker Mead was lectured by her father about "the lawn sprinkler effect," or spraying words over an audience instead of concentrating on one or two listeners. So even after she had earned a large audience for her writing Mead cultivated the particular audience that letter writing provides. While she was in Samoa, Mead would greet a boat arriving every few weeks with seventy or so letters to which she responded with pleasure and detail. Her good habits as a correspondent continued throughout her life as she made her letters a place to contemplate her own experience and the meanings and uses of ethnography.

Like a Tugboat

For poets and novelists the letter has often been a professional as well as a personal occasion. In writers as different as Keats and Flannery O'Connor, letters are often a means of recording reactions to other writers and explaining the background and intentions of their own work. Though we also read letters for biographical information, they are often revealing about the processes of writing itself. We read letters for pleasure and instruction but also for their informality, the opportunity they often provide for observing the observer outside the routines of professional discourse. With Margaret Mead we recognize the continuity between her several voices, the consistency of her "signature."

Still, letters written by scientists and social scientists have not merited critical interest. Freud's are the best known, especially those he wrote to his medical colleague Wilhelm Fliess as he was developing the first principles of psychoanalysis. They are valuable evidence of the ways in which Freud converted his neurobiological background into a new theory of psychology and method of therapy. Freud's rhetorical style has been justifiably called a "veritable psychomachia of dynamic interactions" in which his own self is dramatized even as he directs his own or his audience's attention to the text he is writing (or reading).[5] Freud's letters are an important part of the psychoanalytic canon because they have many of the same qualities of his theoretical and clinical work. They can be taken to be a part of his identity as a writer—his "signature"—and the sense we have of his general ambitions and capacities in prose should be distributed across all the forms in which he wrote.

Perhaps because the social sciences have since Freud sought more science, we would not expect psychologists and others to turn to the apparent informality of correspondence for scholarly purposes. Jane Howard believes that Mead's frequent letter writing was a "luxury" and an "addiction," even a form of "self-indulgence" during fieldwork. And "empty time was something that alarmed her."[6] Mead wrote easily and often, prose being one way her constitutional dynamism found expression. Speaking of his marriage to her, Gregory Bateson confessed: "It was almost a principle of pure energy. I couldn't keep up and she couldn't stop. She was like a tugboat. She could sit down and write three thousand words by eleven o'clock in the morning and spend the rest of the day working at the museum."[7]

But writing was not just a matter of personal habit or, as Howard would have it, surplus or displaced energy, or even as Mead herself once claimed, a form of "dissipation." It was the essence of the scientific vocation as she understood it. There is an unintentional reply to Bateson in an essay she wrote many years after their marriage ended on the special problems of women in the field: "differential self-esteem and competitiveness are very likely to accompany any field work and are particularly likely to complicate a relationship between man and wife. Field work is individualistic; ideally each young anthropologist wants to write a whole book about the whole culture."[8] Indeed, she said with pride once in a letter from Bali, it was clear to the people whom she and Bateson were studying that "we belong to the caste of those who make books, and my arms are beginning to ache as if that were literally true."[9] Mead's zest for inclusiveness also made her an avid letter writer, the form serving to fortify relationships (she was, in today's term, an inveterate "networker") and to expand the opportunities she had for both "signature" and "discourse," professional habits that came to be almost one with her personal life.

The Personal Equation

Mead acknowledged when a selection from her correspondence was published in 1977 that "when I started to write these letters, I had no sense that I was discussing the making of a method" (*LF*, 6). She acknowledged that her letters did provide some relief from the difficulties of fieldwork even as they represented and explained its uses. The audience for her letters, often family and college friends, was in large part a nonprofessional one and the letters a means for finding some perspective on her work. "One must somehow maintain the delicate balance," she said, "between emphatic participation and self-awareness, on which the whole research process depends" (*LF*, 7).

Mead's letters are important for the insight they provide into the inner life of fieldwork. They display artistic intentions as well, at least in the sense that they represent the performative element in her rhetorical stance, the making and maintenance of her "signature" in personal and now public form. The meaning and uses of her letters, therefore, derive from the same frame of mind which informs the Balinese shadow play as Mead herself described it in a 1936 letter: "The Balinese have no sense of a greenroom at all; putting on the make up of dancers, tying the last flowers of a headdress, tuning a musical instrument, putting up decorations, unpacking the puppet box, all are part of the show to be commented on, criticized and enjoyed" (*LF,* 191). So too, Mead's method, including the fieldwork reported in her letters, is fully revealed to her audience, the record of a mind too vigorous to ignore even the slightest experiences and too honest to deny the strong personal feelings that shape their expression.

Mead's method as an anthropologist, one now seen to be typical in its presentation of ambiguities and problems, is her insistence on the authority of the unique data of fieldwork inseparable as it is from the interests and attitudes of the field worker.[10] In a comment on "methodology" appended to *Coming of Age in Samoa,* she compares her work to medicine and psychoanalysis, their concentration on cases, and inability to prove beyond refutation the truth of their ideas. "So the student of the more intangible and psychological aspects of human behavior is forced to illuminate rather than demonstrate a thesis." Further, she admits that her book's conclusions are also "all subject to the limitations of the personal equation."[11] It is, however, part of the appeal of Mead's method that this "limitation" becomes a primary virture. Mead's attitudes toward ethnography and her particular areas of research, and her role in the lives of those she studied, became for her important subjects in their own right.

Still, Mead's first letters, written after she left for Samoa in the summer of 1925, reveal very little about her actual professional circumstances. A letter written from Pago Pago to Franz Boas, the founder of anthropology as an academic discipline in the United States and her teacher at Columbia, is properly deferential—it asks for advice and is reassuring about a young and inexperienced anthropologist's ability to survive in a remote place—but barely suggests the doubts with which Mead understood her field tasks. "How much checking should you consider it necessary and legitimate for me to do?" (*LF,* 30) she asks after reporting that her early informants were mainly tribal chiefs and apparently "well-informed." That kind of question, and its apparent methodological innocence, confirms the memory of her departure for Samoa that Mead included in her autobiography: "When I sailed for Samoa, I realized only very vaguely what a commitment to fieldwork and writing about fieldwork meant." Her academic preparation under Boaz was all theoretical and insufficient for the tasks he had assigned to her. "There was, in fact, no *how* about our education. What we learned was *what* to look for. . . . Nobody really asked what were the young fieldworker's skills and aptitudes—whether he had, for instance, the ability to observe and record accurately or the intellectual discipline to keep at the job, day after day, when there was no one to supervise, no one to compare notes with, to confess delinquencies to, or even to boast to on an especially successful day."[12] It was in her letters that Mead filled some of these gaps in her preparation and adjusted to her new circumstances.

It is no surprise then that the letters from the small island of Tau, where Mead did the fieldwork for *Coming of Age in Samoa* from the fall of 1925 to early spring of the following year, contain the excitement of discovery, the evidence of growing confidence and increasing capability in building an anthropological method. Pride in her acceptance by the Samoans and rapidly developing sophistication as a field worker is not, however, diminished by recognition of the persistent curiosities of participant observation.

> It was a curious scene there at midnight on the edge of a fretting sea, raining a little, at times a sickly moon, the sand sticky and yielding under foot, tiny children escaped from home scurrying here and there, adults with blackened faces in strangely cohesive groups that scattered when anyone approached, shrinking indecisively behind the bordering coconut palms. I had to skip, an unknown accomplishment in Samoa, to the tune of the deafening tin cans on the pulpy sand, and then of course, there were hundreds of salutations, some respectful and some not, it being New Year's Eve. The cut of my dress betrayed my identity, even at midnight. (*LF,* 41).

> It is curious to see these two (household helpers) and half a dozen other boys, clad only in lavalavas (cloth wraps) with hibiscus behind their ears or a graceful fillet of leaves on their hair, sitting on the floor on my room, tremendously at ease amid its various sophistications. The Santa Claus which is weighted at the bottom so that it always stands upright is their favorite plaything or they musingly turn over pages of a *Dial* or a *Mercury* with an air of detached tolerance. But when one of them discovered a letter of Louise Bogan's about the style of Henry James, all neatly typewritten and legible, he admitted himself stumped. (*LF,* 46–7).

Such anomalies are, as Mead of course knew, more than mere curiosities. They are suggestive of the interest in cultural differences that motivated her fieldwork in the first place.

In Spite of Smoke

Mead sought an epistolary style that would accommodate the curiosities, relieve the intellectual and emotional pressures associated with demanding settings in the field, and convey as much as possible of the total character of the native population and her own relation to it. "Gradually I am becoming part of the community" she reported from Samoa after she had been there several months and her longer letters from the island and subsequent fieldwork locations convey not only the details of this achievement but a certain structure and coherence which make them small essays. They display many of the tools of prose artistry: narrative, figurative language, dramatization, and management of tone and point of view. When she undertook original research as a professional anthropologist she no doubt hoped for an influential place in the scientific community; yet her literary interests required that she develop a style that was not simply part of her fieldwork method but actually represented her scientific vigor, imaginative sympathy for cultural difference, and ambitions as a writer, which required a strong sense of immediacy and contact with an audience.

A letter form Alitoa, near Mt. Arapesh in New Guinea, displays these virtues while it provides, together with other letters from this community, an informal ethnographic record supporting the formal findings of *Growing Up in New Guinea* (1930). The letter (sent 20 April 1932) begins with the admission that Mead and her second husband and co-fieldworker, Reo Fortune, faced a very basic methodological problem indeed: "We have still not decided what to call this mountain people for they have no name for themselves, just friendly little nicknames or names for sections of the community, like man-o-bush or poisonous snakes!" A remark then on the weather—that classic epistolary gambit—becomes a comment on Arapesh supernaturalism.

The weather has continued glorious, although now that the northwest monsoon is dying there are bad storms which make the thatch stand up like fur on the back of an angry cat and knock down the more superannuated houses of the village. All wind and rain come from supernatural creatures called *walin* who inflict storms on the entire community whenever unwanted people from another clan invade their domain or when members of the proper clan come and do not speak politely, reminding them of the relationship . . . These people have made the man-o-bush into the devil, the man who traffics in the temporary angers of his nice neighbors, the professional sorcerer. The ghosts they have localized under the care of the *walin* of each clan and you do not have to encounter them if you go hunting elsewhere and are careful where you get your firewood. (*LF,* 117–8).

Conscious of the highly charged atmosphere in which the Arapesh live, Mead portrays ordinary village life with some irony.

So in the village you are free to have a good time—to smoke and chew and yawn and hum little songs under your breath and repeat the name of the nicest baby over and over or sing the baby to sleep by reciting the names of your favorite pig—or if you haven't any baby, a puppy or better still a little pig will do. If you are feeling gay, you can put flowers in your hair and red and white paint on your face; or if you like, you can put the paint on the baby or the pig. If you are feeling cross, you put the black paint of war on the forehead of the ten-year-old. If you have a headache, you tie a piece of bark around your head and go and sit in the *place clear* so that everyone will know how miserable you feel. If your mind runs on feasts, you can get out the hand drum and thump it happily all by yourself. If your pig dies, you can fasten a set of spears in a piece of bark and tie a yam to the bundle and set it in front of your wife's doorway, just to show her what you think of the way she looks after the pigs, and then *she* can take a long bright leaf and tie it into a knot and hang it over the door, just to say that she won't cook any more food for the people whose jealous talk made her pig die until they give her something nice for a present. If you have something important to say, you stalk through the village and everybody knows by your shoulders that something is up and trails along to see what it is. (*LF,* 118).

"For all that," Mead acknowledges, "life is complicated at times," and in a well-timed dramatic detail she suggests something of her own domestic arrangements, again with the irony which is part of her method.

The village is dark, only an occasional flicker of fire shows through the eyelets in the bark walls of the houses. A tense nervous boy appears by the entry to the housecook and stands there staring. We know that he has something important to say and wait. Is the sago bad, or has there been a fight, or has someone run away? He explains: "Gerud would like to work tonight after dinner. Myelahai has lost a big knife and wants Gerud to tell him where it is." Gerud is assistant cook-boy and the only diviner in the village. We assent. Gerud's divining always brings us a fine lot of ethnological detail. . . . He eats a little bone-scraping from the skull of an ancestor mixed with a little ginger. Then he dashes madly about in the dark, plunging up and down the steep slopes at either end of the village until he unearths a bit of bamboo filled with rubbish, which he can allege is a bit of the physical essence of someone which has been placed in a wild taro root to cause a sore. Then he falls flat on the ground, arms outflung in a crucified position, and answers questions and also makes startling remarks about usually unmentionable things and throws in a few dark hints about future disasters. (*LF,* 118–9)

Gerud's divining turns out to be, in this instance at least, harmless, so Mead turns to the difficulties of maintaining a satisfactory food supply and then to the problem of storing a growing collection of Arapesh ceremonial artifacts. "While they are being carried," Mead notes, "I hid in a native house with a woman who spent her time showing me an abortive drug and commenting sharply that men could not see the drug, that they could not even hear the name of it. Thus feminine self-esteem was avenged" (*LF,* 121).

Mead's laconic judgment at a midpoint in this representative letter is "And so it goes." She adds: "A mad world where little bits of taro and little bits of yam are each bought separately for a separately served spoonful of beads or matches, where every misfortune is magically determined and where one sits ready to pounce on the significance of a plate of croquettes being carried by the door" (*LF,* 121). Her detachment, even bemusement, is balanced, however, by the letter's closing sections which reaffirm the centrality of taboos and sorcery in Arapesh culture. Gender separation, as is evident from the above, is the most common theme.

Then there was the night last week when Amito'a and I dyed skirts. This is one of the occasions when the women get back at the men. No men or children can come near, no smell of meat cooking, no knife which has ever touched meat, no feather headdresses can come near. The very sound of men's voices will spoil the dye, just as the sound of women's voices will anger the Tambaran and as the touch of a woman's hand may spoil hunting gear. We squatted in a windswept little leaf shelter and watched the great pot, its top covered with pads of big green leaves, boil over with a bubbling fluid which gradually turned blood red. And once some boys talked, and the skein of sago threads which was being put into the pot caught fire. And Amito'a's husband stayed with Reo until midnight and just to reassert his masculine superiority told Reo all about the nice brain soup which the warriors used to drink, brewed from the scooped-out brains of the enemy, although up to now they had been denying any touch of cannibalism. So Baimal danced about the room, illustrating the savage delight of war, for Baimal is always light and airy even when his talk is of death. And Amito'a and her sister-in-law, Ilautoa, squatted by the watched pot and said: "We feed pigs, we make grass skirts, we dance, two by two we go for firewood, two by two we bring up water, two by two we dye our grass skirts." The wind howled and ruffled the thatch, and I enjoyed it in spite of the smoke in my eyes. (*LF*, 121–2)

And after noting Reo's determination to pursue his data on language whatever the obstacles—he even spoils some of Mead's own research based on doll play to check a small point of pronunciation—Mead closes this letter with a quick glance at the outside world. "Our knowledge of it is fragmentary," she says, and copies of American magazines are "manna in the wilderness." There is a final dramatized comment about the relationship of ethnography to its informants and the relative merits of anthropological research and native wisdom.

On the veranda Reo is doing legend texts and the old men passing by ask: "What are you doing?" "Legends." "Child's play," they snort and pass by. Legends are only for children, you tell them to your children and then heave a sigh of relief and forget the nonsense so that you are free to concentrate on important things like charms, which are just (as it were) "Tweedledum and Tweedledee, Rumpty-dum and Rumpty-dee," male and female. Of one thing these people are very sure and that is "Male and female created he them." But at that, even those who are sophisticated about white people sometimes slip up in talking to me. (*LF*, 123)

To be sure, Reo himself produced authoritative accounts of

Arapesh language and custom but Mead's triumph, as is often revealed in her letters as well as in her books and essays, is what might be called her methodological equilibrium (the solution to "oscillation"). She recognized from the beginning of her career that the relation of subject to object, researcher to researched, is fluid and imprecise and that it required, in addition to descriptive and analytic rigor, the use of stylistic devices more characteristic of art than science. The artistry of Mead's letters is in her integration of setting, incident, and judgment with sufficient variety in diction, syntax, and tone to establish a genuine epistolary voice. Geertz thinks this less careful than expressive in the sense that artists invoke the freedom of imaginative forms to represent the actual workings of their minds. Hence, Mead had "a loose-limbed, improvisational style, saying seventeen things at once and marvelously adaptable to the passing thought, white-line curlicuing if ever there was such."[13]

Mead's best letters include a mix of devices and intentions but even those that are less complete and ambitious contain pointed and sometimes colorful passages of psychological and cultural description. In a letter accounting for some of the "transparent social processes" among New Guineans, she offered with her own bracketed glosses an incisive cross-cultural analysis of incest taboos. "The saying goes: 'Other women, other pigs, other yams, you can eat. [This is literal.] Your own sister, your own mother, your own pigs, your own yams which you have piled up [indicating a surplus], these you cannot eat.' Seen in this light, incest prohibitions can be understood not as some obscure psychological process in the mind of the individual, but as necessary to social cooperation in societies which operate at the kinship level of integration" (*LF*, 130). And Mead also included in her letters, as she did only occasionally in her scholarship, elegant descriptions of scenes of great natural beauty.

> The lake to which we came, through a *baret*, was all black, polished like a mirror, with faraway mountains ringing it all about and on its shining surface floated pink and white lotuses, lying in patches of thousands, their pads still and fixed on the black water, while among them stood, as if posed for a portrait, white ospreys and blue herons. It is all as ordered, as simple in its few contrasting themes, as a

Japanese print, and the lack of miscellaneous, only half-congruent notes makes it seem unreal. It was before sunrise when we slid into the center of the lake and the black irregular arms of water stretched away among further and further patches of lotuses, seeming almost to meet the mountains, and there was no human thing there except ourselves. It is the best this country has to offer and very, very good. (*LF,* 139)

Like Darwin and Thoreau, Mead often depended on such scenic pleasure to fortify her analytic interests.

But by 1938, when she understood her prose to be polished in conventional formats, she was puzzled by her reception from colleagues in anthropology even as she welcomed her growing influence in other fields. Writing to psychologist Gardner Murphy she expresses her impatience with the entire matter of methods, a theme which motivated her letter writing as well as her ethnography. "I've had a pleasant and recreational time writing this letter," she says,

despite the fact that I have at least 200 pages of notes to type up . . . and . . . trying to develop and try out new field techniques in the hope of developing field methods which will appeal more to the type of student which we need to send into the field. . . . It is significant that Psycho-Analysts and Social Workers don't have any difficulty handling my results, but anthropologists, more interested in forms than in people, do. So I've decided it's wasteful to collect material by methods which other people won't use and therefore can't credit and I've set myself the task of overhauling the whole matter. . . . But it's hard to keep your mind on methods when there is so much sheer work to be done.[14]

Still, despite being troubled by the impact of her books, Mead was a tireless worker and determined believer in the benevolent motive and consequences of scholarship. *Letters from the Field* is characteristically buoyant and represents the image Mead herself wished for her career and her self-consciousness in its making and methods. Nonetheless, Mead's daughter Mary Catherine Bateson has proposed that a complete picture of her mother's disposition in professional matters (if not personal ones) will require publication of her letters displaying a less optimistic version of her field experiences.[15]

Conclusion: Anything, Everything, and Nothing

In her later letters, especially those following World War II when she had the opportunity to look back at the development of her method, Mead recognized that her younger contemporaries faced critical artistic dilemmas which reflected the complexity of modern anthropology. Writing from New Guinea again in 1965, she offers a compact explanation of the relation of the scientific imagination—those resources for hypotheses building and the reporting of experimental results—to the data on which it must ultimately depend. And she deftly manages the question of the relations between novel writing and ethnography, emphasizing the responsibilities (one might say constraints) the latter puts on the former even as the anthropologist's artistic sensibility must be cultivated. The choice is not between being an anthropologist and a novelist, between being a scientist and an artist. It is between being accountable to one's material and to one's audience as completely as possible or simply relying, as she complained to Murphy, on the "forms" that any field provides.

> Today we give the fieldworker a whole battery of methods, techniques, tools and theories from which to choose—more than anyone can use, just as the vivid, ongoing life of a people is more than anyone can possible cover in the same detail, with the same vigilance, with the same attention. So the fieldworker must choose, shape, prune, discard this and collect finer detail on that, much as a novelist works who finds some minor character is threatening to swallow up the major theme or that the hero is fast taking him out of his depth. But unlike the novelist . . . the fieldworker is wholly and helplessly dependent on what happens—on the births, deaths, marriages, quarrels, entanglements and reconciliations, depressions and elations of the one small community. . . . One must be continually prepared for anything, everything and—perhaps most devastating—for nothing. (*LF,* 281)

According to Mead, good fieldworkers inevitably find themselves in the artistic situation, dependent finally on creative resources to reveal the meaning of facts as artists do of images and imagined events. For "there are rewards for the individual who likes to work alone, just one mind required to take in a culture that has been hundreds, perhaps thousands of years in the making. . . . All the skills he can employ as a scientist and all the skills he can draw on as an artist are needed here, and he is accountable to no one except to the actuality before him" (*LF*, 282).

While the individual anthropologist is part of the "orchestral realization of the themes of scientific fieldwork she is also one in a "series of minds" who have come before and will come after. The letter is an indispensable form of such an ideal of scholarly communication. So Mead ended a letter to her English colleague Geoffrey Gorer: "Well, now *you* say something."[16]

Notes

1. Haddon is quoted in Meyer Fortes, "Anthropology and the Physiological Disciplines," *Soviet and Western Anthropology*, ed. Ernest Gellner (New York: Columbia University Press, 1980), 124.
2. Clifford Geertz, *Works and Lives: The Anthropologist as Author*. (Stanford, CA: Stanford University Press, 1988), 10.
3. See Jay Ruby, ed. *A Crack in the Mirror: Reflexive Perspectives in Anthropology* (Philadelphia: University of Pennsylvania Press, 1982); George W. Stocking, Jr., ed. *Observers Observed: Essays on Ethnographic Fieldwork* (Madison: University of Wisconsin Press, 1983); and James Clifford and George Marcus, eds. *Writing Culture: The Poetics and Politics of Ethnography* (Berkeley: University of California Press, 1986).
4. Geertz, *Works and Lives*, 4.
5. Patrick J. Mahoney, *Freud as a Writer*, 2nd ed. (New Haven: Yale University Press, 1987), 136-7.
6. Jane Howard, *Margaret Mead: A Life* (New York: Simon and Schuster, 1984), 198, 287. There were times of course when Mead did display such an attitude. In Bali in 1936, after noting that she had completed a particularly difficult piece of ethnographic transcription, she confessed that "I feel entitled to the dissipation of another bulletin" (Margaret Mead, *Letters from the Field 1925–1975* [New York: Harper and Row, 1977], 174).
7. Howard, *Margaret Mead*, 253. Mead was not diffident about her high standards of productivity. As a participant at a symposium she responded this way to the news that a morning session had been postponed: "How *dare* they? Do they know I get up at five o'clock every morning to write a thousand words before breakfast?" (287).
8. Margaret Mead, "Fieldwork in the Pacific Islands, 1925–1967," in *Women in the Field: Anthropological Experiences*, ed. Peggy Goode (Chicago: Aldine, 1970), 326.
9. Margaret Mead, *Letters From the Field: 1925–1975* (New York: Harper and Row, 1977), 182. Future references appear in the text

with the acronym *LF*. Speaking of her childhood in a well-educated, academic family Mead said: "I did my first drawing on galley proofs, glazed paper that only took a pencil mark if you pressed till it scratched—all the mechanics of bookmaking were familiar to me before I could read or write. I don't think I ever had any doubts that making books was what adults did" ("Margaret Mead," in *A History of Psychology in Autobiography,* vol. 6, ed. Gardner Lindzey [Englewood Cliffs, NJ: Prentice-Hall, 1974], 295).

10. See for example Clifford and Marcus, *Writing Culture.*
11. Margaret Mead, *Coming of Age in Samoa* (1925; reprint, New York: Morrow, 1961), 260–1.
12. Margaret Mead, *Blackberry Winter: My Earlier Years* (1972; reprint, New York: Pocket Books, 1975), 151–2.
13. Geertz, *Works and Lives,* 111.
14. Howard, *Margaret Mead,* 205–6.
15. Mary Catherine Bateson, "Continuities in Insight and Innovation: Toward a Biography of Margaret Mead," *American Anthropologist* 82 (1980): 273.
16. Howard, *Margaret Mead,* 200.

10

"A Tune Beyond Us, Yet Ourselves": Medical Science and Lewis Thomas

Like other professionals, physicians depend on acceptance of the historic legitimacy and practical benefits of their authority. And as Paul Starr has proposed, few other groups in American society have managed to establish and maintain their prerogatives as well as doctors. He demonstrates the conversion during the past century of clinical expertise into social and economic privilege, and acknowledges the power of professional authority not only to influence action—its therapeutic dimension—but to evaluate reality and experience. The authority of physicians, he says, "extends to the meaning of things." By defining "health," for instance, physicians shape and control the institutions and practices that maintain or restore it.[1]

Yet within contemporary American medicine as Starr describes it, such meaning is not shaped exclusively by orthodox professionalism. Lewis Thomas, a former dean of the medical schools at New York University and Yale, and former president of the Memorial Sloan-Kettering Cancer Center, has had a considerable stake in the forces that have transformed medicine during his lifetime. He is himself an example of the achievements and hegemony of major medical institutions. At the same time, however, Thomas is a skeptic, devoted to the doctrine of an earlier philosopher of medicine, Maimonides, who asked that he be "contented in everything except in the great science of my profession."

189

Since the mid-1970s, in a series of books that have brought him a large audience within and beyond the medical community, Thomas has displayed confidence in medical science and respect for its limits. His essays are particular and philosophic, technical and accessible, generous and prescriptive all at once. In other words, Thomas has fashioned in his writing a personal and literary format for the expression of the scientific authority of medicine. And he has made of his discontent an unsystematic but revealing analysis of medical science in a prose style suited to the popular presentation of science and its relations to social and moral issues.

The Gift of Affection

According to Thomas, his education began just after World War I, when he observed his father's suburban New York medical practice, which was only a marginal social and financial success. The elder Thomas was devoted to diagnosis and prognosis as the most feasible of medical tasks. He was, in his son's judgment, a "therapeutic nihilist" because he was impressed early with the imperfections of medicine. Nevertheless, his father's professional friendships were instrumental in gaining for Thomas, an indifferent student as a Princeton undergraduate, admission to Harvard Medical School, where he concentrated on several of the dominant clinical problems of the 1930s: tuberculosis, pneumonia, typhoid, rheumatic fever, and syphilis. It was, however, as a fourth-year medical student that Thomas reached the core of the curriculum, and made the same grim discovery as all of his colleagues: "It gradually dawned on us that we didn't know that much that was really useful, that we could do nothing to change the course of the great majority of the diseases we were so busy analyzing, that medicine, for all its facade as a learned profession, was in real life a profoundly ignorant occupation."[2] Finding most hospital medicine "custodial," Thomas became, like his father, a good doctor but a fatalist. What mattered most for the ill were shelter and warmth, for "medicine made little or no difference." As a young physician, therefore, Thomas was inclined toward the "long conversation in which the patient was at the epicenter of concern and knew it" (TYS, 59). He came to believe in the primacy of "the gift of affection," a therapeutic principle he later converted to a rhetorical one in essays that often rely on identification with the welfare of readers.

As a young physician in Boston hospitals Thomas had the advantage of ward rounds with exemplary diagnosticians in internal medicine. His anxiety about medical ignorance abated somewhat as he participated in intellectually satisfying (if not always healing) forms of observation and analysis that might be practiced in his profession. "To watch a master of diagnosis in execution of a complete physical examination," he says, "is something of an aesthetic experience, rather like observing a great ballet dancer or concert cellist" (*TYS,* 30). Recalling the near infallibility of his favorite teacher, however, Thomas also admits that it was only in a handful of cases that correct diagnosis actually resulted in being able to *do* something—usually surgery—to change the course of the illness. The major infectious diseases were untreatable until the redirection of medicine into a technology based on basic research, or what Thomas calls "genuine" science. In 1937 he observed the cure of pneumonia with one of the new sulfanilimide preparations, and thereafter, with the other interns, he fixed his hopes on the apparently boundless possibilities of antibiotics. Raised for one kind of profession, Thomas and his colleagues realized that it had changed radically at the moment of their entry: "It was the opening of a whole new world. . . . We became convinced, overnight, that nothing lay beyond reach for the future" (*TYS,* 35). Thomas has never ceased being an optimist, though he has been chastened by the intellectual parochialism of contemporary medicine and by the arms race.

"I had the guiltiest of wars," Thomas admits, "doing under orders one thing after another that I liked" (*TYS,* 91). Following assignments in research projects on infectious diseases in Guam and Okinawa, he spent periods of a few years each at Johns Hopkins, Tulane, and the University of Minnesota. In 1954 he became chairman of pathology at NYU, the critical step in launching a distinguished administrative career. At the same time that he has led major institutions, Thomas has worked hard on behalf of public health programs, as well as local and federal efforts in biomedical research. As a physician-scientist he has himself benefited from this self-imposed discipline: "The key to a long, contented life in the laboratory is to have a chronic insoluble problem and to keep working at it" (*TYS*, 149). For him that has meant more than four decades of fascination with the still uncompleted study of endotoxin and what it may tell us about how disease is related to breakdowns in the body's mechanisms for protecting itself.

Thomas reports on his parallel careers by bringing the lessons of each to the other. Thus when he admits that "the greatest difficulty in trying to reason your way scientifically through the problems of human disease is that there are so few solid facts to work with" (*TYS*, 179), he reveals the sources of his occasional heresies in matters of the medical curriculum (it needs more liberal arts), university governance (medical schools are too powerful), and federal support for science (it is meager and misguided). He leaves more room for imagination and intellectual play than the standard bureaucrat not because he is an ambivalent policymaker. For he recognizes that our understanding of facts depends on our taste for fiction, the reach of the mind in imagining—in myths, laboratory hypotheses, or personal essays—the neglected meanings of what is already known. After music he loves poetry most; after Bach, Wallace Stevens, whose "Man with the Blue Guitar" is to Thomas "a tale of the earth itself, and hence a source for his mission and method.

> The man bent over his guitar,
> A shearsman of sorts. The day was green.
>
> They said, "You have a blue guitar,
> You do not play things as they are."
>
> The man replied, "Things as they are
> Are changed upon the blue guitar."
>
> And they said then, "But play, you must,
> A tune beyond us, yet ourselves.
>
> A tune upon the blue guitar
> Of things exactly as they are."

A prescriptive exactness has never satisfied Thomas, who has tried to find the "serenade" in science.

No Method at All

Though a lifelong admirer of Montaigne, Thomas became an essayist by accident. As an immunologist and part-time worker in other fields he wrote nearly two hundred essays in the conventional forms of laboratory science. Because he sought "absolute unambiguity in every word," he now finds the diction and syntax of these pieces "hideous." A 1970 paper on inflammation, however, employing a multi-vehicle collision as a metaphor brought an invitation from *The New England Journal of Medicine* to write some brief essays in a similar style. The terms were attractive: an unpaid one thousand words a month which could be rejected but not edited. Thomas relished the chance to break free of orthodox scientific prose and the lifelong habit of carefully outlining his thoughts. "I changed the method," he says, "to no method at all, picked out some suitable times late at night, usually on the weekend two days after I'd already passed the deadline, and wrote without an outline or planning in advance, as fast as I could" (*TYS*, 243). The first satisfactory product was "The Lives of a Cell," first published in the *Journal* in 1971 and then again in 1974 as the title essay in the volume, still his best, which brought Thomas a large audience outside science.

Thomas speaks not only as a physician but as a colleague, neighbor, and citizen. He displays in "The Lives of a Cell" the technique which accounts for the appeal and durability of his best essays: collaboration with his readers in recognizing what a professional knowledge of science can tell us about ordinary life. In this characteristic paragraph he also demonstrates his ability to bind technical and general vocabularies in explaining the consequences of our biological history.

> A good case can be made for our nonexistence as entities. We are not made up, as we had always supposed, of successively enriched packets of our own parts. We are shared, rented, occupied. At the interior of our cells, driving them, providing the oxidative energy that sends us out for the improvement of each shining day, are the mitochondrias, and in a strict sense they are not ours. They turn out to be little separate creatures, the colonial posterity of migrant prokaryocytes, probably primitive bacteria that swam into ancestral precursors of our

eukaryotic cells and stayed there. Ever since, they have maintained themselves and their ways, replicating in their own fashion, privately, with their own DNA and RNA quite different from ours. They are as much symbionts as the rhizobial bacteria in the roots of beans. Without them, we would not move a muscle, drum a finger, think a thought.[3]

Written and read from the inside out, the technical knowledge is at the service of the most ordinary of ideas: all living things are continuous with all others.

There is in Thomas's work a moral logic as well which offers the lessons of biological solidarity as the answer to problems of political and technological competition. Thomas would ask those "practical" national leaders who make arms policy, and who believe in life as a competition of systems driven by force and aggression, to observe the example of the protozoan myxotricha paradoxa which inhabits the inner part of the digestive tract of the Australian termite. This small piece of life, like many others in *Lives of a Cell,* is a key actor in one of Thomas's fables of relational benevolence. The "termite ecosystem" which depends on the union of the myxotricha with the termite is, for Thomas, the world—biological, social, and political—in a grain of sand. For "if we could understand this tendency, we would catch a glimpse of the process that brought single separate cells together for the construction of metozoans, culminating in the invention of roses, dolphins and, of course, ourselves. It might turn out that the same tendency underlies the joining of organisms into communities, communities into ecosystems, and ecosystems into the biosphere" (*LOC,* 33). Eager to claim that this "drift of things" is indeed the way of the world, Thomas suggests that aggression and defense might be redefined as secondary features of life which only regulate and modulate the universal tendencies toward symbiosis. Such was his faith in the early 1970s in science as a moral model, and in the scientific method as a medium for the resolution of disputes, that Thomas hoped this computer-produced message might be sent to the enemy in the first few minutes of nuclear confrontation: "Request more data. How are spirochetes attached? Do not fire" (*LOC,* 34).

Yet *Lives of a Cell* showed that Thomas is a more convincing optimist than ironist. He was willing to risk sentimentality in his search for the essential unity of living things, a theme now as prone to banality as it is to inspiration. More than anything else Thomas wants evidence from basic research for organic solidarity and for his belief in the rhythmic orderliness of living and dying. He believes in the homeostasis of the earth, the universe's most complicated coordinated mechanism for the regulation of growth and decay. Each part in the system is both a medium and a target for what needs to be known about its relation with others: "In this immense organism, chemical signals might serve the function of global normones, keeping balance and symmetry in the operation of various interrelated working parts, informing tissues in the vegetation of the Alps about the state of eels in the Sargasso Sea, by long, interminable relays of interconnected messages between all kinds of other creatures" (*LOC,* 48). The relays connect but they also conceal, and as Thomas appears to know (he would not insist so often on unity if he didn't) there is a paradox in his work: devotion at once to diversity and synthesis as the most instructive result of modern biology.

Near the end of *Lives of a Cell* he tells us that we are individually the most improbable of entities, statistically considered on physical terms. The organized structures of life, human and animal, are the products of the random distribution of matter, the "amorphous middle" of the universe. "We violate probability," he says, "by our nature. To be able to do this systematically, and in such wild varieties of form, from viruses to whales, is extremely unlikely; to have sustained the effort successfully for the several billion years of our existence, without drifting back into randomness, was nearly a mathematical impossibility" (*LOC,* 166). Yet as differentiation between and within species appears to be the "goal" of physical evolution, so the binding of thoughts, ideas, and feelings is evidence for the unity transcending differences. Once again Thomas questions our belief in ourselves as "entities," biologically private individuals, related only by choice and chance to others.

Necessity and evolution, Thomas believes, suggest manifold possibilities for the future. Modern world culture, the arts and scientific research for instance, constantly intensified and transformed by technical advances in communications and transportation, causes him to imagine the reorganization of the brain itself.

It is perhaps "the primitive precursor of more complicated, poly-merized structures that will come later, analogous to the prokar-yotic cells that drifted through shallow pools in the early days of biological evolution. Later, when the time is right, there may be fusion and symbiosis among the bits, and then we will see eukary-otic thought, metazoans of thought, huge interliving coral shoals of thought" (*LOC,* 168). As he looks ahead to greater unification, however, Thomas also celebrates "mutations," especially those in the arts and learning, which are models for science, as science is the unexpected model for morals. Montaigne and Bach, for exam-ple, "process" the information they share with others (language and music) in ways that produce novel forms with new meanings. "Bach was able to do this," Thomas says in assimilating his achievement to biological evolution, "and what emerged in the current were primordia in the music." Hence the Art of the Fugue and the St. Matthew Passion "were, for the evolving organism of human thought, feathered wings, opposing thumbs, new layers of frontal cortex" (*LOC,* 169). Thomas's own essays are distant cousins of such work—a thought that would be discomforting to his natural modesty—because they collapse conventional dis-tinctions between science and art. They contribute in their way to the interactive evolution at least of medical thought, and its affiliations, Thomas hopes, with the other sciences and arts.

Music is for Thomas the best available metaphor for organic forms of communication. Convinced that the urge to make music is a fundamental biological function, Thomas proposes that "rhythmic sounds might be the recapitulation of something else— an earliest memory, a score for the transformation of inanimate random matter in chaos into the improbably ordered dance of living forms" (*LOC,* 27). It is, however, language itself which comes to dominate Thomas's proposals for a science more reflec-tive of human history and wishes. Lacking laboratory evidence for many of his hypotheses, Thomas offers the resources of speaking and writing as a rationale for his unusual method. For him the human meanings in science are in its expressive capacities and achievements which are needlessly limited by professional conven-tions, especially the reluctance to capitalize on the ambiguity of language to represent how science is at once incomplete and loaded with meaning. Because Thomas recognizes the genetic capacity for language (he was an early enthusiast for Noam Chomsky's views) he insists upon seeing the sources of science as dynamic and creative.

In a passage with apparent personal meaning he tries to convey the actual experience of scientific experimentation and expression as first biological and then dramatic events:

> We start out our lives with templates, and attach to them, as we go along, various things that fit. There are neural centers for generating, spontaneously, numberless hypotheses about the facts of life. We store up information the way cells store energy. When we are lucky enough to find a direct match between a receptor and a fact, there is a deep explosion in the mind; the idea suddenly enlarges, rounds up, bursts with new energy, and begins to replicate. At times there are chains of reverberating explosions, shaking everything: the imagination, as we say, is staggered. (*LOC,* 108)

With perhaps his own essays in mind Thomas asserts that we live by transforming energy into words, storing some, releasing some in "controlled explosions." Moreover, the peculiarities of human language, compared to other biological systems of communication, make ambiguity its indispensable element. Meaning depends, in Thomas's view, on our understanding of the "strangeness" and "askewness" of language, its tendency to direct thought in unexpected and idiosyncratic ways. Human communication, therefore, is a sign that we are biologically unique.

> The specifically locked-on antigen at the surface of a lymphocyte does not send the cell off in search of something totally different; when a bee is tracking sugar by polarized light, observing the sun as though consulting his watch, he does not veer away to discover an unimaginable marvel of a flower. Only the human mind is designed to work in this way, programmed to drift away in the presence of locked-on information, straying from each point in a hunt for a better, different point. (*LOC,* 111)

The result is "layers of counterpoint in meaning," evidence of the difficulty in sticking to the matter at hand and of the desirability of making scientific discourse more pliable and even explosive.

For Thomas, language tends toward the binding of diverse forms of nature and experience. Ideas and words, like living things, must "get along" to preserve and enhance their separate identities. And while language evolves so slowly that it is difficult to feel a personal sense of participating in morphological change, speaking (and, for some, writing) is a sign, like our origins in cellular matter, that we are bound to and depend on others. "The earth," Thomas says simply, "is a lovely, formed, spherical organism with all its working parts linked in symbiosis" (*LOC*, 122). We are, therefore, not only dependent but responsible and in need of science as a guide to our moral as well as our biological circumstances.

Hankering for Friends

The *Journal* essays collected in *The Medusa and the Snail* reaffirmed, in themes and spirit, Thomas's pathmaking earlier work. The examples change—ponds, committees, cloning, for instance—but the essential points are repeated, reflecting Thomas's confidence in having found an audience for his efforts to make scientific information cohere around his moral speculations. And writing itself becomes a major subject. In an essay on thinking he describes the processes of sorting and selecting, what writing teachers call "invention," as one in which "many aggregates are simultaneously in flight and the separate orbits are arranged in shimmering membranes very close to each other like a complicated, meticulously ordered dance."[4] The motion is ceaseless yet patterned, like Bach's Brandenburg concertos, as the mind becomes capable of purposeful directed movement, in Thomas's case, prose. The mind seeks "something similar, with matching receptors, *outside.*" The audience Thomas imagines for himself is now in fact accustomed to his unusual analogies, the large lessons he finds in small things, the leaps from the analysis of matter to morals. Warts are "wonderful structures" he says, because of the classical medical problems they present in understanding the cellular and chemical participants in tissue rejection and the unexpected role of the unconscious in the management of disease. For it turns out, to Thomas's astonishment, that under hypnosis some sufferers of warts have apparently willed their disappearance.

The powers and limits of Thomas's own mind are the subject of one of his most disarming and morally suggestive essays, an account of a visit to the Tucson zoo. There his investigative or analytical intentions are usurped by his observation, in the unusually intimate surroundings provided by inventive zoo designers, of adjoining pools of otters and beavers.

> I was transfixed. As I now recall it, there was only one sensation in my head: pure elation mixed with amazement at such perfection. Swept off my feet, I floated from one side to the other, swiveling my brain, staring astounded at the beavers, then at the otters. I could hear shouts across my corpus callosum, from one hemisphere to the other. I remember thinking, with what was left in charge of my consciousness, that I wanted no part of the science of beavers and otters; I wanted never to know how they performed their marvels; I wished for no news about the physiology of their breathing, the coordination of their muscles, their vision, their endocrine systems, their digestive tracts. I hoped never to have to think of them as collections of cells. All I asked for was the full hairy complexity, then in front of my eyes, of whole, intact beavers and otters in motion.[5]

Deep in experience and at the limits of formal knowledge, Thomas relies on his candor to maintain his authority as a scientist. He confesses a "surprised affection" for creatures he has only thought about as subjects. As a scientist he admits to having learned nothing about beavers and otters in Tucson but much about himself and his readers. The evidence for genetic altruism, now one of Thomas's favorite themes, is readily available in the observation of patterns of human response blocked by consciousness but awaiting release: "Left to ourselves, mechanistic and autonomic, we hanker for friends."

Like Montaigne, also the subject of an essay in *The Medusa and the Snail,* Thomas enjoys a form of sovereignty denied most modern professionals. In his best essays, Thomas notes in admiration, Montaigne "simply turns his mind loose and writes whatever he feels like writing." It is, of course, only Thomas's background in traditional science that makes him capable still of astonishment at this creative commonplace. But for him the essence of Montaigne's example is the moralism and honesty typified in his assertion that there is no "science so arduous as to know how to live this life of ours well and naturally" and his admission that "I have nothing to say about myself absolutely, simply and solidly, without confusion and without mixture, or in one word." Thomas's achievement is to have come to the same conclusions through a contemporary medical science burdened with claims for the pure truth of facts and the necessity of moral neutrality.

Montaigne is exuberant, modest and consistent, at least in his inconsistencies. Thomas is now known for these traits and others. Many readers share his pleasure in etymology as a source of insight into the history of scientific and humanistic inquiry. The technical term "stochastic," for instance, gets special treatment in *The Youngest Science* since its contemporary use signifying absolute randomness conceals its origins as a term referring to precise targets. This secret of language tells us that the only possible accuracy is a function of trial and error. "It is being in motion, at random, that permits us to get things done" (*TYS*, 83). Having also defended the usefulness of error, not merely in laboratory experiments but in all sorts of actions and judgments, Thomas has by now built a strong case for his method as a scientist and essayist.

And in *The Youngest Science* he charges to a Panglossian bias his belief in what is known as the Gaia hypothesis (after J. E. Lovelock's *Gaia: A New Look at Earth* [1979]). As stated at the conclusion of his most personal book, where Thomas resists the charge that he is unscientifically teleogical, the proposal is that "the conjoined life of the planet not only comprises a sort of organism but succeeds in regulating itself, maintaining stability in the relative composition of the constituents of its atmosphere and waters, achieving something like the homeostasis familiar to students of conventional complex organisms, man himself for example" (*TYS*, 245). Even "bad dreams" of modern life and the future—overpopulation, pollution, deforestation and thermonuclear war—cannot quite dim Thomas's native optimism, at least as far as it is represented in his autobiography.

That is not the case, however, in *Late Night Thoughts on Listening to Mahler's Ninth Symphony,* where only a minority of the essays display the learned geniality which has contributed to Thomas's appeal. The possibility of nuclear war has made him angry. He addresses the dangers of the arms race and military policies generally in several essays, including a bitterly ironic one in which he finds the budgetary dominance of the military an expression of the surreptitious redefinition in our society of arms research as "basic" science. Behind militarism, however, is nationalism, which Thomas sees now as the most dangerous historical form of human activity. We are at once the most social and youngest of species, still experimenting, mainly out of good will, with forms of civilization. Essentially altruistic, we are driven by the urge to be useful, a genetic trait which, according to Thomas, also produces our myth, poetry, and music. Yet contemporary patriotism reveals how difficult it is to shape this urge for social and international purposes. The modern nation, Thomas claims, is "probably the most stupefying example of biological error since the age of the great reptiles, wrong at every turn, but always felicitating itself loudly."[6] We are slow learners, he admits, but the risks of ignoring the human consequences of the nuclear arms race are greater than any other form of scientific ignorance.

Thinking of Mahler, and the mixture of pleasure and melancholy he provides, Thomas no longer finds reassurance in the eternal rhythms of nature. With his inspiration threatened, Thomas's despair is too deep even for expression. The example at hand is a civil defense analyst calmly presenting data on evacuation, radiation, and death ratios. Now in the last phase of his career, Thomas says "If I were sixteen or seventeen years old and had to listen to that, or read things like that, I would want to give up listening and reading. I would begin thinking up new kinds of sounds, different from any music heard before, and I would be twisting and turning to rid myself of human language."[7]

Conclusion: Scientific Optimism

A decade ago Thomas proposed that language is the core of human life, "holding us together, moving us in meaning." Contemplating, if not quite expecting the death of language itself, Thomas has been more recently an openly political writer. He joined a number of scientific and literary intellectuals stressing "nuclearism" in their social criticism. By conservative writers they are rejected, even ridiculed, as naive or worse. Thomas has been charged with falsifying biology in order to "wrest" political lessons from nature.[8]

Within the scientific community Thomas has been criticized, as he acknowledges in *The Youngest Science,* for promoting a modern version of deism in his enthusiasm for the Gaia hypothesis. He has been called a sentimental advocate of the "current cult of natural things" who has mobilized an ancient feeling for union and community (what Freud dismissed as the "oceanic feeling") on behalf of a new scientific morality. "The optimist figures that this drive, which used to be toward God, could be directed to some product of science, or even to science itself. Part of the work of progress is making this substitution, so that the soul of the race is invested in it."[9] Accordingly, Thomas carries the stigma of contributing to the obscure New Age philosophy with its forms of mystical anti-intellectualism. It falsifies science as moral and progressive and misrepresents scientists as putative poets needing to be as hospitable to trends in the epistemological status of language as literary critics. This is a steep price to pay for trying to "humanize" scientific rationalism.

Thomas himself claims that his disagreements with scientists, at least, derive not from disputes about facts but from different points of view about them. For him altruism is not simply a question of biology or even choice, but is a human necessity because we cannot rationalize our obligations away. Altruism "is there, maybe in our genes for the recognition of cousins, or, if not, it ought to be there in our intellects from having learned about the matter."[10] Violations, past and potential, or partnership have brought Thomas to the point where morals and hence politics are continuous with science.

The limits of Thomas's optimism, however, are revealed politically in his strong attacks throughout *Late Night Thoughts* on national defense policies. A fully realized modern science, he says, would offer ways of "getting rid of thermonuclear weapons, patriotic rhetoric and nationalism all at once." In the strength of his indignation is evidence that what Thomas has given up in pure research has been replaced by moral criticism of the consequences of "value-free" science. What he has learned as a writer, added to what he knew as a scientist, has made Thomas a citizen with claims to professional authority of a sort not always welcome in medicine and the professions generally. They would, out of conviction sometimes, but also out of caution or expediency, isolate scholarship from opinion, especially in politics. It is, however, Thomas's achievement to have reasserted their relation as an urgent and permanent necessity.

"Throw away the lights, the definitions," Stevens says near the end of "The Man with the Blue Guitar," "and say of what you see in the dark." But Thomas's is more than a poetic gesture. For even as an essayist he is still doing essential work in science according to the standards proposed by Victor Weisskopf. He defends Thomas's approach (without naming him) because important parts of human experience cannot be evaluated by science alone. Hence we need forms of writing, in science and other fields, that display the "complementarities" obscured by their parochial and professional habits. We need rational talk about feeling, he says, and emotional discussions of science and its meanings. "Within each approach," Weisskopf states, "there is a specific type of discourse; it appears lucid and concise within its own intrinsic scale of values, but fragile and indefinite when judged by the peculiar requirements of a complementary approach. One view complements the other, and we must use all of them in order to get the full significance of our experiences."[11]

Thomas's gift has been to make of complementary elements of science and the humanities a unique style of scientific discourse. The undertaking began in unusually favorable circumstances, the importance of which should not, according to Thomas himself, be underestimated. Professional motives, he remarked in an essay on "Natural Science," cannot be programmed. "If you want a bee to make honey, you do not issue protocols in solar navigation of carbohydrate chemistry, you put him together with other bees and do what you can to arrange the general environment around the hive. If the air is right, the science will come in its own season, like pure honey" (*LOC*, 120). Now the air has changed, for Thomas and for us, and science, at least as he practices it, will have to struggle with the products of its own instinctive idealism.

Notes

1. Paul Starr, *The Social Transformation of American Medicine: The Rise of a Sovereign Profession and the Making of a Vast Industry* (New York: Basic Book, 1982), 13.

2. Lewis Thomas, *The Youngest Science: Notes of a Medicine Watcher* (New York: Viking, 1983), 29. Future references appear in the text with the acronym *TYS*.
3. Lewis Thomas, *The Lives of a Cell: Notes of a Biology Watcher* (1974; reprint New York: Bantam, 1975), 2. Future references appear in the text with the acronym *LOC*.
4. Lewis Thomas, *The Medusa and the Snail: More Notes of a Biology Watcher* (New York: Viking, 1979), 153.
5. Thomas, *The Medusa and the Snail*, 8.
6. Lewis Thomas, *Late Night Thoughts on Listening to Mahler's Ninth Symphony* (New York: Viking, 1983), 161.
7. Ibid., 168.
8. Ronald Bailey, "Politics of the Cell," *Commentary* 78 (September 1984): 72–4.
9. Alan G. Wasserstein, "Scientific Optimism: A Progress Report," *Raritan* 9 (1989): 126.
10. Thomas, *Late Night Thoughts,* 106.
11. Victor Weisskopf, "The Frontiers and Limits of Science," *Daedalus* 113 (1984): 193.

11

History and the Rhetoric of Inquiry: the Example of Dominick LaCapra

Critics of the organization of the university often identify academic departments as the chief problem. But even while reformers are contemplating the renovation of the disciplines by reorganizing their institutional structure, a promising change has taken place for at least some scholars in the way that they understand their work. They now refer to their fields as "discourse communities" to signify their recognition that disciplines are actually sites for distinctive rhetorical traditions and practices. Whether the lesson comes from within one's own research, from a pathmaking critic like Kenneth Burke, or from colleagues in English composition, rhetoric itself is now widely understood to be a form of knowing and the forms of scholarly discourse are seen now to be worth as much attention as their subjects.[1]

Historian J. H. Hexter's contribution to this change (though it was slow to be recognized) was based on his aversion to the application of scientific standards of coherence and explanatory adequacy to history writing. In his view the "denotative univocal vocabulary" and "strict deductive entailment" of natural science are unsatisfactory for history (and for the social sciences generally) because of the absolute claims made on their behalf. "The vocabulary of modes of explanation," he says, "is not something that exists *in vacuo,* but only in relation to what particular inquirers at particular moments, seek to know." He values the loyalty of history to logical argument but also to rhetoric as a measure of its contingency. Effective history writing—essentially narrative—is guided by principles of "proportion" and "tempo" and makes a virtue of its "indispensable imprecision." Hexter would convert the neglect among historians of their own rhetoric as story tellers to a more self-conscious methodological advantage. "It is part of the task of the writer of history," he says, "to mediate understanding and confirmation by the devices of the rhetoric of history less direct but more compelling, more to the purpose than the simple maximizing of completeness, accuracy and exactness."[2]

Similar proposals are now available in other fields, including anthropology, sociology, and economics.[3] Dominick LaCapra's *History and Criticism* is an authoritative guide to thinking about the uses of rhetoric in history, bringing Hexter's proposals for historiography to recent developments in literary and critical theory. Moreover, at a time when claims are often made for the priority of rhetoric in past and present practices in the academic disciplines, LaCapra offers some "provisional" directions for demonstrating the rhetorical aspects of both creative and critical texts across the curriculum.

LaCapra is interested not only in the history of ideas—the conventional territory of his subdiscipline, intellectual history—but also in the relations of historiography with other forms of intellectual practice. He hopes to prompt his colleagues toward greater self-consciousness of interpretive techniques and their contexts (the putative domain of the social historians). His taste for the liveliness of methodological debate, as it has developed in literary (and composition) theory, is accompanied by the wish to make a place for historiography in them, "not simply as a repository of facts or a neopositivist stepchild of social science, and certainly not as a mythological locus for some prediscursive image of 'reality,' but as a critical voice in the disciplines addressing problems of understanding and explanation."[4] LaCapra knows the obstacles:

> Historians tend to pride themselves on their immunity to the wormlike doubt and self-reflective scrutiny that have appeared in other areas of inquiry, notably those infiltrated by recent French thought. Far from seeing recent critical initiatives as holding forth the angelic promise of a reformation or even a renaissance in historical studies, many historians have been seized with what might almost be

called a counter-reformational zeal in reasserting orthodox procedures. (46)

With such evidence for his own rhetorical gifts, it is no surprise
that LaCapra sees opportunities for enlarging the personal dimension of scholarship.

Styles in History

Historians, of course, have long attended to the methodological
foundations of their work, even occasionally for audiences outside
the profession. But in LaCapra's view these efforts lack the
concrete attention to ideas about language available from rhetorical theory. His own reformer's zeal, however, deserves some
context. In *Style in History,* for example, Peter Gay compares not
only the rhetorical techniques of Gibbon, Ranke, Macaulay, and
Burkhardt, but also presents a nascent theory of writing based on
familiar propositions about the nature of language. The relation in
history of style to truth is a perplexing matter because no account
of the past can be an actual copy of it. Writing imposes linearity
though events occur simultaneously. Yet for Gay, narrative and
scholarly conventions in history and other fields are more than
inconveniences. They are themselves part of the truth they are
used to represent. "While the stylist's shaping hand appears to be
imposing order on disparate, often seemingly disconnected past
realities," he says, "his act of ordering is formal, exacted by the
requirements of presentation. The order itself is something the
historian does not make; he finds it. So controversial an activity as
the carving out of a historical period is not a construction but a
discovery. The order, the period, are there."[5]
Gay appears to be resisting without quite acknowledging the
epistemological radicalism—originating outside of historiography
as LaCapra would have it—of the last decade. His confidence in
the transparency of narrative stands out in a time when precisely
that feature of historical writing has become the object of some
skepticism. At the same time Gay can be said to have anticipated
what has come to be called "the revival of narrative," or the
reaction to the atomization of historical methods.[6] In the conduct

of their internal debate historians are demonstrating some heretofore unexpressed relations with both theory and practice in rhetoric and composition.[7]

The gift Gay finds in his favorite rhetorical models is the one often proposed as the goal for students seeking to move from the personal or freshman essay to work in a discipline of the liberal arts curriculum—the assimilation of an authentic personal voice to the authority derived from even very limited mastery of the contents and conventions of a particular field. The task is not of course simply a matter of technique. If that were so, the process could be taught more confidently than it is. For though Gay characterizes any work of history as "a report, often with aesthetic merit," he finds the good ones plausible because he believes in the power of the rhetorical conventions behind them to guide the writer to the truths in complex phenomena. His is the bias of work in all disciplines that justify their authority in the selection and interpretation of events and behavior, of ideas and documents, by relying on both rhetorical conventions and innovations. Hence, even if expert practitioners are unaware of their rhetorical tools, their work may still be effective.

Most theorists of rhetoric and writing, whatever their familiarity with history or historiography (or for that matter with other disciplines and their systems of self-analysis), will grant as much. The issue for them, however, is not only competence, but self-consciousness. Historians do not usually think about their writing, except within the routines of scholarship, that is, within the organization of evidence and inference and the relation of new work (their own primarily) to old. And indeed, Gay's book and now a few others like it in other disciplines suggest that style in scholarship is still something of a surprise—even for the scholar.

This qualification is justified by the examples of traditional historians and inventive critics of history alike. Speaking in the Depression about the uses of academic scholarship (he was the president of the American Historical Association), Carl Becker had to know something about effective rhetoric. He wondered about the consequences of specialized vocabularies and stressed what could be learned about the past from "ordinary people." It was, paradoxically, professional arrogance and intellectual naivete, specifically about writing, that prompted historians to believe that the facts in history somehow speak for themselves and could be restated without being reshaped.

> To set forth historical facts is not comparable to dumping a barrow of bricks. A brick retains its form and pressure wherever placed; but the form and substance of historical facts, having a negotiable existence only in literary discourse, vary with the words employed to convey them. Since history is not a part of the external material world, but an imaginative reconstruction of vanished events, its forms and substance are inseparable: in the realm of literary discourse substance, being an idea, *is* form; and form, conveying the idea, *is* substance.[8]

Becker later made a sideline of speaking to college and public audiences about "The Art of Writing" (the title of an essay in a posthumous collection of his work).[9] His Strunk and Whiteisms have by now been absorbed with others of the period into the writing handbooks, but his insistence on the authority of form and the making of a scholarly voice is still fresh. And "imaginative reconstruction" is now a byword among historians.

Fact and Fiction

Since Becker, influential statements about historical writing have, like Gay's, stressed similar themes, though within the framework of a more sophisticated historiography. Most have been motivated as well by the hegemony of science (or perhaps scientism) in intellectual life, a burden for LaCapra and others. Hayden White, for example, finds undue respect for scientific methods to be an obstacle in understanding the inner workings of historical writing. Today's most influential critic of historiography *outside* the historical professions, White shares Gay's belief in the arts of history and Hexter's skepticism about historians' confidence in their scholarly vocabularies. But White is less sure than Hexter about the control historians have over their materials and methods, for he believes in the durability of rhetorical forms and the unconscious power they have over all users. White is an adept reader of historical texts and a persuasive theorizer whose taste for classification has introduced into historiography some terms from literary criticism. Yet what he has adapted from Northrop Frye, for example, is less important than what he has done to bring the discourses of history, philosophy, and criticism together on behalf of a more complete understanding of language use and ethical intent.

In his ambitious account of the great nineteenth-century historians White takes up Gay's subject, but he relies on the technical vocabularies of poetry, criticism, and political philosophy. By his own admission (when he is thinking perhaps of traditional historians as an audience), White's approach to historical styles can appear "mystifying." He justifies it on the basis of what might be called a psychology of scholarship. In the rhetorical analysis of texts, therefore, the goal is "first to identify the manifest—epistemological, aesthetic and moral—dimensions of the historical work and then to penetrate to the deeper level on which these historical operations found their implicit, precritical sanctions." Accordingly, White opens new territory for rhetorical analysis, for "formal argument" is just one way historians carry out their explanatory projects. Some (to suggest just a few of White's favored categories) use "emplotment," others rely on "ideological implication," and many on a mix of all three though typically with little choice in the matter. "I believe," White says, "the historian performs an essentially poetic act, in which he prefigures the historical field and constitutes it as a domain upon which to bring to bear the specific theories he will use to explain 'what was really happening' in it."[10]

White's purpose is to rescue the artistry of history from those who would make their operations orderly, conscious, and scientific. Hence the goals and methods of history, and of other disciplines, can be found among the resources of literary study. "The modes in which theory is articulated in the different sciences," White says in a later book with literature as a main theme, "represents theoretical formulations of the tropes of natural language."[11] Moreover, works of history achieve their effects and durability much the same way that literature does, at least as the case has been made by influential literary critics like Frye and Harold Bloom.

> We can speak of the metaphorical, metonymic, synecdochic, and ironic modes of historical discourse. And because these modes correspond to the readers' modalities of language use (and therefore to their ways of conceptualizing the world), they provide the ground for

the communication of understanding and meanings between specific 'schools' of historians, on the one side, and specific publics, on the other. Because there is a generally poetic element in all historical writing, an element that appears in prose discourse as rhetoric, great historical works . . . retain vividness and authority long after they have ceased to count as contributions to "science."[12]

Writing history reflects moral and aesthetic choices (those "prefigured" and those not) rather than merely empirical ones. Accordingly, White finds historiographic uses for Frye's archetypal plot structures:

Tragedy and Satire are modes of emplotment which are consonant with the interest of those historians who perceive behind or within the welter of events contained in the chronicle an ongoing structure of relationships or an eternal return of the Same in the Different. Romance and Comedy stress the emergence of new forces or conditions out of processes that appear at first glance to be changeless in their essence or to be changing only in their phenomenal forms."[13]

In the essays collected in *Tropics of Discourse* White elaborates his point of view within the context of current activities in critical theory generally. By stressing history's interpretive and imaginative capacities, he writes straightforwardly of "The Historical Text as Literary Artifact" and even a bit ironically of "The Fictions of Factual Representation." As he says, "[W]hen it is a matter of speaking about human consciousness, we have no absolute theory to guide us; everything is under contention."[14]

Yet White protests that "radical skepticism" is not his intent (as some have charged) but the tracing of rhetorical relations between the disciplines and the maintenance of variety even as techniques for classifying the forms and goals of historical thought improve. Achieving the latter might make it possible "to provide protocols for translating between alternative modes which, because they are taken for granted either as natural or as established truth, had hardened into ideologies." Historical rhetoric, therefore, may be claimed as a research tool for its own heuristic and representational uses. With White's program in place, "we would recognize that it is not a matter of choosing between objectivity and distortion, but rather between different strategies for constituting 'reality' in thought so as to deal with it in different ways, each of which has its own ethical implications."[15] And in another of White's contributions to the debate over narrative he explains how he sees in the uses of language moral choices lying beyond the routines of academic discourse.[16]

In the complex arenas of critical theory in the human sciences White is particularly helpful because he captures at once the necessity of tradition and the force of today's trends. Hence, in an essay on "The Absurdist Moment in Contemporary Literary Theory," he can find what is timely in Derrida and other influential figures and then admit the defect of his own critical discourse, it having "become infected by the sickness of those whose condition we wished to account for."[17] By contemplating, with appropriate rhetorical flourish, his own status as yet another "mandarin" critic of culture and by choosing himself to employ (largely) familiar diction and syntax, he is skeptical and accessible enough to promote the sort of "translation" across disciplines needed for the discovery and use of shared rhetorical resources.

The Dialogue with the Past

For LaCapra, explaining the relations of "Rhetoric and History" (the title of the key essay in *History and Criticism*) means answering this question: "How may the necessary components of a documentary model without which historiography would be unrecognizable be conjoined with rhetorical features in a broader, interactive understanding of historical discourse?" (35). He offers these reasons why the traditional documentary model is itself now under pressure:

> An inclination to rely on a social definition of context as an explanatory matrix; a shift toward an interest in popular culture; a reconceptualization of culture in terms of collective discourses, mentalities, world views, and even "languages"; a redefinition of intellectual history as the study of social meaning as historically constituted; and archivally based documentary realism that treats artifacts as quarries for facts in the reconstitution of societies and cultures of the past. (46)

Widely acclaimed historians like Carlo Ginzburg (*The Cheese and the Worms* [1980]) and Robert Darnton *(The Literary Underground of the Old Regime* [1982]), therefore, deserve credit for their "progressive" contributions to historiography. Yet LaCapra notes that novelty itself can produce its own dogma, often today in the form of a misguided "methodological populism." Hence Ginzburg's account of the private cosmology of a sixteenth-century Italian miller yields two significant rhetorical problems. First, based as it is on sources inaccessible to its readers, it falls short in what LaCapra calls its "cognitive responsibilities." So thoroughly mingled are the voices of its author and its subject that the coherence of the presentation masks rhetorical confusion, much the way, it might be added, the mingled voices do in this country's documentary psychologists and social critics like Robert Coles and Studs Terkel.

A second problem also appears in the kind of subject-author relations typical of texts like Ginzburg's. As the bearer of an oral, popular culture, the miller represents a newly privileged source, at least in relation to traditional historiographic standards. In LaCapra's view this populist rhetorical pattern leads many of today's historians into the presumption that those who study and present such sources are the most authentic scholars, focusing on the most important things. "The result," he says ruefully, "is a bizarre and vicious paradox whereby a vicarious relation to the oppressed of the past serves as a pretext for contemporary pretensions to dominance" (69).

Less politically troublesome but still rhetorically problematic for LaCapra is the historical approach favored by Darnton whose books—acclaimed by both professional and general readers—are based on inventive archival research. Darnton's "narrow empiricism," dismissive attitude toward high culture, and insufficient interest in the interactions between levels of culture, yield in LaCapra's view "a patronizingly anti-intellectual populism and a sociopsychological reductionism" (90). There is here, unmistakably, a serious intradisciplinary quarrel in the form of a nascent debate over historiographic rhetoric. In other words, as LaCapra both argues and demonstrates, rhetoric is not an addition to historical argument but an inseparable part of its distinctive forms and goals.

Like White, LaCapra offers an estimate of developments in literary criticism and also a companion essay on the novel and history. His grasp of these forms is sure, but he is not optimistic about enlarging the audience for them among historians. Hence,

with examples of rhetorical innovation in history found to be not
so exemplary after all (though in a note he hedges on Darnton),
and with the uses for historians of literature and criticism limited
by their formal demands and, in the case of criticism, its increasingly specialized vocabulary, rhetorical practices in history and
inquiry into them will depend on the redistribution of interests
among traditional historians. By virtue of his own methods in
intellectual history, LaCapra reflects devotion to texts as primary
historical sources calling for intensive rhetorical study. Accordingly, he assumes that the texts he and his colleagues produce
depend on their interpretive capacities and display the results in
diverse forms of scholarship. LaCapra would now restore historical rhetoric as a contribution from intellectual history to other
specialties of the discipline.

It is as false, LaCapra insists, to hold science and rhetoric to be
opposites as it is to claim that a plain style is the only acceptable
one for truth-seeking in prose. To be scientific and anti-rhetoric,
he says, amounts to "a self-denying quest for a certain rhetoric, a
rhetoric unadorned by figures, unmoved by emotion, unclouded
by images, and universalistic in its conceptual or mathematical
scope" (42). Scholars who know this (or who should) would also
recognize the rhetorical aspects of their work as they are enumer-
ated by LaCapra in the core section of *History and Criticism* (I
have collapsed some categories and added emphasis for purposes
of this summary): 1) the *dialogical:* historians must be skeptical of
the ideal of a "unified authorial voice providing an ideally exhaus-
tive and definitive account of a fully mastered object of knowledge" (36), and they must be attentive to "disconcerting 'voices'
of the past" without projecting self-serving demands on them; 2)
the *performative:* all writers want to claim the interest of readers
and to provoke them by finding occasions for the festive, even
carnivalesque capacities of language; 3) the *critical:* since scholarly writing entails reading and historians must recognize significant texts as important events posing problems in interpretation and contextualization, they also must welcome the terms of
rhetoric and criticism since "devices of composition and arrangement generate resistances to the construal of texts in terms of their
'representational' or narrowly documentary functions, and . . .
disclose how texts have critical or even potentially transformative

relations to phenomena 'represented' in them" (38); 4) the *psy-chological:* the power of transference relations in the study of the past accounts for the tendency of writers to transfer onto objects of study their own needs, wishes, and fantasies and to experience some ambivalence and role tension in managing the relations of sympathy for one's subject and critical distance from it; 5) the *contextual:* the relations of history and historiography as institutions to social, political, and economic interests must be clarified and their experimental forms justified in terms of increased access to intellectual and educational resources, for "without a self-critical attempt to come to terms with its own insertion in this setting . . . even the most insistent dialogue with the past is condemned to be a dead letter" (43).

The mark of Bakhtin is plain in the injunction to "dialogize" and "carnivalize," and he is indeed a central figure in LaCapra's other work.[18] LaCapra is also candid about his ambivalence about White, though he welcomes recent signs of the latter's abandonment of "genetic structuralism" (or his debt to Frye). For while he has pioneered in the application of rhetorical ideas to historiography, White's approach actually has represented, in its elaborate systems of classification, a science of rhetoric in which usage is a matter of codes. LaCapra wants more art, but not too much more, for he is equally cautious about rhetorical innovation for its own, or publicity's sake: "Rhetorical power that rides roughshod over the demands of empirical accuracy and rigorous proof may at times be more objectionable than complacent business as usual" (41). His taste for the radical transformation of history is modified by recognition of its institutional and scholarly relations and a pragmatic grasp of its ideals, uses, and limits.

History and Criticism ends with LaCapra's acknowledgement that he may have overstated the flaws of conventional history and the virtues of a transformed version, but he has done so, he insists, on behalf of the very methodological change he favors most, the incorporation of "contestatory voices" into the central work of the discipline. There is no qualification, however, for the actual working problem to which colleagues must now turn, that is

> the way all documents are texts that rework what they "represent" and thus make a difference in the sociopolitical and discursive context in which they are inserted. The transferential dimension of research

makes this a problem not only in the phenomena of the past that we study but in the very way in which we study them—the language we use and abuse in coming to terms with them. (141)

Conclusion: History Toward Rhetoric

Evidence that LaCapra is less isolated than he may think is available now in recent work in which the transferential aspects of historiography and close reading of texts are central themes.[19] It is still true of course that important accounts of the status of historiography can neglect rhetorical dimensions of theory.[20] But such interests are now more often assumed to be central to synthesizing efforts.[21] LaCapra has written (with irony) of his poor treatment at the hands of colleagues who resist the argument for rhetoric.[22] What is at stake is more than the addition of another methodological tool for the working historian. For his own field of intellectual history is by its very nature a rhetorical enterprise, or a "mechanism for the preservation and reinterpretation of [a culture's] exceptional products."[23] The question of what is "exceptional" carries with it of course the debate of the past two decades between intellectual and social historians about the primacy of some kinds of historical sources in relation to others. For in addition to the texts that intellectual historians have favored, the writing of history now requires attention to institutional practices and the many forms of social discourse distributed throughout a pluralist society of speakers and writers. To be sure, influential theorists have attempted to construe all activities and events as textual.[24] Though he shares something of this point of view, LaCapra also takes the traditional position on behalf of the role of the text itself in what can be called "textuality."

LaCapra's belief in the importance of rhetoric is also made plain in a tactful account of what he takes to be the essential division in scholarly and intellectual life today. Indeed, LaCapra presents the two positions as representing the traditional *"erudit"* or scholar and the "critical intellectual." The first aims at producing accounts of experience, including texts, that display its orderliness and coherence. It may recognize a measure of chaos within order but it relies on the necessity of determinate meanings and the basic unity of cultural expression for its authority. The second approach seeks to apply a sort of "shock therapy" to the first by disclosing what is indeterminate, incoherent, marginal, or disorienting about a text and the value of "deconstructing" it. LaCapra, an erudite interpreter of this second (and contemporary) school of thought nonetheless (like White) displays his own uneasiness about it and the danger of it remaining fixed at the level of shock. "In doing so," he warns, "it may aggravate what its proponents would see as undesirable tendencies in the larger society, become symptomatic where it would like to be critical, and confuse ordinary equivocation and evasiveness—or even slipshod research—with the kind of transformative interaction between self and other (or language and world) it would like to reactivate."[25] In effect, LaCapra is recommending another "mechanism," this one being the rhetorical study of scholarship across the disciplines. Aimed at correcting overemphases in either the traditional or experimental (some would say "postmodern") camps it would show where the goals of scholars and intellectuals meet and diverge in a reciprocal discourse, the rhetoric of inquiry.[26]

Notes

1. See John S. Nelson, Allan Megill, and Donald McCloskey, *The Rhetoric of Inquiry: Language and Argument in Scholarship and Public Affairs* (Madison: University of Wisconsin Press, 1987).
2. J. H. Hexter, *Doing History* (Bloomington: Indiana University Press, 1971), 31, 59. The essay was first published in the *International Encyclopedia of the Social Sciences* (1968).
3. See James Clifford and George Marcus, eds. *Writing Culture: The Poetics and Politics of Ethnography* (Berkeley: University of California Press, 1986) and Clifford Geertz, *Works and Lives: The Anthropologist as Author* (Stanford, CA: Stanford University Press, 1988); Richard H. Brown, *A Poetic for Sociology: Toward a Logic of Discovery for the Human Sciences* (Cambridge: Cambridge University Press, 1977); Donald McCloskey, *The Rhetoric of Economics* (Madison: University of Wisconsin Press, 1985). An important book that addresses rhetorical themes in several fields is Charles Bazerman, *Shaping Written Knowledge: The Genre and Activity of the Experimental Article in Science* (Madison: University of Wisconsin Press, 1988).
4. Dominick LaCapra, *History and Criticism* (Ithaca: Cornell University Press, 1985), 10. Future references appear in the text.
5. Peter Gay, *Style in History* (New York: McGraw-Hill, 1974), 217.

6. See Lawrence Stone, "The Revival of Narrative: Reflections on a New Old History," *Past and Present* 85 (1979): 3–24 and Mark Phillips, "The Revival of Narrative: Thoughts on a Current Debate,"*University of Toronto Quarterly* 53 (1983): 140–65.
7. See Theodore K. Rabb, "Coherence, Synthesis and Quality in History," *Journal of Interdisciplinary History* 12 (1981): 315–32; James West Davidson, "The New Narrative History: How New? How Narrative?" *Reviews in American History* 12 (1984): 322–34; and Stephen Bann, "Towards a Critical Historiography," *Philosophy* 56 (1981): 365–85 and "Analyzing the Discourse of History," *Dalhousie Review* 64 (1984): 376–400.
8. Carl Becker, *Everyman His Own Historian: Essays on History and Politics* (New York: Crofts, 1935), 251.
9. Carl Becker, *Detachment and the Writing of History: Essays and Letters,* ed. Philip L. Snyder (Ithaca: Cornell University Press, 1958).
10. Hayden White, *Metahistory: The Historical Imagination in Nineteenth-Century Europe* (Baltimore: Johns Hopkins University Press, 1973), x.
11. Hayden White, *Tropics of Discourse: Essays in Cultural Criticism* (Baltimore: John Hopkins University Press, 1978), 116.
12. Ibid.
13. White, *Metahistory,* 11.
14. White, *Tropics of Discourse,* 22.
15. Ibid., 22.
16. Hayden White, "The Question of Narrative in Contemporary Historical Theory," *History and Theory* 23 (1984): 1–33.
17. White, *Tropics of Discourse,* 281.
18. See Dominick LaCapra, *Rethinking Intellectual History: Texts, Contexts, Language* (Ithaca: Cornell University Press, 1983).
19. See for example David W. Noble, *The End of American History: Democracy, Capitalism and the Metaphor of Two Worlds in Anglo-American Historical Writing, 1880-1990* (Minneapolis: University of Minnesota Press, 1986) and C. Vann Woodward, *Thinking Back: The Perils of Writing History* (Baton Rouge: Louisiana State University Press, 1986).
20. See for example William H. Goetzmann, "Time's American Adventures: American Historians and their Writing Since 1776," *Social Science Quarterly* 57 (1976): 3–48; Bernard Bailyn, "The Challenge of Modern Historiography," *American Historical Review* 87 (1982): 1–24; and Alan Brinkley, "Writing the History of Contemporary America: Dilemmas and Challenges," *Daedalus* 113 (1984): 121–41.
21. See for example Fred Matthews, "'Hobbesian Populism': Interpretive Paradigms and Moral Vision in American Historiography," *Journal of American History* 72 (1985): 92–115; John Patrick Dig-

gins, "Comrades and Citizens: New Mythologies in American Historiography," *American Historical Review* 90 (1985): 614–38.

22. Dominick LaCapra, "On Grubbing in My Personal Archives," *Boundary 2* 13 (1985): 43–67.

23. LaCapra, *Rethinking Intellectual History,* 67. For a similar view from a specialist in American history see David Hollinger, "Historians and the Discourse of Intellectuals," *New Directions in American Intellectual History,* ed. John Higham and Paul K. Conkin (Baltimore: Johns Hopkins University Press, 1979), 42–63.

24. See for example Paul Ricoeur, "The Model of the Text: Meaningful Action Considered as a Text," in *Hermeneutics and the Human Sciences,* ed. and trans. John B. Thompson (Cambridge: Cambridge University Press, 1981), 197–221.

25. LaCapra, *Rethinking Intellectual History,* 68–9.

26. An unsympathetic view of LaCapra's work, emphasizing its loyalty to critical innovations (especially Derrida's), can be found in Anthony Pagden, "Rethinking the Linguistic Turn: Current Anxieties in Intellectual History," *Journal of the History of Ideas* 49 (1988): 519–30. See also LaCapra's response in "A Review of a Review," *Journal of the History of Ideas* 49 (1988): 677–85.

12

How to Speak Wittgenstein: Clifford Geertz and the Uses of Anthropology

For someone who has referred to his own scholarly method as "vagrant erudition" the study of his field's pioneers as writers was a bold step. But Clifford Geertz's inquiry hardly had as a goal the discovery of rhetorical standards for anthropology. Indeed, he compares the criticism of anthropological writing to criticism of literature which should resist imported ideas about form. So too in the case of anthropology: criticism "ought to grow out of a similar engagement with *it,* not out of preconceptions of what it must look like to qualify as a science."[1] The question of his predecessors turns out also to be an invitation to think about Geertz himself who is—for his erudition and more—a guide to the motives, making, and uses of scholarship in his own field and those he has aligned with it.

The Career of "Culture"

In the mid-1950s anthropology was still a distant enough enterprise to teachers and scholars in literature that Margaret Mead devoted her address at a meeting of the Modern Language Association to a rudimentary summary of a few of the discipline's major themes and tasks. She wished to make a strong but tactful case for the uses of anthropology in literary study, and so she stressed its capacity to discover significant facts about the history of everyday life in remote societies. She also addressed a related matter, the potential in primitive societies for the kinds of achievements most admired in advanced ones.

> Human cultures, like the individual personalities whose capacities they both express and underwrite, may be stabilized at very different levels of symbolic expression—may vary from the type of culture in which *"essen trinken schlafen Schluss"* consumes man's efforts and all that is left of their imaginations, to cultures as neatly calibrated to the physical environment as a perfectly designed tool, where men catch the most fish possible in the best way their technological level permits, to cultures in which nine-tenths of men's time is devoted to elaborations of art and ritual, pursued with delight and creativity.[2]

Her analysis was meant to prompt her audience to see its pedagogical and scholarly efforts against the backdrop of enormous and as yet barely recorded human variety. Not yet a hundred years old as a discipline when she spoke, anthropology has in the ensuing decades achieved substantial influence among the other fields of the humanities and the social sciences. It is at the heart of what is often called "the interpretive turn" in these intellectual domains.[3] And indeed, when Susan Sontag declared Claude Levi-Strauss an example of the "anthropologist as hero" she termed anthropology a "total occupation" whose critical and creative techniques, and spiritual and moral commitments, are the most inclusive in scholarship.[4]

Its potential for heroism (or as skeptics might suggest celebrity) aside, one reason for current interest in anthropology is its apparent ownership of the term "culture" and the constellation of related ideas and themes. Mead defined culture as one of her central interests because it is probably the most suggestive category for work in what is now often called the "human sciences." In their comprehensive survey, the distinguished anthropologists Alfred Kroeber and Clyde Kluckholn state that "in explanatory importance and in generality of application culture is comparable to such categories as gravity in physics, disease in medicine, evolution in biology."[5] Culture of course is something we all live in and observe. Scholars study it under the names history, philosophy, and literary criticism, critics under the names art, film, and even food. Yet as a subject in search of its own rules of inquiry, culture, or Culture, has been the occasion for much confusion. The dozens of definitions offered by Kroeber and Kluckholn are reminiscent of a similar scholarly struggle to define "Romanticism." Matthew Arnold, the apostle of "culture" in traditional literary studies, did not have in mind all that Mead did when she proposed this definition to the MLA: "Culture may be seen as a system of tradition within which the crude sensations originating within the body—the quickened pulse beat, the tautened throat muscles, the clammy hand—and those originating outside the body—the slowly rising moon or the sudden flash of an electric light bulb, the line of a tree or lamp post against a wintry sky, the cry of a bird or the grinding machinery of a garbage truck—are given meaning."[6] Yet Arnold's understanding of the shaping force of tradition resembles Mead's view enough to suggest that "culture" can be used with the expectation of relative consistency of understanding. Writers as diverse as Cambridge don, critic, and novelist Raymond Williams (in *Culture and Society* [1958]) and Kentucky farmer, poet, and essayist Wendell Berry (*A Continuous Harmony: Essays Cultural and Agricultural* [1972]) use the term to mean the whole way of life of a nation or group, but both are aware of, and occasionally even employ, more specialized uses.[7]

Describing Description

Geertz's widely cited essay "Thick Description: Toward an Interpretive Theory of Culture" is a point from which the study of "culture" and the uses of anthropology might begin. According to Geertz theories of culture have suffered needless diffusion. In their efforts to be as inclusive as possible—pluralistic in method, subject matter, and theory—anthropologists have created a "conceptual morass" in their theorizing about culture. "Eclecticism is self-defeating," he says, "not because there is only one direction in which it is useful to move, but because there are so many: it is necessary to choose."[8] Geertz favors a concept of culture he terms "semiotic." "Man is an animal suspended in webs of significance he himself has spun," he says, and "I take culture to be those webs." He accepts, moreover, the methodological limits suggested by this view because the semiotic analysis of culture cannot be "an experimental science in search of law but an interpretive one in search of meaning" (*IC*, 5). Geertz prefers ethnography to anthropology to describe the kind of interpretation he is after. Yet textbook ethnography, like the traditional uses of the term culture, also will not do. The popularly understood tasks of ethnographic fieldwork—establishing rapport, selecting informants, transcribing texts, taking genealogies, mapping the terrain, keeping a diary—do not adequately define the activity. What defines it, Geertz says, is "the kind of intellectual effort it is: an elaborate venture in thick description" (*IC*, 6). This term, borrowed from Oxford philosopher Gilbert Ryle, represents the results of Geertz's lifelong ethnographic project, carried out mainly in Indonesia, North Africa, and Bali, and enormously suggestive across cultures, nationalities, and disciplines. "It is explication I am after," he says, "construing social expressions on their surface enigmatical" (*IC*, 5).

Speaking to interpreters in other fields Geertz explains that apart from routinized data collection, what the ethnographer faces is "a multiplicity of complex conceptual structures, many of them superimposed upon or knotted into one another, which are at once strange, irregular and inexplicit, and which we must contrive somehow first to grasp and then to render" (*IC*, 10). While he recognizes the similarity of this activity to other kinds of intellectual work, he also emphasizes its characteristic obstacle, for "doing ethnography is like trying to read (in the sense of 'construct a reading') a manuscript—foreign, faded, full of elipses, incoherencies, suspicious emendations and tendentious commentaries written not in conventionalized graphs of sound but in transient examples of shaped behavior" (*IC*, 10). As Geertz recognizes, however, the obscurity of ethnographic materials and the complexities of the societies in which they originate are two reasons anthropologists have differed about the structure and meaning of culture, about whether it is essentially "subjective" or "objective," a body of local information and a system of beliefs and values, or the expression of material circumstances like geography, food, clothing, and technology. Both views, according to Geertz, can be unnecessarily reductive when they lead to the pursuit of systematic ethnographic

rules for the description of culture. Behind this goal, he says, is
a style of ethnography relying on this misguided definition: "A
society's culture consists of whatever it is one has to know or
believe in order to operate in a manner acceptable to its members" (*IC,* 11). The practice of this functionalist principle
ignores symbols and their complicated meanings for the surface
of experience and its more readily codifiable ones.

In setting out, therefore, to thickly describe a culture,
anthropologists must eschew both formalism and impression-
ism in favor of principles of explication that unify all aspects of
life and communications. "Once human behavior is seen as
symbolic action—action which like phonation in speech, pig-
ment in painting, line in writing, or sonance in music, signifies—the question as to whether culture is patterned conduct or
a frame of mind, or even the two somehow mixed together,
loses sense" (*IC,* 10). Organizing examples of behavior is secondary to explaining their meaning. "Looked at in this way,"
Geertz insists, "the aim of anthropology is the enlargement of
the universe of human discourse" (*IC,* 14). He recognizes other
aims, of course—instruction, practical advice, and the discovery, perhaps, of a natural order in human behavior—and the
utility of other disciplines in pursuing them. The power of
anthropology, however, lies in its unique descriptive capacities. "As interworked symbols of construable signs [or symbols]
culture is not a power, something to which social events, behav-
iors, institutions, or processes can be casually attributed; it is a
context, something within which they can be intelligibly—that
is thickly—described" (*IC,* 14). Good ethnography, therefore,
offers examples of human behavior rich in meaning because
they are set in the patterns of domestic, social, and institutional
life that inform them. Variations in cultures and hence in the
meaning of ordinary acts tell us not that societies different from
our own are arbitrary or quixotic, as some may think, but
simply that they are different. Ethnographers must be exacting
in observing and describing these differences but also alert to
those forms of culture that bind societies. "Understanding a
people's culture exposes their normalness without reducing
their particularity . . . it renders them accessible: setting them
in the frame of their own banalities, it dissolves their opacity"

(*IC,* 14). The more an anthropologist gets to know a foreign culture the more logical and singular it appears. And approaching it by way of its signs and symbols provides anthropologists, Geertz says, with access to the conceptual world of their subjects so that we can "converse with them." This conversation is a complicated one and ultimately includes, through its semiotic interpretations, a conversation with the large interpretive community of historians, linguists, philosophers, and literary critics.

Yet "thick description" is both a prerequisite for and an impediment to cultural theory. For while theory is "unseverable from the immediacies thick description presents, its freedom to shape itself in terms of its internal logic is rather limited. What generality it contrives to achieve grows out of the delicacy of its distinctions, not the sweep of its abstractions" (*IC,* 25). It is a mistake, therefore, to try to build a theory of culture by codifying social rules. The prior task is the systematization of the techniques for their description. Theory can be used to "ferret out the unapparent import of things," and anthropologists should seek "not to generalize across cases but within them" (*IC,* 26).

In arguing for a modest but still technically arduous method, Geertz is well aware that it is often the large-scale interpretations of societies and world events, of the history and meaning of grand ideas like Faith, Power, and Beauty, that earn for anthropology attention outside its own scholarly boundaries. He confesses that "finding our feet . . . is what ethnographic research consists of as a personal experience; trying to formulate the basis on which one imagines, always excessively, one has found them is what anthropological writing consists of as a scientific endeavor" (*IC,* 13). Reconciling the need for ethnographers to be patient and precise—"microscopic" is his word—in their work with their natural instinct to match other disciplines in their apparent profundities is a major problem. Moving from local knowledge to general ideas probably cannot be resisted—indeed much of Geertz's own work is an example—but the interpretive priority, and ultimately the validity, in ethnographic work must finally reside in the former. With this emphasis anthropology can play a unique role among the disciplines whose ambitions Geertz only grudgingly acknowledges.

> The important thing about the anthropologists' findings is their complex specific-ness, their circumstantiality. It is with the kind of material produced by long-term, mainly (though not exclusively) qualitative, highly participative, and almost obsessively fine-comb field study in confined contexts that the mega-concepts with which contemporary social science is afflicted—legitimacy, modernization, integration, conflict, charisma, structure . . . meaning—can be given the sort of sensible actuality that makes it possible to think not only realistically and concretely *about* them, but, what is more important, creatively and imaginatively *with* them. (*IC,* 23)

Yet Geertz is careful about endorsing wholesale application of the products of "thick description" to all manner of social issues and problems. "Where an interpretation comes from does not determine where it can be impelled to go" (*IC,* 23). It is origins that count, the professional motives of fieldwork. The history of an ethnographic detail or the interpretation of the relations between groups of them is unpredictable and problematic.

Negara: Pomp and Power

The relation of parochial understandings based on microscopic fieldwork to comprehensive ones motivated by the desire to interpret as well as to report has been one of Geertz's major interests. He acknowledged in *Islam Observed* that fieldwork was "the source not just of discrete hypotheses but of whole patterns of social and cultural interpretation: the bulk of what I have seen (or thought I have seen) or the broad sweep of social history I have seen (or thought I have seen) first in the narrow confines of country towns and peasant villages." The parenthetical modesty is his characteristic hedge against definitiveness. The risks of unearned generalizations are always there: "What was private domain, neatly fenced and intimately known, becomes foreign ground, heavily traversed but personally unfamiliar."[9]

Yet early in his career Geertz found in the idea of culture, and in what he came to call the "blurred genre" of anthropology as he practiced it, a format for giving closely observed particulars the meanings which would lead eventually to more ambitious statements about the uses of ethnography and the import of different styles of social organization. In an epilogue to *The Social History of an Indonesian Town* Geertz reflected on the meaning of a local election he described in considerable detail.

> The actual course of action was at no point a mere reflex of cultural categories and the distinctions giving rise to them. But at no point, also, was it free of their ordering impact. . . . This is the paradox of the role of culture or, if you will, systems of ideas—in social activity. No actual event (or sequence of events) can be predicted from them, and no actual event (or sequence of events) can be explained without them."[10]

The essays collected in *The Interpretation of Cultures* (1973) and *Local Knowledge* (1983), on evolution, religion, art, Third World politics, law and other subjects, are testimony to the power of that paradox.

In *Negara,* neglected by partisans of Geertz's approach on behalf of his well-known essays, he synthesized his major themes and theories. Mindful of his own suggestion that good scholarship exhibits many of the qualities of creative work, he produced in *Negara* a book of great stylistic novelty and achievement. Organized so that it may be used by different kinds of readers, *Negara* is one-half unfootnoted text (a brief one at that) aimed at scholars who are not anthropologists or even at the elusive general reader. The second half consists of the detailed citation of sources and discussion of the history and current state of Indonesian and Balinese ethnography.

Still, methodological problems are one of the central themes of even the first part of *Negara.* Bookend-like opening and closing chapters consider the relation of anthropological study of Bali to historical method and to political theory. Like other proponents of the "new history," Geertz contrasts history writing which describes wars, revolutions, and great events, the succession of dates, places, and influential individuals, with scholarship devoted to the discernment of patterns of social or cultural change. "The period approach," he says, "distributes clusters of concrete events along a time continuum in which the major distinction is prerequisite and outcome." Naturally he recognizes the complementarity of these styles: "The flow of particular events, chronicled in full detail, gives substance to the schematic outline of structural change; and the constructed phases of developmental history—themselves frames for historical perception, not segments of historical reality—give intelligible form to the recorded flux of actual occurrences."[11] *Negara* is an effort to contribute to such a history.

What we know of Bali is fragmented and ambiguous. As an anthropologist, Geertz defines his task as the construction of a precise and empirically based model of Balinese culture. Such a model, fortified by thickly described details, will provide an interpretive device for historical, and in the case of *Negara,* political generalization. Though it meets Geertz's standards for cultural interpretation, he admits that the model is abstract. It will also demonstrate its utility in a relatively esoteric area of scholarship.

> On the one hand, it is a simplified, necessarily unfaithful, theoretically tendentious representation of a relatively well-known sociocultural institution: the nineteenth-century Balinese state [the negara]. On the other it is a guide, a sort of sociological blueprint, for the construction of representations, not necessarily or even probably identical to it in structure, of a whole set of relatively less well-known but presumptively similar institutions: the classical Southeast Asian Indic states of the fifth to fifteenth centuries. (*N,* 9–10)

The interest of many literary critics, philosophers, and historians in *Negara,* therefore, will be less in its ethnographic findings than in the methods that demonstrate that in anthropology are synthesized many of the enduring problems of interpretation common to other disciplines.

Geertz begins boldly. The opening paragraphs of *Negara's* first chapter (following the introductory one on "Bali and Historical Method") suggest not only the ritualistic quality of Balinese history but also Geertz's decision to make his own scholarly style as expressive or dramatic as its material. The passage deserves quotation for these reasons and also because it suggests the narrative gift Geertz brings to all of his interpretive work.

> In 1891 what was to be the last of the dozen or so kings of Mengwi, an inland Balinese palatinate some fifteen kilometers north of the present capital, Den Pasar, found his capital besieged by his two most familiar enemies, Tabanan and Badung, allied at last against him. His army routed, his nobles all fled or fallen, and Badung troops headed by a small but, against defenders armed with only lances and daggers, terribly proficient company of mercenary Bugis riflemen waiting at the edge of town, he was an end-game chess king left without pawns or pieces. Old, sick, unable to walk, he commanded his servants to carry him on the royal litter from the palace toward the invaders. The Bugis gunners, who had been expecting such an appearance, shot his bearers and he rolled helplessly on the ground. The Badung troops (largely low-caste Sudras) moved to take him, but he refused capture and they were obliged, out of due respect, to kill him. The seven principal kingdoms of the south Bali heartland—Tabanan, Badung, Gianyar, Klungkung, Karengasem, Banglie, and Mengwi—were thus reduced to six.
>
> But the victors' glory was only momentarily enjoyed. In 1906, the Dutch army appeared, for reasons of its own, at Sanur on the south coast and fought its way into Badung, where the king, his wives, his children, and his entourage marched in a splendid mass suicide into the direct fire of its guns. Within the week, the king and crown prince of Tabanan had been captured, but they managed to destroy themselves, the one by poison, the other by knife, their first evening in Dutch custody. Two years later, in 1908, this strange ritual was repeated in the most illustrious state of all, Klungkung, the nominal "capital" of traditional Bali; the king and the court again paraded, half entranced, half dazed with opium, out of the palace into the reluctant fire of the by now thoroughly bewildered Dutch troops. It was quite literally the death of the old order. It expired as it had lived: absorbed in a pageant. (*N*, 11)

Spectacle and ceremony dominated Balinese culture. Military martyrdom was only one expression of a culture which also dramatized social status and inequality, according to Geertz the "ruling obsessions." In this theater state "court ceremonialism was the driving force of court politics; and mass ritual was not a device to shore the state, but rather the state, even in its final gasp, was a device for the enactment of mass ritual" (*N*, 13). The foreignness of Balinese culture lies not only in its exotic setting and domestic customs, its public artistry and elegance, familiar from travelogues and *The National Geographic,* but in its reversal of aspects of the modern political state. "Power served pomp, not pomp power" (*N,* 13), Geertz claims, and in *Negara* he presents a society in which public and private life share central motives.

A second important factor in Balinese history and politics is the island's peculiar topography: steep strips of fertile land under rice cultivation lying at the feet of volcanic mountains and separated by deep ravines. "If ever there was a forcing house for the growth of a singular civilization, this snug little amphitheater was it; and if what was produced turned out to be a rather special orchid, perhaps we should not be altogether surprised" (*N,* 20). One way of seeing life as the Balinese have seen it is to accommodate the extremes of its compact landscape. Geertz offers a series of contrasts that represent the dynamics of Balinese cultural history, beginning in the "animal barbarism" of ancient Bali later to be transformed into "the renascent Bali of aesthetic elegance and liturgical splendor." Yet as Bali became more "civilized," its original unity broke down, and the Balinese, according to Geertz, see their history as "not a relentless progress toward the good society but a gradual fading from view of a classical model of perfection" (*N,* 15). He also finds economic struggles organized around the lengthwise and crosswise character of the topography, "horizontal and vertical" extensions of patterns of social status and politics. They express the tension between the historical force of exemplary state ritual and the modernizing force of state structure. The argument is brief but dense, and in the "diverse and mobile field" of Balinese political history, Geertz's account is more suggestive than complete, a composite portrait telescoping many decades and making the "model" perhaps more coherent than the actuality.

The Exemplary Center

The middle chapters of *Negara* are devoted to detailed explanations of Balinese systems of kinship, local and regional politics, and irrigation, the last a matter of critical importance to the national economy. These chapters display the "thick description" Geertz takes to be the goal of anthropology and are evidence for the major thesis of *Negara,* that for several centuries all aspects of Balinese life were carried out in an essentially ceremonial framework. The intricacies of each system—domestic, inter-familial, political, and economic—expressed and institutionalized the unique Balinese cosmology.

The presentation is dense and carefully organized and will likely slow the pace of *Negara* for many readers. The technical languages of Balinese kinship, of political and economic clientship, and of the complicated geometry of irrigation must, however, be understood if not mastered in order that Geertz's explanation of the organization of the Balinese state—the negara—be appreciated. Unwilling to capitalize on a lay reader's ignorance of Bali and of enthnographic techniques, Geertz wisely includes enough detail to sustain his general argument. He is trying to solve the persistent problem of the relation of generalizations to particulars. But as in *Islam Observed,* in which he also sought an audience outside anthropology, Geertz displays a problem unique to anthropological scholarship. Speaking to a group of literary critics he noted once that anthropologists can take it as an advantage that few readers have any independent knowledge of the facts or observations on which their arguments are based. Critics, philosophers, and historians, conversely, typically consider materials widely known or at least readily available. The anthropologist, however, is "faced with an unattractive choice of boring his audience with a great deal of exotic information or attempting to make his argument in an empirical vacuum."[12] Geertz makes the same point in *Negara* when he notes that understanding the intricate irrigation network is the key to seeing how a system of ritual obligations was also a medium for economic coordination.

When he turns to Balinese ceremonies and spectacles, Geertz relies on a second narrative episode. This time it is a long and suggestive quotation from an eyewitness account of the funeral in 1847 of a Rajah who was followed voluntarily into the pyre by three concubines. The description mingles awe for the beauty, mystery, and grandeur of the ceremony as a whole and dismay over the barbarism of the sacrifice, the "suttee." The ritual, the costumes and actions, even the apparent attitudes of the participants are described in impressive, even ethnographic appearing detail (if based on secondary sources).

This account of mid-nineteenth-century Bali provides evidence for Geertz's assertion about connections between social rank and religion, and between Balinese attitudes about these matters (and others) and their expression in symbolic forms. "The Balinese," he says, "cast their most comprehensive ideas of the way things ultimately are, and the way that men should therefore act, into immediately apprehended sensuous symbols—into a lexicon of carvings, flowers, dances, melodies, gestures, chants, ornaments, temples, postures, and masks—rather than into a discursively apprehended, ordered set of explicit 'beliefs'" (*N*, 103). Such habits of expression have produced a richly expressive society but one that can confound its interpreters, until very recently all foreign visitors and scholars.

Geertz's analysis of the nineteenth-century ceremony (modern versions of which, free of suttee, he has himself witnessed) illustrates his interpretive principles: "Neither the precise description of objects and behavior that is associated with traditional ethnography, nor the careful tracing of stylistic motifs that is traditional philology are themselves enough. They must be made to converge in a such a way that the concrete immediacy of enacted theater yields the faith enclosed within it." Hence the many symbols associated with the cremation ceremony—historically the most elaborate and dramatic in Bali—are explained from several points of view. As Geertz says, they are "polysemic," and it is necessary to recognize their "significance spreading out profusely in an embarrassment of directions" (*N*, 104). In short, Balinese religious symbols, like the signs that constitute any culture, "reek of meaning." In illustrating the symbolism of state power epitomized in the cremation rite, Geertz emphasizes the ways in which the pattern of Balinese symbols is repeated again and again, beginning with the most elementary and universal ones which are then organized architecturally to give meaning to the design of the royal palace and spatially to give structure to the myriad elements of the cremation procession. All is shaped by a network of fixed relations, between "buwana agung" and "buwana alit," which can only roughly be approximated in English as macrocosm and microcosm, or better yet in Geertz's view as "outside" and "inside." As in other religious and philosophical systems, they are not definitive categories of experience but expressions of the relation of its aspects, each "inside" particular having its "outside" and more inclusive counterpart.

Geertz's selective but revealing approach to Balinese symbolism can be seen in this discussion (an explanation, he would say, is impossible) of one of the basic animating objects and ideas.

> Literally, padmasana means "lotus seat." It is used to refer to the throne of the supreme god, Siva (or Surya, the Sun), who sits unstirring in the center of a lotus (padma), surrounded on four petals to the north, east, west, and south by Wisnu, Iswara, Mahadewa, and Brahma, each associated with a particular color, day of the week, part of the body, weapon, metal, magical syllable, and form of supernatural power. It is used to refer to the small stone column, surmounted by a high-back chair (also of stone) set cater-cornered on the most sacred spot in Balinese temples, upon which offerings to the supreme god are placed during temple ceremonies when, enticed out of one version of heaven into another by his dancing worshippers, he comes there to sit. It is used to refer to the posture, a kind of infolded squat, one adopts when meditating upon the divine. It is used to refer to the act and the experience of mediation itself. It is a coital position, it is one of the many names of the supreme god, it is an iconic picture of the cosmos, it is the receptacle upon which the remains of a high priest are conducted to his cremation. And it is the innermost reaches of the human heart. (*N*, 104–5)

The goal of all royal ceremonies symbolically is to fuse the "buwana agung" and "buwana alit." Their union amounts to a sweeping "metapolitical" claim: "the cultural forms that the negara celebrates in rituals and the institutional ones that it takes in society are the same forms. . . . All the enormous gorgeousness [of the cremation ceremony and less elaborate ones] was an attempt to set up, in terms of drama and decoration, an authoritative pattern of political analogy" (*N*, 108). Palace and procession, family and irrigation society, religious philosophy, and traditions of daily life all repeat the pattern: "The more sacred/central/interior/private/formal/elevated/ primary/hermetic/mysterious . . . against the less" (*N*, 112). The entire system, again, is based on the emulation in state-craft, regional governance, economic pursuits, and domestic life of an "exemplary center," the Balinese vision of perfection, of divinely inspired kingship. Its genius (and to us its strangeness) was its consistency, captured by Geertz in compact and elegant descriptions of the internal organization of the royal palace and the cremation ceremony. "From a small offering on a minor holiday by the priest in charge of the royal temple at its padmasana, a bare ritual gesture routinely observed, to the mass festivals on major occasions in and around the palace as a whole, great public enterprises involving the entire society, the props and settings of the theater state were, like its dramas, at base the same. What varied was the number of people caught up in the performance, the elaborateness with which the unchanging themes were developed, and the practical impact of the event upon the general course of Balinese life" (*N*, 113).

Readers of *Negara* will observe, however, that there is always a methodological outside to Geertz's descriptive inside. Even the chapter on "Spectacle and Ceremony" is shaped by his professional self-consciousness. Anthropology, Geertz says, is like literary criticism when it seeks to interpret cultural materials as complicated as those offered by the Balinese: "The message here is so deeply sunk in the medium that to transform it into a network of propositions is to risk at once both of the characteristic crimes of exegesis: seeing more in things than is really there, and reducing a richness of particular meaning to a drab parade of generalities" (*N*, 103). These are the inevitable tendencies of two kinds of understanding converging in the interpretation of cultures: the description of the symbolic meanings of acts, objects, and institutions, and their placement in the social, political, economic, and domestic settings that define their use and meaning. Geertz recognizes this process as "nothing but the by-now-familiar trajectory of the hermeneutic circle: a dialectical tacking between the parts in such a way as to bring parts and whole simultaneously into view" (*N*, 103).

Negara closes (its ethnographic first half) with an essay on "Bali and Political Theory" in which Geertz insists again on the need to interpret the symbolic dimensions of state power in a way which recognizes the "ordering force of display, regard, and drama." Accordingly, all modern theories of the state have only incompletely acknowledged the importance of this aspect of politics. Their mistake has been to assume that all forms of political symbolism and ceremony merely serve the practical interest of the state. Geertz points out that modern political theory beginning with Max Weber has produced a useful taxonomy of political power but its limits are revealed in the study of the remote Balinese system. "What was high centralization representationally was enormous dispersion institutionally, so that an intensely competitive politics, rising from the specifics of landscape, custom and local history, took place in an idiom of static order emerging from the universalizing symbology of myth, rite, and political drama" (*N*, 132). What is wanting in familiar models of political theory is the imaginative capacity to see that every state has a poetics as well as a mechanics of power.

The negara is an integrated political system with a nearly seamless relation between the symbolic and the real. The Balinese, in other words, do not make such a distinction. As Mead reminded her MLA audience, "We may think of human societies as existing in various degrees of balance between the needs and capacities of their individual members and the elaborated imaginative material on which these members are fed."[13] Simultaneously abstract and concrete, the Balinese system is a natural medium for demonstrating an integrated approach to the humanities and social sciences.

Cultures of Interpretation

Geertz favors ideas found in recent literary theory. His designation of his method as "semiotic" is consistent with his assertion in *Negara* and in essays that have followed it that "arguments and melodies, formulas and maps and pictures are not idealities to be stared at but texts to be read; so are rituals, palaces, technologies and social formations" (*N*, 135). As a catalogue of interpretive interest, this one resembles the many recently presented by critics, philosophers, and others who have enlarged the subject matter of criticism as they have pursued the contingencies of language and meaning, the nature of "textuality" and of "authorship."[14] As it was put early in the period of critical theory's (and postmodernism's) influence on intellectual life: "We know that criticism is about the impossibility of anything being about life . . . or about anything. Criticism has taken the very idea of 'aboutness' away from us. It has taught us that language is tautological, it is not nonsense, and that to the extent that it is about anything it is about itself. Mathematics is about mathematics, poetry is about poetry, and criticism is about the impossibility of its own existence."[15]

Geertz himself comes close to saying that anthropology is only about anthropology, that it can claim no objective knowledge of the world, no access to aspects of living other than itself. He notes an aspect of method that often escapes professional attention: "Although culture exists in the trading post, the hill fort, or the sheep run, anthropology exists in the book, the article, the lecture, the museum display, or sometimes nowadays, the film." In other words, the border between interpretation and its subject matter is often unclear and resists firm definition. That ambiguous relation poses a threat to the objective status of anthropological knowledge as it does of course to the results of historical or philosophical inquiry or to the products of the literary imagination and their mediation through criticism. "It does threaten it," Geertz admits, but "the threat is hollow" (*IC,* 16). His reasons are consistent with the resistance to some current trends represented by critics like Gerald Graff who have argued against criticism in which "everything is swallowed up in an infinite regress of textuality."[16]

Unlike others who employ semiotic techniques in literary or ethnographic study, Geertz is confident that ethnographic information tells us about people and the lives they lead and not merely about signs, language, and the structure of observation and interpretation. "The claim to attention of an ethnographic account does not rest in its author's ability to capture primitive facts in faraway places and carry them home like a mask or a carving, but in the degree to which he is able to clarify what goes on in such places, to reduce the puzzlement—what manner of men are these—to which unfamiliar acts emerging out of unknown backgrounds naturally give rise" (*IC,* 16). "Thick Description," therefore, contributes to our "appraisal" (one of Geertz's favored terms) of cultural particulars. Discriminating among ethnographic accounts of foreign cultures for the truth they tell and not just the meanings they reveal about their subjects is the responsibility and pleasure of anthropologists and their scholarly allies. Such discrimination does not take place in a closed universe of learned discourse but in a world of many styles of interpretation having as their subject life as it is lived even when we are not thinking, talking, or writing. "It is not against a body of uninterpreted data, radically thinned descriptions, that we must measure the urgency of our explications, but against the power of the scientific imagination to bring us into touch with the lives of strangers" (*IC,* 16). And in a pleasing aside on criticism dominated by obscure theory at the expense of accessible knowledge, Geertz in "Thick Description" endorses Thoreau's attitude toward scholarship made marginal by excessive if expert attention to methodological virtuosity: it is not worth it to go round the world to count the cats in Zanzibar.

For Geertz the best products of scholarship, cultural analysis, or ethnography are those that respect "the informed logic of actual life" which can make sense to the actor and critical observer alike. Significance, the meaning of symbols and signs, is a product of social action—the behavior of individuals and groups, families, and nations. Ethnography is a suggestive model for interpretation when it is exact in observation and worldly in its interests.

> If anthropological interpretation is constructing a reading of what happens, then to divorce it from what happens—from what, in this time or that place, specific people say, what they do, what is done to them, from the whole vast business of the world—is to divorce it from its applications and render it vacant. A good interpretation of any-thing—a poem, a person, a history, a ritual, an institution, a society—takes us into the heat of that of which it is the interpretation. When it does not do that, but leads us instead somewhere else—into an admiration of its own elegance, of its author's cleverness, or of the

beauties of Euclidean order—it may have its intrinsic charms; but it is something else than what the task at hand calls for. (*IC,* 18)

Wary of some kinds of semiotic interpretation, Geertz groups its doctrinaire practitioners with those whose work suggests that an "advanced form of thought is going to enable us to understand men without knowing them" (*IC,* 30). Not surprisingly, the form of thought he admires most is represented by Lionel Trilling and similar critics. Differences of discipline and subject matter count for less, he says, than intentions and results. "It doesn't really matter much in the end whether one trains one's attention on Joseph Conrad or on suttee: the social history of the moral imagination is a single subject" (*LK,* 40).

An adept if infrequent critic of both literature and criticism, Geertz offers Faulkner's *Absalom, Absalom* and Paul Fussell's *The Great War and Modern Memory* (1975) as examples of the "translation" of experience into literature and the subsequent translation of literature by generations of critics and other readers into the understanding of historical or culturally remote life. In his comment on this process, Geertz states his own intentions and the relation of ethnography to literature, indeed the essential continuity of all scholarly work in the humanities and the social sciences.

> This is how anything imaginational grows in our minds, is transformed, socially transformed, from something we merely know to exist or have existed, somewhere or other, to something which is properly ours, a working force in our common consciousness. In the Balinese case, it is not a matter (not for us at least) of the past recaptured, but of the strange construed. Yet this is only a genre detail—a fiction framed as ethnography rather than history; a complicating matter but not a decisive one. When major cultural lines are traversed in the process of interpretive reworking, a different sense of discovery is produced: one more of having come across something than of having remembered it, of an acquisition than of an inheritance. But the movement from some scene of singular experience . . . through groping representations of what went on there raised to figurations of collective life is the same. Nor is the matter seriously otherwise when the originating scene is artifactual rather than, as we say, "real"—*Emma* or *Mansfield Park;* or, for that matter, suttee. That but alters vocabulary. The passage is still from the immediacies of one form of life to the metaphors of another. (*LK,* 47–8)

As "passage" or "translation" the process embodies a convincing argument against what Graff quotes from Susan Sontag's *Against Interpretation* as the typical "denunciation" of traditional criticism: "to interpret is to impoverish, to deplete the world—in order to set up a shadow world of meanings." As a self-declared "semiotician," Geertz is an unexpected but welcome interpreter of the stable relation of texts to life.

Inevitably Geertz also advocates making more of the natural overlap and interplay of disciplines. Knowledge of literature and the history of ideas can contribute to our understanding of events, and sociological and political knowledge includes at least the nascent understanding of symbolic structures. To "refigure" literary and social thought in such a way is not, he insists, to confuse art and life. "It is the proper method for a study dedicated to getting straight how the massive fact of cultural and historical particularity comports with the equally massive fact of cross-cultural and cross-historical accessibility—how the deeply different can be deeply known without becoming any less different" (*LK,* 48). Yet Geertz's interest in the negara reflects more than a desire to enhance political theory or to demonstrate that history, literary criticism, and other disciplines can benefit from assimilating ethnographic techniques. For "thick description" is more than a technique to record and interpret meanings. Interpreting the politics of the negara, for instance, can make a foreign culture less opaque, more deeply known, by being thickly described. Our own culture, meanwhile, will appear more opaque as our interpretation of a freshly discovered culture makes us less sure that we know the precise or complete meanings of our own texts and symbols, history and politics.

Such readings not only bring us closer to acts and artifacts but to the actuality of the culture in which the texts originate. The goal as always is to get as close as possible to the experience of living in another place, another time. Accepting Geertz's method means eschewing misleading distinctions between figurative and literal, aesthetic and practical, mystical and mundane, and the like. In the negara the expressions of the theater state were the essence of the state itself; the dramaturgy of power was the actual structure of its workings. "The state drew its force . . . from its imaginative energies, its semiotic capacity to make inequality enchant" (*N,* 123). Geertz himself is a somewhat enchanted observer, impressed by the elegance and coherence of Balinese life, but also hardheaded enough to recognize the implications and shortcomings of his own observations.[17]

Conclusion: Speaking Wittgenstein

All of Geertz's work is actually a denial of the simple division of motives, like enchantment and hardheadedness; it is an invitation to blur not only the genres (as his famous essay on "Blurred Genres" would have it) but their sources. "The relation between thought and action in social life can no more be conceived of in terms of wisdom than it can in terms of expertise. How it is to be conceived, how the games, dramas or texts which we do not just invent or witness but live, have the consequences they do remains very far from clear. It will take the wariest of wary reasonings, on all sides of all divides, to get it clearer" (*LK,* 35). Even so, the demands of the subjects of ethnography themselves will often stand in the way of such a goal. Speaking of the problems entailed in defining and then presenting the "legal sensibility" in three different cultures, Geertz cites a remark by Wittgenstein: "A veridical picture of an indistinct object is not after all a clear but an indistinct one" (*LK,* 215).

Whatever Geertz's motives, what is plain for his admirers is his highly adaptive learning and talent for moving among cultural materials apparently (or until he looks at them) unrelated. To anthropologists and others with more modest—some might say realistic—scholarly goals, this strategy is elusive and may seem to be no more than "accumulated cunning." But that is Geertz's own phrase, meant not to be coy with regard to his methods but modest about their results thus far. Critics may claim that he sometimes shows more strategy than sense, that he exemplifies a Moroccan proverb he himself cites in his interpretation of the royal procession: "Roam and you confound adversaries, sit and they will confound you" (*LK,* 137). Jonathan Leiberson, for example, admires the range and ambition of Geertz's work at the same time that he finds it, at crucial points, "incomplete" and "obscure."[18] Yet it was the condition of his subjects that brought his method into being, with consequences Geertz himself acknowledges. It is part of the "turn toward examining the ways in which the world is talked about—depicted, charted, represented—rather than the way it intrinsically is." He and like-minded colleagues across the disciplines, have "been speaking Wittgenstein all along" (*LK,* 4).

Other critics have made politics or "praxis" the issue. William Roseberry has asked that we pay more attention, in cases like Bali and its cockfighting (the subject of another of Geertz's widely cited essays), to the role of state formation and colonialism than to the meaning-making structures Geertz proposes.[19] And for Sherry Ortner, Geertz does indeed lack a "systematic sociology." Yet compensation can be found, as Ortner proposes in an authoritative survey of anthropological theory including Geertz's formative place in it, in his redirection of anthropology in the 1980s toward "diachronic, processual" analyses. Hence *Negara* is classified with those contributions that "delineate forces of both stability and change at work within a given system, as well as the social and cultural filters operating to select and/or reinterpret whatever may be coming in from outside."[20]

Still, what Roseberry is after are the political consequences of history and the commitment of anthropology to advocacy and mediation through its particular practices. In some ways his essay on the "seductions" of interpretive anthropology is a plea for someone to play Habermas to Geertz's version of Gadamer. In their disagreement over the social meaning of hermeneutics, its role in the critique of ideology as a determinant of culture, is contained the framework for a host of scholarly debates, in anthropology and other fields, which turn on the tasks of scholarship in relation to politics, or as Habermas put it, on the matter of "Modernity Versus Postmodernity."[21] Geertz's historicism (in *Negara*) does not satisfy Roseberry who is convinced that this method amounts to the "removal of culture from the wellings-up of action, interaction, power and praxis."[22]

Geertz may be cool to the idea of advocacy but he does not, as Roseberry implies, obscure it. In fact his approach locates the actual (including the historical) experience of politics, inescapable as that is from the experience of culture. As Ortner says of anthropology as a model and moral form of social inquiry:

The attempt to view other systems from ground level is the basis, perhaps the only basis, of anthropology's distinctive contribution to the human sciences. It is our capacity, largely developed in fieldwork, to take the perspective of the folks on the shore, that allows us to learn anything at all—even in our own culture—beyond what we already know. . . . It is our location "on the ground" that puts us in a position to see people not simply as passive reactors to and enactors of some "system," but as active agents and subjects in their own history.[23]

Geertz has succeeded not only in helping to form and carry out this program but in making it a format for affiliations among the disciplines leading to interpretations of culture that include if they do always begin with the example of ethnography.

Yet Geertz's admirers, all those trying for "thick description" in the study of history, health care, writing and many other areas, still have to cope with his insistence that the very things that have brought him a large audience are still to his mind propositions awaiting particulars. "To an ethnographer sorting through the machinery of distant ideas," he reminds us, "the shapes of knowledge are always ineluctably local, indivisible from their instruments and their encasements. One may veil this fact with ecumenical rhetoric or blur it with strenuous theory, but one cannot really make it go away" (LK, 4). His problem and ours, in other words, is the success of an original idea whose limits contain some of its powers.

The matter of the origins, construction, and circumstances (including the reception) of Geertz's work might also be approached from the point of view of his relations with ethnographic tradition. In an essay on Evans-Pritchard he singles out his style—"unmodified and undecorated . . . flat declarative"—and the problems its characteristic confidence and sturdy realism pose for today's ethnographers. They are "confronted . . . by an army of wildly contrasting approaches to description and analysis . . . and harassed by grave inner uncertainties, amounting almost to a sort of epistemological hypochondria, concerning how one knows that anything one says about other forms of life is as a matter of fact so."[24] Geertz of course has made what he says are missing in Evans-Pritchard ("quizzical interrogatives, hedging conditionals, or musing apostrophes") a vital part of his own prose in order to represent the relation of ethnography to the problems of discourse in general. He is no less realistic or descriptive than Evans-Pritchard, only more aware of the problems of technique and how any description represents more than the objects of observation.

Geertz is also devoted to the moral uses of anthropology and the forms of inquiry it influences. He has reacted sharply to assertions that his style of interpretation is simply redesigned relativism.[25] Though he speaks Wittgenstein he defends his "particularism" as an epistemological and moral necessity, and he dismisses the beliefs of colleagues that interpretive anthropology—pluralistic, skeptical, and democratic—is a threat to the "moral fiber" of scholars and their readers.[26] His reasons are pragmatic and principled since the issue is not just reading and writing but living, where the ability to imagine other lives, in other times and other places, is crucial.

> To see ourselves as others see us can be eye-opening. To see others as sharing a nature with ourselves is the merest decency. But it is from the far more difficult achievement of seeing ourselves amongst others, as a local example of the forms human life has locally taken, a case among cases, a world among worlds, that the largeness of mind, without which objectivity is self-congratulation and tolerance a sham, comes. (*LK*, 16)

It is for such capacities that Richard Rorty has identified anthropology as a discipline "enlarging and deepening our sense of community."[27] And it is this "fugitive truth," in Geertz's words, that animates and justifies interpretation as the characteristic activity in anthropology—its own local knowledge—and the instrument of learning and living within and beyond it.

Notes

1. Clifford Geertz, *Works and Lives: the Anthropologist as Author* (Stanford, CA: Stanford University Press, 1988), 6.
2. Margaret Mead "The Cultural Basis for Understanding Literature," *PLMA* 68 (1953): 14.
3. See Paul Rabinow and William M. Sullivan, eds. *Interpretive Social Science: A Second Look* (Berkeley: University of California Press, 1987).
4. Susan Sontag, *Against Interpretation* (New York: Farrar, Strauss, Giroux, 1966), 70.
5. Alfred Kroeber and Clyde Klukholn, *Culture: A Critical Review of Concepts and Definitions* (New York: Random House, 1963), 3.
6. Mead, "The Cultural Basis for Understanding Literature," 13.
7. See Williams's brief but suggestive account of the history of the term in *Keywords: A Vocabulary of Culture and Society,* rev. ed. (New York: Oxford University Press, 1983), 87–93.
8. Clifford Geertz, *The Interpretation of Cultures* (New York: Basic Books, 1973), 5. Future references appear in the text with the initials *IC.*
9. Clifford Geertz, *Islam Observed* (New Haven, CT: Yale University Press, 1968), vi, viii.
10. Clifford Geertz, *The Social History of an Indonesian Town* (Cambridge, MA: MIT Press, 1965), 203.
11. Clifford Geertz, *Negara: The Theater State in Nineteenth Century Bali* (Princeton, NJ: Princeton University Press, 1980), 5. Future references appear in the text with the initial *N.*
12. Clifford Geertz, *Local Knowledge: Further Essays in Interpretive Anthropology* (New York: Basic Books, 1983), 36. Future references appear in the text with the initials *LK.*
13. Mead, "The Cultural Basis for Understanding Literature," 16.
14. The theoretical literature is already vast. A selection Geertz himself cites is *Works and Lives* is J. V. Harari, ed., *Textual Strategies* (Ithaca: Cornell University Press, 1979). A widely used guide to the field is Terry Eagleton, *Literary Theory: An Introduction* (Minneapolis: University of Minnesota Press, 1983).
15. Robert Scholes, "The Fictional Criticism of the Future," *TriQuarterly* 18 (1970): 101.
16. Gerald Graff, *Literature Against Itself* (Chicago: University of Chicago Press, 1980), 61.
17. He has not, however, been quite good enough for his distinguished British colleague Edmund Leach who, while acknowledging the stylistic virtues of *Negara,* termed its central argument "rubbish" on the basis of his own theoretical position that genetic predisposition and not culture form and dominate behavior (*The New Republic* [4

April 1981]: 30–33). For a fully enthusiastic view see Quention Skinner, "The World as a Stage," (*New York Review of Books* [16 April 1981]: 35–37).

18. Jonathan Lieberson, "Interpreting the Interpreter," *New York Review of Books* (15 March 1984): 39–45.

19. William Roseberry, "Balinese Cockfights and the Seduction of Anthropology," *Social Research* 49 (1982): 1013–28.

20. Sherry B. Ortner, "Theory in Anthropology Since the Sixties," *Comparative Studies in Society and History* 26 (1984): 108, 159.

21. The essay appeared with that title in *New German Critique* (1981). It appears with the title "Modernity—An Incomplete Project" (endorsed by Habermas) in Rabinow and Sullivan, *Interpretive Social Science,* 141–56.

22. Roseberry, "Balinese Cockfights," 1027.

23. Ortner, "Theory in Anthropology," 143.

24. Geertz, *Works and Lives,* 60, 71.

25. Geertz, *The Interpretation of Cultures,* 4. See also on this point Geertz's "Distinguished Lecture" to the American Anthropological Association, "Anti-Anti-Relativism," *American Anthropologist* 86 (1984): 263–78 and the important exchange between Geertz and philosopher Richard Rorty on "The Uses of Diversity" in the *Michigan Quarterly Review* 26 (1986): 105–23 and 525–34.

26. Such is the implication of an essay by Ernest Gellner in which Geertz is the unnamed but clearly identifiable villain ("The Stakes in Anthropology," *American Scholar* 57 [1988]: 15–30).

27. Richard Rorty, *Consequences of Pragmatism* (Minneapolis: University of Minnesota Press, 1982), 203.

Index

247